The Complete Works Of Friedrich Nietzsche

THE COMPLETE WORKS

OF

FRIEDRICH NIETZSCHE

The First Complete and Authorised English Translation

EDITED BY

Dr. OSCAR LEVY

VOLUME SEVEN

HUMAN, ALL-TOO-HUMAN

PART TWO

FRIEDRICH NIETZSCHE

HUMAN
ALL-TOO-HUMAN

A BOOK FOR FREE SPIRITS

PART II

TRANSLATED BY

PAUL V. COHN, B.A.

NEW YORK
THE MACMILLAN COMPANY
1913

Printed by MORRISON & GIBB LIMITED, *Edinburgh*

CONTENTS

INTRODUCTION

THE publication of *Human, all-too-Human* extends over the period 1878–1880. Of the two divisions which constitute the Second Part, "Miscellaneous Maxims and Opinions" appeared in 1879, and "The Wanderer and his Shadow" in 1880, Nietzsche being then in his thirty-sixth year. The Preface was added in 1886. The whole book forms Nietzsche's first lengthy contribution to literature. His previous works comprise only the philological treatises, *The Birth of Tragedy*, and the essays on Strauss, Schopenhauer, and Wagner in *Thoughts out of Season.*

With the volumes of *Human, all-too-Human* Nietzsche appears for the first time in his true colours as philosopher. His purely scholarly publications, his essays in literary and musical criticism —especially the essay on Richard Wagner at Bayreuth—had, of course, foreshadowed his work as a thinker.

These efforts, however, had been mere fragments, from which hardly any one could observe that a new philosophical star had arisen on the horizon. But by 1878 the period of transition had definitely set in. Outwardly, the new departure is marked by Nietzsche's resignation in that year of his professorship at Bâle—a resignation due partly to ill-health, and partly to his conviction that his was a voice that should speak not merely to students of philology, but to all mankind.

Nietzsche himself characterises *Human, all-too-Human* as "the monument of a crisis." He might as fitly have called it the first-fruits of a new harvest. Now, for the first time, he practises the form which he was to make so peculiarly his own. We are told —and we may well believe—that the book came as a surprise even to his most intimate friends. Wagner had already seen how matters stood at the publication of the first part, and the gulf between the two probably widened on the appearance of the Second Part.

Several aphorisms are here, varying in length as in subject, and ranging over the whole human province—the emotions and aspirations, the religions and cultures and philosophies, the arts and literatures and politics of mankind. Equally varied is the range of style, the incisive epigram and the passage of pure poetry jostling each other on the same page. In this curious power of alternating between cynicism and lyricism, Nietzsche appears as the prose counterpart of Heine.

One or two of the aphorisms are of peculiar interest to English readers. The essay (as it may almost be called) on Sterne (p. 60, No. 113) does ample justice, if not more than justice, to that wayward genius. The allusion to Milton (p. 77, No. 150) will come as somewhat of a shock to English readers, especially to those who hold that in Milton Art triumphed over Puritanism. It should be remembered, however, that Nietzsche's view coincides with Goethe's. The dictum that Shakespeare's gold is to be valued for its quantity rather than its quality (p. 81, No. 162) also betrays a certain exclusiveness—a legacy from that eighteenth-century France which appealed so strongly to Nietzsche on its intellectual side. To Nietzsche, as to Voltaire, Shakespeare is after all "the great barbarian."

The title of the book may be explained from a phrase in *Thus Spake Zarathustra*: "Verily, even the greatest I found—all-too-human." The keynote of these volumes is indeed disillusion and destruction. Nor is this to be wondered at, for all men must sweep away the rubbish before they can build. Hence we find here little of the constructive philosophy of Nietzsche—so far as he had a constructive philosophy. The Superman appears but faintly, the doctrine of Eternal Recurrence not at all. For this very reason, *Human, all-too-Human* is perhaps the best starting-point for the study of Nietzsche. The difficulties in style and thought of the later work— difficulties that at times become well-nigh insuperable in *Thus Spake Zarathustra*—are here practically absent. The book may, in fact, almost be described as "popular," bearing the same relation to Nietzsche's later productions as Wagner's *Tannhäuser* and *Lohengrin* bear to the *Ring*.

The translator's thanks are due to Mr. Thomas Common for his careful revision of the manuscript and many valuable suggestions.

P. V. C.

PREFACE.

I.

ONE should only speak where one cannot remain silent, and only speak of what one has *conquered*— the rest is all chatter, "literature," bad breeding. My writings speak only of my conquests, "I" am in them, with all that is hostile to me, *ego ipsissimus*, or, if a more haughty expression be permitted, *ego ipsissimum*. It may be guessed that I have many below me. . . . But first I always needed time, convalescence, distance, separation, before I felt the stirrings of a desire to flay, despoil, lay bare, "represent" (or whatever one likes to call it) for the additional knowledge of the world, something that I had lived through and outlived, something done or suffered. Hence all my writings,—with one exception, important, it is true,—must be *ante-dated*—they always tell of a "behind-me." Some even, like the first three *Thoughts out of Season*, must be thrown back before the period of creation and experience of a previously published book (*The Birth of Tragedy* in the case cited, as any one with subtle powers of observation and comparison could not fail to perceive). That wrathful outburst against the Germanism, smugness, and raggedness of speech of old David Strauss, the

contents of the first *Thought out of Season*, gave a
vent to feelings that had inspired me long before, as
a student, in the midst of German culture and cultured Philistinism (I claim the paternity of the now
much used and misused phrase "cultured Philistinism "). What I said against the "historical disease " I said as one who had slowly and laboriously
recovered from that disease, and who was not at
all disposed to renounce "history" in the future because he had suffered from her in the past. When
in the third *Thought out of Season* I gave expression
to my reverence for my first and only teacher, the
great Arthur Schopenhauer—I should now give it a
far more personal and emphatic voice—I was for my
part already in the throes of moral scepticism and
dissolution, that is, as much concerned with the
criticism as with the study of all pessimism down to
the present day. I already did not believe in "a
blessed thing," as the people say, not even in Schopenhauer. It was at this very period that an un-
published essay of mine, " On Truth and Falsehood
in an Extra-Moral Sense," came into being. Even
my ceremonial oration in honour of Richard Wagner,
on the occasion of his triumphal celebration at
Bayreuth in 1876—Bayreuth signifies the greatest
triumph that an artist has ever won—a work that
bears the strongest stamp of "individuality," was in
the background an act of homage and gratitude to a
bit of the past in me, to the fairest but most perilous
calm of my sea-voyage . . . and as a matter of fact
a severance and a farewell. (Was Richard Wagner
mistaken on this point? I do not think so. So
long as we still love, we do not paint such pictures,

we do not yet "examine," we do not place ourselves so far away as is essential for one who "examines." "Examining needs at least a secret antagonism, that of an opposite point of view," it is said on page 46 of the above-named work itself, with an insidious, melancholy application that was perhaps understood by few.) The composure that gave me the *power* to speak after many intervening years of solitude and abstinence, first came with the book, *Human, All-too Human*, to which this second preface and apologia * is dedicated. As a book for "free spirits" it shows some trace of that almost cheerful and inquisitive coldness of the psychologist, who has *behind* him many painful things that he keeps *under* him, and moreover establishes them for himself and fixes them firmly as with a needle-point. Is it to be wondered at that at such sharp, ticklish work blood flows now and again, that indeed the psychologist has blood on his fingers and not *only* on his fingers?

2.

The *Miscellaneous Maxims and Opinions* were in the first place, like *The Wanderer and His Shadow*, published separately as continuations and appendices to the above-mentioned human, all-too human *Book for Free Spirits*: and at the same time, as a continuation and confirmation of an intellectual cure, consisting in a course of anti-romantic self-treatment, such as my instinct, which had always remained

---

* "Foreword" and "forword" would be the literal rendering of the play on words.—Tr.

healthy, had itself discovered and prescribed against a temporary attack of the most dangerous form of romantics. After a convalescence of six years I may well be permitted to collect these same writings and publish them as a second volume of *Human, All-too Human*. Perhaps, if surveyed together, they will more clearly and effectively teach their lesson— a lesson of health that may be recommended as a *disciplina voluntatis* to the more intellectual natures of the rising generation. Here speaks a pessimist who has often leaped out of his skin but has always returned into it, thus, a pessimist with goodwill towards pessimism—at all events a romanticist no longer. And has not a pessimist, who possesses this serpentine knack of changing his skin, the right to read a lecture to our pessimists of to-day, who are one and all still in the toils of romanticism? Or at least to show them how it is—done?

3.

It was then, in fact, high time to bid farewell, and I soon received proof. Richard Wagner, who seemed all-conquering, but was in reality only a decayed and despairing romantic, suddenly collapsed, helpless and broken, before the Christian Cross. . . . Was there not a single German with eyes in his head and sympathy in his heart for this appalling spectacle? Was I the only one whom he caused—suffering? In any case, the unexpected event illumined for me in one lightning flash the place that I had abandoned, and also the horror that is felt by every one who is unconscious of a great danger until he has passed through it. As I went forward alone, I shuddered, and not long afterwards I was ill, or rather more than ill—weary: weary from my ceaseless disappointment about all that remained to make us modern men enthusiastic, at the thought of the power, work, hope, youth, love, flung to all the winds: weary from disgust at the effeminacy and undisciplined rhapsody of this romanticism, at the whole tissue of idealistic lies and softening of conscience, which here again had won the day over one of the bravest of men : last, and not least, weary from the bitterness of an inexorable suspicion—that after this disappointment I was doomed to mistrust more thoroughly, to despise more thoroughly, to be alone more thoroughly than ever before. My task—whither had it flown ? Did it not look now as if my task were retreating from me and as if I should for a long future period have no more right to it ? What was I to do to endure this most terrible privation ?—I began by entirely forbidding myself all romantic music, that ambiguous, pompous, stifling art, which robs the mind of its sternness and its joyousness and provides a fertile soil for every kind of vague yearning and spongy sensuality. " Cave musicam " is even to-day my advice to all who are enough of men to cling to purity in matters of the intellect. Such music enervates, softens, feminises, its " eternal feminine " draws us—*down*! * My first suspicion, my most immediate precaution, was directed against romantic music. If I hoped for anything at all from music, it

---

* The allusion is to the ending of the Second Part of Goethe's *Faust*—" das Ewig Weibliche Zieht uns *hinan* ! "— " The Eternal Feminine Draweth us *on* ! "—TR.

was in the expectation of the coming of a musician bold, subtle, malignant, southern, healthy enough to take an immortal revenge upon that other music.

4.

Lonely now and miserably self-distrustful, I took sides, not without resentment, *against* myself and *for* everything that hurt me and was hard to me. Thus I once more found the way to that courageous pessimism that is the antithesis of all romantic fraud, and, as it seems to me to-day, the way to " myself," to my task. That hidden masterful Something, for which we long have no name until at last it shows itself as our task—that tyrant in us exacts a terrible price for every attempt that we make to escape him or give him the slip, for every premature act of self-constraint, for every reconciliation with those to whom we do not belong, for every activity, however reputable, which turns us aside from our main purpose, yes, even for every virtue that would fain protect us from the cruelty of our most individual responsibility. " Disease " is always the answer when we wish to have doubts of our rights to our own task, when we begin to make it easier for ourselves in any way. How strange and how terrible ! It is our very alleviations for which we have to make the severest atonement ! And if we want to return to health, we have no choice left—we must load ourselves *more heavily* than we were ever laden before.

5.

It was then that I learnt the hermitical habit of

speech acquired only by the most silent and suffering. I spoke without witnesses, or rather indifferent
to the presence of witnesses, so as not to suffer from
silence, I spoke of various things that did not concern me in a style that gave the impression that
they did. Then, too, I learnt the art of showing myself cheerful, objective, inquisitive in the presence
of all that is healthy and evil—is this, in an invalid,
as it seems to me, his "good taste"? Nevertheless,
a more subtle eye and sympathy will not miss what
perhaps gives a charm to these writings—the fact
that here speaks one who has suffered and abstained
in such a way as if he had never suffered or abstained. Here equipoise, composure, even gratitude
towards life *shall* be maintained, here rules a stern,
proud, ever vigilant, ever susceptible will, which has
undertaken the task of defending life against pain
and snapping off all conclusions that are wont to
grow like poisonous fungi from pain, disappointment, satiety, isolation and other morasses. Perhaps
this gives our pessimists a hint to self-examination?
For it was then that I hit upon the aphorism, "a
sufferer has as yet no right to pessimism," and that
I engaged in a tedious, patient campaign against
the unscientific first principles of all romantic pessimism, which seeks to magnify and interpret individual, personal experiences into "general judgments," universal condemnations—it was then, in
short, that I sighted a new world. Optimism for
the sake of restitution, in order at some time to
have the right to become a pessimist—do you understand that? Just as a physician transfers his patient
to totally strange surroundings, in order to displace

him from his entire "past," his troubles, friends, letters, duties, stupid mistakes and painful memories, and teaches him to stretch out hands and senses towards new nourishment, a new sun, a new future: so I, as physician and invalid in one, forced myself into an utterly different and untried zone of the soul, and particularly into an absorbing journey to a strange land, a strange atmosphere, into a curiosity for all that was strange. A long process of roaming, seeking, changing followed, a distaste for fixity of any kind—a dislike for clumsy affirmation and negation: and at the same time a dietary and discipline which aimed at making it as easy as possible for the soul to fly high, and above all constantly to fly away. In fact a minimum of life, an unfettering from all coarser forms of sensuality, an independence in the midst of all marks of outward disfavour, together with the pride in being able to live in the midst of all this disfavour: a little cynicism perhaps, a little of the "tub of Diogenes," a good deal of whimsical happiness, whimsical gaiety, much calm, light, subtle folly, hidden enthusiasm—all this produced in the end a great spiritual strengthening, a growing joy and exuberance of health. Life itself rewards us for our tenacious will to life, for such a long war as I waged against the pessimistic weariness of life, even for every observant glance of our gratitude, glances that do not miss the smallest, most delicate, most fugitive gifts. . . . In the end we receive Life's great gifts, perhaps the greatest it can bestow—we regain *our* task.

6.

Should my experience—the history of an illness and a convalescence, for it resulted in a convalescence —be only my personal experience? and merely just my "Human, All-too-human"? To-day I would fain believe the reverse, for I am becoming more and more confident that my books of travel were not penned for my sole benefit, as appeared for a time to be the case. May I, after six years of growing assurance, send them once more on a journey for an experiment?—May I commend them particularly to the ears and hearts of those who are afflicted with some sort of a "past," and have enough intellect left to suffer even intellectually from their past? But above all would I commend them to you whose burden is heaviest, you choice spirits, most encompassed with perils, most intellectual, most courageous, who must be the *conscience* of the modern soul and as such be versed in its *science*:* in whom is concentrated all of disease, poison or danger that can exist to-day: whose lot decrees that you must be more sick than any individual because you are not "mere individuals": whose consolation it is to know and, ah! to walk the path to a new health, a health of to-morrow and the day after: you men of destiny, triumphant, conquerors of time, the healthiest and the strongest, you *good Europeans*!

7.

To express finally in a single formula my op-

---

* It has been attempted to render the play on "Gewissen" and "Wissen."—TR.

position to the romantic pessimism of the abstinent, the unfortunate, the conquered : there is a will to the tragic and to pessimism, which is a sign as much of the severity as of the strength of the intellect (taste, emotion, conscience). With this will in our hearts we do not fear, but we investigate ourselves the terrible and the problematical elements characteristic of all existence. Behind such a will stand courage and pride and the desire for a really great enemy. That was *my* pessimistic outlook from the first—a new outlook, methinks, an outlook that even at this day is new and strange? To this moment I hold to it firmly and (if it will be believed) not only *for* myself but occasionally *against* myself. . . . You would prefer to have that proved first ? Well, what else does all this long preface— prove ?

SILS-MARIA, UPPER ENGADINE,
        September, 1886.

HUMAN, ALL-TOO-HUMAN.

PART I.

MISCELLANEOUS MAXIMS AND OPINIONS.

1.

TO THE DISILLUSIONED IN PHILOSOPHY.—If you hitherto believed in the highest value of life and now find yourselves disillusioned, must you immediately get rid of life at the lowest possible price?

2.

OVERNICE.—One can even become overnice as regards the clearness of concepts. How disgusted one is then at having truck with the half-clear, the hazy, the aspiring, the doubting! How ridiculous and yet not mirth-provoking is their eternal fluttering and straining without ever being able to fly or to grasp!

3.

THE WOOERS OF REALITY.—He who realises at last how long and how thoroughly he has been befooled, embraces out of spite even the ugliest reality. So that in the long run of the world's history the best men have always been wooers of reality, for the best have always been longest and most thoroughly deceived.

4.

ADVANCE OF FREETHINKING.—The difference
between past and present freethinking cannot better
be characterised than by that aphorism for the recognition and expression of which all the fearlessness of
the eighteenth century was needed, and which even
then, if measured by our modern view, sinks into an
unconscious naïveté. I mean Voltaire's aphorism,
" croyez-moi, mon ami, l'erreur aussi a son mérite."

5.

A HEREDITARY SIN OF PHILOSOPHERS.—Philosophers have at all times appropriated and *corrupted*
the maxims of censors of men (moralists), by taking
them over without qualification and trying to prove
as necessary what the moralists only meant as a
rough indication or as a truth suited to their fellow-
countrymen or fellow-townsmen for a single decade.
Moreover, the philosophers thought that they were
thereby raising themselves above the moralists !
Thus it will be found that the celebrated teachings
of Schopenhauer as to the supremacy of the will
over the intellect, of the immutability of character,
the negativity of pleasure—all errors, in the sense
in which he understands them—rest upon principles
of popular wisdom enunciated by the moralists.
Take the very word "will," which Schopenhauer
twisted so as to become a common denotation of
several human conditions and with which he filled
a gap in the language (to his own great advantage,
in so far as he was a moralist, for he became free to

speak of the will as Pascal had spoken of it). In the hands of its creator, Schopenhauer's "will," through the philosophic craze for generalisation, already turned out to be a bane to knowledge. For this will was made into a poetic metaphor, when it was held that all things in nature possess will. Finally, that it might be applied to all kinds of disordered mysticism, the word was misused by a fraudulent convention. So now all our fashionable philosophers repeat it and seem to be perfectly certain that all things have a will and are in fact One Will. According to the description generally given of this All-One-Will, this is much as if one should positively try to have the stupid Devil for one's God.

6.

AGAINST VISIONARIES.—The visionary denies the truth to himself, the liar only to others.

7.

ENMITY TO LIGHT.—If we make it clear to any one that, strictly, he can never speak of truth, but only of probability and of its degrees, we generally discover, from the undisguised joy of our pupil, how greatly men prefer the uncertainty of their intellectual horizon, and how in their heart of hearts they hate truth because of its definiteness.—Is this due to a secret fear felt by all that the light of truth may at some time be turned too brightly upon themselves? To their wish to be of some consequence, and accordingly their concealment from the world of what they are?   Or is it to be traced to their horror of the all-too brilliant light, to which their crepuscular, easily dazzled, bat-like souls are not accustomed, so that hate it they must?

8.

CHRISTIAN SCEPTICISM.—Pilate, with his question, " What is Truth ? " is now gleefully brought on the scene as an advocate of Christ, in order to cast suspicion on all that is known or knowable as being mere appearance, and to erect the Cross on the appalling background of the Impossibility of Knowledge.

9.

" NATURAL LAW," A PHRASE OF SUPERSTITION. —When you talk so delightedly of Nature acting according to law, you must either assume that all things in Nature follow their law from a voluntary obedience imposed by themselves—in which case you admire the morality of Nature : or you are enchanted with the idea of a creative mechanician, who has made a most cunning watch with human beings as accessory ornaments.—Necessity, through the expression, " conformity to law," then becomes more human and a coign of refuge in the last instance for mythological reveries.

10.

FALLEN FORFEIT TO HISTORY.—All misty philosophers and obscurers of the world, in other words all metaphysicians of coarse or refined texture are seized with eyeache, earache, and toothache when they begin to suspect that there is truth in the saying : " All philosophy has from now fallen forfeit to history." In view of their aches and pains we may pardon them for throwing stones and filth at him who talks like this, but this teaching may itself thereby become dirty and disreputable for a time and lose in effect.

II.

THE PESSIMIST OF THE INTELLECT.—He whose intellect is really free will think freely about the intellect itself, and will not shut his eyes to certain terrible aspects of its source and tendency. For this reason others will perhaps designate him the bitterest opponent of free thought and give him that dreadful, abusive name of "pessimist of the intellect" : accustomed as they are to typify a man not by his strong point, his pre-eminent virtue, but by the quality that is most foreign to his nature.

12.

THE METAPHYSICIANS' KNAPSACK. — To all who talk so boastfully of the scientific basis of their metaphysics it is best to make no reply. It is enough to tug at the bundle that they rather shyly keep hidden behind their backs. If one succeeds in lifting it, the results of that "scientific basis" come to light, to their great confusion : a dear little "God," a genteel immortality, perhaps a little spiritualism, and in any case

a complicated mass of poor-sinners'-misery and
pharisee-arrogance.

13.

OCCASIONAL HARMFULNESS OF KNOWLEDGE.—
The utility involved in the unchecked investigation of
knowledge is so constantly proved in a hundred
different ways that one must remember to include in
the bargain the subtler and rarer damage which
individuals must suffer on that account. The chemist
cannot avoid occasionally being poisoned or burnt
at his experiments. What applies to the chemist,
is true of the whole of our culture. This, it may be
added, clearly shows that knowledge should provide
itself with healing balsam against burns and should
always have antidotes ready against poisons.

14.

THE CRAVING OF THE PHILISTINE.—The Philistine thinks that his most urgent need is a purple
patch or turban of metaphysics, nor will he let it
slip. Yet he would look less ridiculous without
this adornment.

15.

ENTHUSIASTS.—With all that enthusiasts say in
favour of their gospel or their master they are defending themselves, however much they comport
themselves as the judges and not the accused:
because they are involuntarily reminded almost at
every moment that they are exceptions and have
to assert their legitimacy.

16.

THE GOOD SEDUCES TO LIFE.—All good things, even all good books that are written against life, are strong means of attraction to life.

17.

THE HAPPINESS OF THE HISTORIAN.—"When we hear the hair-splitting metaphysicians and prophets of the after-world speak, we others feel indeed that we are the 'poor in spirit,' but that ours is the heavenly kingdom of change, with spring and autumn, summer and winter, and theirs the after-world, with its grey, everlasting frosts and shadows." Thus soliloquised a man as he walked in the morning sunshine, a man who in his pursuit of history has constantly changed not only his mind but his heart. In contrast to the metaphysicians, he is happy to harbour in himself not an "immortal soul" but many *mortal* souls.

18.

THREE VARIETIES OF THINKERS.—There are streaming, flowing, trickling mineral springs, and three corresponding varieties of thinkers. The layman values them by the volume of the water, the expert by the contents of the water—in other words, by the elements in them that are not water.

19.

THE PICTURE OF LIFE.—The task of painting the picture of life, often as it has been attempted by poets and philosophers, is nevertheless irrational. Even in the hands of the greatest artist-thinkers, pictures and miniatures of one life only—their own —have come into being, and indeed no other result is possible. While in the process of developing, a thing that develops, cannot mirror itself as fixed and permanent, as a *definite object.*

20.

TRUTH WILL HAVE NO GODS BEFORE IT.—The belief in truth begins with the doubt of all truths in which one has previously believed.

21.

WHERE SILENCE IS REQUIRED.—If we speak of freethinking as of a highly dangerous journey over glaciers and frozen seas, we find that those who do not care to travel on this track are offended, as if they had been reproached with cowardice and weak knees. The difficult, which we find to be beyond our powers, must not even be mentioned in our presence.

22.

HISTORIA IN NUCE.—The most serious parody I ever heard was this: "In the beginning was the nonsense, and the nonsense was with God, and the nonsense was God." *

---

* Cf. John i. 1.—TR.

23.

INCURABLE.—The idealist is incorrigible: if he be thrown out of his Heaven, he makes himself a suitable ideal out of Hell. Disillusion him, and lo! he will embrace disillusionment with no less ardour than he recently embraced hope. In so far as his impulse belongs to the great incurable impulses of human nature, he can bring about tragic destinies and later become a subject for tragedy himself, for such tragedies as deal with the incurable, implacable, inevitable in the lot and character of man.

24.

APPLAUSE ITSELF AS THE CONTINUATION OF THE PLAY.—Sparkling eyes and an amiable smile are the tributes of applause paid to all the great comedy of world and existence—but this applause is a comedy within a comedy, meant to tempt the other spectators to a *plaudite amici.*

25.

COURAGE FOR TEDIUM.—He who has not the courage to allow himself and his work to be considered tedious, is certainly no intellect of the first rank, whether in the arts or in the sciences.—A scoffer, who happened for once in a way to be a thinker, might add, with a glance at the world and at history: "God did not possess this courage, for he wanted to make and he made all things so interesting."

26.

FROM THE MOST INTIMATE EXPERIENCE OF THE THINKER.—Nothing is harder for a man than to conceive of an object impersonally, I mean to see in it an object and not a person. One may even ask whether it is possible for him to dispense for a single moment with the machinery of his instinct to create and construct a personality. After all, he associates with his thoughts, however abstract they may be, as with individuals, against whom he must fight or to whom he must attach himself, whom he must protect, support and nourish. Let us watch or listen to ourselves at the moment when we hear or discover a new idea. Perhaps it displeases us because it is so defiant and so autocratic, and we unconsciously ask ourselves whether we cannot place a contradiction of it by its side as an enemy, or fasten on to it a " perhaps " or a "sometimes": the mere little word "probably" gives us a feeling of satisfaction, for it shatters the oppressive tyranny of the unconditional. If, on the other hand, the new idea enters in gentle shape, sweetly patient and humble, and falling at once into the arms of contradiction, we put our autocracy to the test in another way. Can we not come to the aid of this weak creature, stroke it and feed it, give it strength and fulness, and truth and even unconditionality? Is it possible for us to show ourselves parental or chivalrous or compassionate towards our idea?—Then again, we see here a judgment and there a judgment, sundered from each other, never looking at or making any movement towards each other. So we are tickled by the thought, whether it be not here feasible to make a match, to draw a *conclusion*, with the anticipation that if a consequence follows this conclusion it is not only the two judgments united in wedlock but the matchmakers that will gain honour. If, however, we cannot acquire a hold upon that thought either on the path of defiance and ill-will or on that of good-will (if we hold it to be true)—then we submit to it and do homage to it as a leader and a prince, give it a chair of honour, and speak not of it without a flourish of trumpets: for we are bright in its brightness. Woe to him who tries to dim this brightness! Perhaps we ourselves one day grow suspicious of our idea. Then we, the indefatigable "king-makers" of the history of the intellect, cast it down from its throne and immediately exalt its adversary. Surely if this be considered and thought out a little further, no one will speak of an "absolute impulse to knowledge"!

Why, then, does man prefer the true to the untrue, in this secret combat with thought-personalities, in this generally clandestine match-making of thoughts, constitution-founding of thoughts, child-rearing of thoughts, nursing and almsgiving of thoughts? For the same reason that he practises honesty in intercourse with real persons : *now* from habit, heredity, and training, *originally* because the true, like the fair and the just, is more expedient and more reputable than the untrue. For in the realm of thought it is difficult to assume a power and glory that are built on error or on falsehood. The feeling that such an edifice might at some time collapse is

humiliating to the self-esteem of the architect—he is
ashamed of the fragility of the material, and, as he
considers himself more important than the rest of
the world, he would fain construct nothing that is
less durable than the rest of the world. In his longing for truth he embraces the belief in a personal
immortality, the most arrogant and defiant idea
that exists, closely allied as it is to the underlying thought, *pereat mundus, dum ego salvus sim!*
His work has become his "ego," he transforms
himself into the Imperishable with its universal
challenge. It is his immeasurable pride that will
only employ the best and hardest stones for the
work—truths,' or what he holds for such. Arrogance has always been justly called the "vice of
the sage"; yet without this vice, fruitful in impulses, Truth and her status on earth would be in
a parlous plight. In our propensity to fear our
thoughts, concepts and words, and yet to honour
ourselves in them, unconsciously to ascribe to
them the power of rewarding, despising, praising,
and blaming us, and so to associate with them as
with free intellectual personalities, as with independent powers, as with our equals—herein lie the
roots of the remarkable phenomenon which I have
called "intellectual conscience." Thus something
of the highest moral species has bloomed from a
black root.

27.

THE OBSCURANTISTS.—The essential feature of
the black art of obscurantism is not its intention
of clouding the brain, but its attempt to darken

the picture of the world and cloud our idea of existence. It often employs the method of thwarting all illumination of the intellect, but at times it uses the very opposite means, seeking by the highest refinement of the intellect to induce a satiety of the intellect's fruits. Hair-splitting metaphysicians, who pave the way for scepticism and by their excessive acumen provoke a distrust of acumen, are excellent instruments of the more subtle form of obscurantism.—Is it possible that even Kant may be applied to this purpose? Did he even *intend* something of the sort, for a time at least, to judge from his own notorious exposition : "to clear the way for belief by setting limitations to knowledge"?—Certainly he did not succeed, nor did his followers, on the wolf and fox tracks of this highly refined and dangerous form of obscurantism—the most dangerous of all, for the black art here appears in the garb of light.

28.

BY WHAT KIND OF PHILOSOPHY ART IS CORRUPTED.—When the mists of a metaphysical-mystical philosophy succeed in making all æsthetic phenomena *opaque*, it follows that these phenomena cannot be comparatively valued, inasmuch as each becomes individually inexplicable. But when once they cannot be compared for the sake of valuation, there arises an entire absence-of-criticism, a blind indulgence. From this source springs a continual diminution of the enjoyment of art (which is only distinguished from the crude satisfaction of a need

by the highest refinement of taste and appreciation).
The more taste diminishes, the more does the desire
for art change and revert to a vulgar hunger, which
the artist henceforth seeks to appease by ever coarser
fare.

29.

ON GETHSEMANE.—The most painful thing a
thinker can say to artists is: "Could ye not *watch*
with me one hour?"

30.

AT THE LOOM.—There are many (artists and
women, for instance) who work against the few
that take a pleasure in untying the knot of things
and unravelling their woof. The former always
want to weave the woof together again and en-
tangle it and so turn the conceived into the un-
conceived and if possible inconceivable. Whatever
the result may be, the woof and knot always look
rather untidy, because too many hands are working
and tugging at them.

31.

IN THE DESERT OF SCIENCE.—As the man of
science proceeds on his modest and toilsome
wanderings, which must often enough be journeys
in the desert, he is confronted with those brilliant
mirages known as "philosophic systems." With
magic powers of deception they show him that
the solution of all riddles and the most refreshing
draught of true water of life are close at hand. His
weary heart rejoices, and he well-nigh touches with

his lips the goal of all scientific endurance and hardship, so that almost unconsciously he presses forward. Other natures stand still, as if spellbound by the beautiful illusion : the desert swallows them up, they become lost to science. Other natures, again, that have often experienced these subjective consolations, become very disheartened and curse the salty taste which these mirages leave behind in the mouth and from which springs a raging thirst —without one's having come one step nearer to any sort of a spring.

32.

THE SO-CALLED "REAL REALITY."—When the poet depicts the various callings—such as those of the warrior, the silk-weaver, the sailor—he feigns to know all these things thoroughly, to be an expert. Even in the exposition of human actions and destinies he behaves as if he had been present at the spinning of the whole web of existence. In so far he is an impostor. He practises his frauds on pure ignoramuses, and that is why he succeeds. They praise him for his deep, genuine knowledge, and lead him finally into the delusion that he really knows as much as the individual experts and creators, yes, even as the great world-spinners themselves. In the end, the impostor becomes honest, and actually believes in his own sincerity. Emotional people say to his very face that he has the "higher" truth and sincerity—for they are weary of reality for the time being, and accept the poetic dream as a pleasant relaxation and a night's rest for head and heart. The visions of the dream

now appear to them of more value, because, as has
been said, they find them more beneficial, and mankind has always held that what is apparently of
more value is more true, more real. All that is
generally called reality, the poets, conscious of this
power, proceed with intention to disparage and to
distort into the uncertain, the illusory, the spurious,
the impure, the sinful, sorrowful, and deceitful. They
make use of all doubts about the limits of knowledge,
of all sceptical excesses, in order to spread over everything the rumpled veil of uncertainty. For they
desire that when this darkening process is complete
their wizardry and soul-magic may be accepted
without hesitation as the path to "true truth " and
" real reality."

33.

THE WISH TO BE JUST AND THE WISH TO BE
A JUDGE.—Schopenhauer, whose profound understanding of what is human and all-too-human and
original sense for facts was not a little impaired by
the bright leopard-skin of his metaphysic (the skin
must first be pulled off him if one wants to find the
real moralist genius beneath)—Schopenhauer makes
this admirable distinction, wherein he comes far
nearer the mark than he would himself dare to admit : " Insight into the stern necessity of human
actions is the boundary line that divides philosophic from other brains." He worked against that
wonderful insight of which he was sometimes
capable by the prejudice that he had in common
with the moral man (not the moralist), a prejudice
that he expresses quite guilelessly and devoutly as

follows : " The ultimate and true explanation of the inner being of the entirety of things must of necessity be closely connected with that about the ethical significance of human actions." This connection is not "necessary" at all: such a connection must rather be rejected by that principle of the stern necessity of human actions, that is, the unconditioned non-freedom and non-responsibility of the will. Philosophic brains will accordingly be distinguished from others by their disbelief in the metaphysical significance of morality. This must create between the two kinds of brain a gulf of a depth and un-bridgeableness of which the much-deplored gulf between "cultured" and "uncultured" scarcely gives a conception. It is true that many back doors, which the "philosophic brains," like Schopenhauer's own, have left for themselves, must be recognised as useless. None leads into the open, into the fresh air of the free will, but every door through which people had slipped hitherto showed behind it once more the gleaming brass wall of fate. For we are in a prison, and can only dream of freedom, not make ourselves free. That the recognition of this fact cannot be resisted much longer is shown by the despairing and incredible postures and grimaces of those who still press against it and continue their wrestling-bout with it. Their attitude at present is something like this: " So no one is responsible for his actions? And all is full of guilt and the consciousness of guilt? But some one *must* be the sinner. If it is no longer possible or permissible to accuse and sentence the individual, the one poor wave in the inevitable rough-and-tumble of the

waves of development—well, then, let this stormy
sea, this development itself, be the sinner.   Here is
free will : this totality can be accused and sentenced,
can atone and expiate.   *So let God be the sinner and
man his redeemer.*   Let the world's history be guilt,
expiation, and self-murder.   Let the evil-doer be his
own judge, the judge his own hangman."   This
Christianity strained to its limits—for what else is
it?—is the last thrust in the fencing-match between
the teaching of unconditioned morality and the
teaching of unconditioned non-freedom.   It would
be quite horrible if it were anything more than a
logical pose, a hideous grimace of the underlying
thought, perhaps the death-convulsion of the heart
that seeks a remedy in its despair, the heart to which
delirium whispers: " Behold, thou art the lamb
which taketh away the sin of God."   This error lies
not only in the feeling," I am responsible," but just as
much in the contradiction, " I am not responsible,
but some one must be."   That is simply not true.
Hence the philosopher must say, like Christ, " Judge
not," and the final distinction between the philosophic brains and the others would be that the
former wish to be just and the latter wish to be
judges.

34.

SACRIFICE.—You hold that sacrifice is the hall-
mark of moral action ?—Just consider whether in
every action that is done with deliberation, in the
best as in the worst, there be not a sacrifice.

35.

AGAINST THE "TRIERS OF THE REINS" OF MORALITY.—One must know the best and the worst that a man is capable of in theory and in practice before one can judge how strong his moral nature is and can be. But this is an experiment that one can never carry out.

36.

SERPENT'S TOOTH.—Whether we have a serpent's tooth or not we cannot know before some one has set his heel upon our necks. A wife or a mother could say : until some one has put his heel upon the neck of our darling, our child.—Our character is determined more by the absence of certain experiences than by the experiences we have undergone.

37.

DECEPTION IN LOVE.—We forget and purposely banish from our minds a good deal of our past. In other words, we wish our picture, that beams at us from the past, to belie us, to flatter our vanity— we are constantly engaged in this self-deception. And you who talk and boast so much of "self-oblivion in love," of the "absorption of the ego in the other person"—you hold that this is something different? So you break the mirror, throw yourselves into another personality that you admire, and enjoy the new portrait of your ego, though calling it by the other person's name—and this whole proceeding is not to be thought self-deception, self-seeking, you marvellous beings?—It seems to me that those who hide something of themselves from themselves, or hide their whole selves from themselves, are alike committing a theft from the treasury of knowledge.   It is clear, then, against what transgression the maxim "Know thyself" is a warning.

38.

TO THE DENIER OF HIS VANITY.—He who denies his own vanity usually possesses it in so brutal a form that he instinctively shuts his eyes to avoid the necessity of despising himself.

39.

WHY THE STUPID SO OFTEN BECOME MAL-IGNANT.—To those arguments of our adversary against which our head feels too weak our heart replies by throwing suspicion on the motives of his arguments.

40.

THE ART OF MORAL EXCEPTIONS.—An art that points out and glorifies the exceptional cases of morality—where the good becomes bad and the unjust just—should rarely be given a hearing : just as now and again we buy something from gipsies, with the fear that they are diverting to their own pockets much more than their mere profit from the purchase.

41.

ENJOYMENT AND NON-ENJOYMENT OF POISONS. —The only decisive argument that has always deterred men from drinking a poison is not that it is deadly, but that it has an unpleasant taste.

42.

THE WORLD WITHOUT CONSCIOUSNESS OF SIN. —If men only committed such deeds as do not give rise to a bad conscience, the human world would still look bad and rascally enough, but not so sickly and pitiable as at present.—Enough wicked men without conscience have existed at all times, and many good honest folk lack the feeling of pleasure in a good conscience.

43.

THE CONSCIENTIOUS.—It is more convenient to follow one's conscience than one's intelligence, for at every failure conscience finds an excuse and an encouragement in itself. That is why there are so many conscientious and so few intelligent people.

44.

OPPOSITE MEANS OF AVOIDING BITTERNESS.— One temperament finds it useful to be able to give vent to its disgust in words, being made sweeter by speech. Another reaches its full bitterness only by speaking out: it is more advisable for it to have to gulp down something—the restraint that men of this

stamp place upon themselves in the presence of
enemies and superiors improves their character and
prevents it from becoming too acrid and sour.

45.

NOT TO BE TOO DEJECTED.—To get bed-sores
is unpleasant, but no proof against the merits of the
cure that prescribes that you should take to your
bed.   Men who have long lived outside themselves,
and have at last devoted themselves to the inward
philosophic life, know that one can also get sores of
character and intellect.   This, again, is on the whole
no argument against the chosen way of life, but
necessitates a few small exceptions and apparent
relapses.

46.

THE HUMAN "THING IN ITSELF."—The most
vulnerable and yet most unconquerable of things
is human vanity : nay, through being wounded its
strength increases and can grow to giant propor-
tions.

47.

THE FARCE OF MANY INDUSTRIOUS PERSONS.
—By an excess of effort they win leisure for themselves, and then they can do nothing with it but
count the hours until the tale is ended.

48.

THE POSSESSION OF JOY ABOUNDING.—He that
has joy abounding must be a good man, but perhaps

he is not the cleverest of men, although he has reached the very goal towards which the cleverest man is striving with all his cleverness.

49.

IN THE MIRROR OF NATURE.—Is not a man fairly well described, when we are told that he likes to walk between tall fields of golden corn: that he prefers the forest and flower colours of sere and chilly autumn to all others, because they point to something more beautiful than Nature has ever attained: that he feels as much at home under big broad‑leaved walnut trees as among his nearest kinsfolk: that in the mountains his greatest joy is to come across those tiny distant lakes from which the very eyes of solitude seem to peer at him: that he loves that grey calm of the misty twilight that steals along the windows on autumn and early winter evenings and shuts out all soulless sounds as with velvet curtains: that in unhewn stones he recognises the last remaining traces of the primeval age, eager for speech, and honours them from childhood up‑wards: that, lastly, the sea with its shifting serpent skin and wild‑beast beauty is, and remains to him, unfamiliar?—Yes, something of the man is described herewith, but the mirror of Nature does not say that the same man, with (and not even "in spite of") all his idyllic sensibilities, might be disagreeable, stingy, and conceited. Horace, who was a good judge of such matters, in his famous *beatus ille qui procul negotiis* puts the tenderest feeling for country life into the mouth of a Roman money-lender.

50.

POWER WITHOUT VICTORY.—The strongest cognition (that of the complete non-freedom of the human will) is yet the poorest in results, for it has always had the mightiest of opponents—human vanity.

51.

PLEASURE AND ERROR.—A beneficial influence on friends is exerted by one man unconsciously, through his nature ; by another consciously, through isolated actions. Although the former nature is held to be the higher, the latter alone is allied to good conscience and pleasure—the pleasure in justification by good works, which rests upon a belief in the volitional character of our good and evil doing —that is to say, upon a mistake.

52.

THE FOLLY OF COMMITTING INJUSTICE.—The injustice we have inflicted ourselves is far harder to bear than the injustice inflicted upon us by others (not always from moral grounds, be it observed). After all, the doer is always the sufferer—that is, if he be capable of feeling the sting of conscience or of perceiving that by his action he has armed society against himself and cut himself off. For this reason we should beware still more of doing than of suffering injustice, for the sake of our own inward happiness—so as not to lose our feeling of well-being—quite apart from any consideration of the precepts of religion and morality. For in suffering injustice we have the consolation of a good conscience, of hope and of revenge, together with the sympathy and applause of the just, nay of the whole of society, which is afraid of the evil-doer. Not a few are skilled in the impure self-deception that enables them to transform every injustice of their own into an injustice inflicted upon them from without, and to reserve for their own acts the exceptional right to the plea of self-defence. Their object, of course, is to make their own burden lighter.

53.

ENVY WITH OR WITHOUT A MOUTHPIECE.— Ordinary envy is wont to cackle when the envied hen has laid an egg, thereby relieving itself and becoming milder. But there is a yet deeper envy that in such a case becomes dead silent, desiring that every mouth should be sealed and always more and more angry because this desire is not gratified. Silent envy grows in silence.

54.

ANGER AS A SPY.—Anger exhausts the soul and brings its very dregs to light. Hence, if we know no other means of gaining certainty, we must understand how to arouse anger in our dependents and adversaries, in order to learn what is really done and thought to our detriment.

55.

DEFENCE MORALLY MORE DIFFICULT THAN ATTACK.—The true heroic deed and masterpiece of

the good man does not lie in attacking opinions and
continuing to love their propounders, but in the far
harder task of defending his own position without
causing or intending to cause bitter heartburns to
his opponent. The sword of attack is honest and
broad, the sword of defence usually runs out to a
needle point.

56.

HONEST TOWARDS HONESTY.—One who is
openly honest towards himself ends by being rather
conceited about this honesty. He knows only too
well why he is honest—for the same reason that
another man prefers outward show and hypocrisy.

57.

COALS OF FIRE.—The heaping of coals of fire on
another's head is generally misunderstood and falls
flat, because the other knows himself to be just as
much in the right, and on his side too has thought
of collecting coals.

58.

DANGEROUS BOOKS.—A man says: "Judging ·
from my own case, I find that this book is harmful."
Let him but wait, and perhaps one day he will confess that the book did him a great service by thrust-
ing forward and bringing to light the hidden disease
of his soul.—Altered opinions alter not at all (or
very little) the character of a man: but they illuminate individual facets of his personality, which
hitherto, in another constellation of opinions, had
remained dark and unrecognisable.

59.

SIMULATED PITY.—We simulate pity when we wish to show ourselves superior to the feeling of animosity, but generally in vain. This point is not noticed without a considerable enhancement of that feeling of animosity.

60.

OPEN CONTRADICTION OFTEN CONCILIATORY. —At the moment when a man openly makes known his difference of opinion from a well-known party leader, the whole world thinks that he must be angry with the latter. Sometimes, however, he is just on the point of ceasing to be angry with him. He ventures to put himself on the same plane as his opponent, and is free from the tortures of suppressed envy.

61.

SEEING OUR LIGHT SHINING.—In the darkest hour of depression, sickness, and guilt, we are still glad to see others taking a light from us and making use of us as of the disk of the moon. By this roundabout route we derive some light from our own illuminating faculty.

62.

FELLOWSHIP IN JOY.*—The snake that stings us means to hurt us and rejoices in so doing: the lowest animal can picture to itself the *pain* of others.

---

* The German word *Mitfreude*, coined by Nietzsche in opposition to *Mitleid* (sympathy), is untranslateable.—TR.

But to picture to oneself the *joy* of others and to rejoice thereat is the highest privilege of the highest animals, and again, amongst them, is the property only of the most select specimens—accordingly a rare "human thing." Hence there have been philosophers who denied fellowship in joy.

63.

SUPPLEMENTARY PREGNANCY.—Those who have arrived at works and deeds are in an obscure way, they know not how, all the more pregnant with them, as if to prove supplementarily that these are their children and not those of chance.

64.

HARD-HEARTED FROM VANITY.—Just as justice is so often a cloak for weakness, so men who are fairly intelligent, but weak, sometimes attempt dissimulation from ambitious motives and purposely show themselves unjust and hard, in order to leave behind them the impression of strength.

65.

HUMILIATION.—If in a large sack of profit we find a single grain of humiliation we still make a wry face even at our good luck.

66.

EXTREME HEROSTRATISM.*—There might be

---

* Herostratus of Ephesus (in 356 B.C.) set fire to the temple of Diana in order (as he confessed on the rack) to gain notoriety.—TR.

Herostratuses who set fire to their own temple, in which their images are honoured.

67.

A WORLD OF DIMINUTIVES.—The fact that all that is weak and in need of help appeals to the heart induces in us the habit of designating by diminutive and softening terms all that appeals to our hearts—and accordingly *making* such things weak and clinging to our imaginations.

68.

THE BAD CHARACTERISTIC OF SYMPATHY.— Sympathy has a peculiar impudence for its companion. For, wishing to help at all costs, sympathy is in no perplexity either as to the means of assistance or as to the nature and cause of the disease, and goes on courageously administering all its quack medicines to restore the health and reputation of the patient.

69.

IMPORTUNACY.—There is even an importunacy in relation to works, and the act of associating oneself from early youth on an intimate footing with the illustrious works of all times evinces an entire absence of shame.—Others are only importunate from ignorance, not knowing with whom they have to do—for instance classical scholars young and old in relation to the works of the Greeks.

70.

THE WILL IS ASHAMED OF THE INTELLECT.—
In all coolness we make reasonable plans against
our passions. But we make the most serious mistake in this connection in being often ashamed,
when the design has to be carried out, of the coolness and calculation with which we conceived it.
So we do just the unreasonable thing, from that
sort of defiant magnanimity that every passion involves.

71.

WHY THE SCEPTICS OFFEND MORALITY.—He
who takes his morality solemnly and seriously is
enraged against the sceptics in the domain of morals.
For where he lavishes all his force, he wishes others
to marvel but not to investigate and doubt. Then
there are natures whose last shred of morality is
just the belief in morals. They behave in the same
way towards sceptics, if possible still more passionately.

72.

SHYNESS.—All moralists are shy, because they
know they are confounded with spies and traitors,
so soon as their penchant is noticed. Besides, they
are generally conscious of being impotent in action,
for in the midst of work the motives of their activity
almost withdraw their attention from the work.

73.

A DANGER TO UNIVERSAL MORALITY.—People
who are at the same time noble and honest come

to deify every devilry that brings out their honesty, and to suspend for a time the balance of their moral judgment.

74.

THE SADDEST ERROR.—It is an unpardonable offence when one discovers that where one was convinced of being loved, one is only regarded as a household utensil and decoration, whereby the master of the house can find an outlet for his vanity before his guests.

75.

LOVE AND DUALITY.—What else is love but understanding and rejoicing that another lives, works, and feels in a different and opposite way to ourselves? That love may be able to bridge over the contrasts by joys, we must not remove or deny those contrasts. Even self-love presupposes an irreconcileable duality (or plurality) in one person.

76.

SIGNS FROM DREAMS.—What one sometimes does not know and feel accurately in waking hours —whether one has a good or a bad conscience as regards some person—is revealed completely and unambiguously by dreams.

77.

DEBAUCHERY.—Not joy but joylessness is the mother of debauchery.

78.

REWARD AND PUNISHMENT.—No one accuses without an underlying notion of punishment and revenge, even when he accuses his fate or himself. All complaint is accusation, all self-congratulation is praise. Whether we do one or the other, we always make some one responsible.

79.

DOUBLY UNJUST.—We sometimes advance truth by a twofold injustice : when we see and represent consecutively the two sides of a case which we are not in a position to see together, but in such a way that every time we mistake or deny the other side, fancying that what we see is the whole truth.

80.

MISTRUST.—Self-mistrust does not always proceed uncertainly and shyly, but sometimes in a furious rage, having worked itself into a frenzy in order not to tremble.

81,

PHILOSOPHY OF PARVENUS.—If you want to be a personality you must even hold your shadow in honour.

82.

KNOWING HOW TO WASH ONESELF CLEAN.— We must know how to emerge cleaner from unclean conditions, and, if necessary, how to wash ourselves even with dirty water.

83.

LETTING YOURSELF GO.—The more you let yourself go, the less others let you go.

84.

THE INNOCENT ROGUE.—There is a slow, gradual path to vice and rascality of every description. In the end, the traveller is quite abandoned by the insect-swarms of a bad conscience, and although a thorough scoundrel he walks in innocence.

85.

MAKING PLANS.—Making plans and conceiving projects involves many agreeable sentiments. He that had the strength to be nothing but a contriver of plans all his life would be a happy man. But one must occasionally have a rest from this activity by carrying a plan into execution, and then comes anger and sobriety.

86.

WHEREWITH WE SEE THE IDEAL.—Every efficient man is blocked by his efficiency and cannot look out freely from its prison. Had he not also a goodly share of imperfection, he could, by reason of his virtue, never arrive at an intellectual or moral freedom. Our shortcomings are the eyes with which we see the ideal.

87.

DISHONEST PRAISE.—Dishonest praise causes many more twinges of conscience than dishonest blame, probably only because we have exposed our capacity for judgment far more completely through excessive praise than through excessive and unjust blame.

88.

HOW ONE DIES IS INDIFFERENT.—The whole way in which a man thinks of death during the prime of his life and strength is very expressive and significant for what we call his character. But the hour of death itself, his behaviour on the death-bed, is almost indifferent. The exhaustion of waning life, especially when old people die, the irregular or insufficient nourishment of the brain during this last period, the occasionally violent pain, the novel and untried nature of the whole position, and only too often the ebb and flow of superstitious impressions and fears, as if dying were of much consequence and meant the crossing of bridges of the most terrible kind—all this forbids our using death as a testimony concerning the living. Nor is it true that the dying man is generally more honest than the living. On the contrary, through the solemn attitude of the bystanders, the repressed or flowing streams of tears and emotions, every one is inveigled into a comedy of vanity, now conscious, now unconscious. The serious way in which every dying man is treated must have been to many a poor despised devil the highest joy of his whole life and a sort of compensation and repayment for many privations.

89.

MORALITY AND ITS SACRIFICE.—The origin of morality may be traced to two ideas: " The community is of more value than the individual," and " The permanent interest is to be preferred to the temporary." The conclusion drawn is that the permanent interest of the community is unconditionally to be set above the temporary interest of the individual, especially his momentary well-being, but also his permanent interest and even the prolongation of his existence. Even if the individual suffers by an arrangement that suits the mass, even if he is depressed and ruined by it, morality must be maintained and the victim brought to the sacrifice. Such a trend of thought arises, however, only in those who are *not* the victims—for in the victim's case it enforces the claim that the individual might be worth more than the many, and that the present enjoyment, the " moment in paradise," * should perhaps be rated higher than a tame succession of untroubled or comfortable circumstances. But the philosophy of the sacrificial victim always finds voice too late, and so victory remains with morals and morality : which are really nothing more than the sentiment for the whole concept of morals under which one lives and has been reared—and reared not as an individual but as a member of the whole, as a cipher in a majority. Hence it constantly happens that the individual makes himself into a majority by means of his morality.

90.

THE GOOD AND THE GOOD CONSCIENCE.—You hold that all good things have at all times had a

* Quotation from Schiller, *Don Carlos*, i. 5.—TR.

good conscience? Science, which is certainly a
very good thing, has come into the world without
such a conscience and quite free from all pathos,
rather clandestinely, by roundabout ways, walking
with shrouded or masked face like a sinner, and
always with the feeling at least of being a smuggler.
Good conscience has bad conscience for its stepping-
stone, not for its opposite. For all that is good has
at one time been new and consequently strange,
against morals, immoral, and has gnawed like a
worm at the heart of the fortunate discoverer.

91.

SUCCESS SANCTIFIES THE INTENTIONS.—We
should not shrink from treading the road to a virtue,
even when we see clearly that nothing but egotism,
and accordingly utility, personal comfort, fear, considerations of health, reputation, or glory, are the
impelling motives. These motives are styled ignoble
and selfish. Very well, but if they stimulate us to
some virtue—for example, self-denial, dutifulness,
order, thrift, measure, and moderation—let us listen
to them, whatever their epithets may be! For if
we reach the goal to which they summon us, then
the virtue we have attained, by means of the pure
air it makes us breathe and the spiritual well-being
it communicates, ennobles the remoter impulses of
our action, and afterwards we no longer perform
those actions from the same coarse motives that
inspired us before.—Education should therefore force
the virtues on the pupil, as far as possible, according
to his disposition. Then virtue, the sunshine and

summer atmosphere of the soul, can contribute her own share of work and add mellowness and sweetness.

92.

DABBLERS IN CHRISTIANITY, NOT CHRISTIANS.—So that is your Christianity !—To annoy humanity you praise "God and His Saints," and again when you want to praise humanity you go so far that God and His Saints must be annoyed.—I wish you would at least learn Christian manners, as you are so deficient in the civility of the Christian heart.

93.

THE RELIGIOUS AND IRRELIGIOUS IMPRESSION OF NATURE.—A true believer must be to us an object of veneration, but the same holds good of a true, sincere, convinced unbeliever. With men of the latter stamp we are near to the high mountains where mighty rivers have their source, and with believers we are under vigorous, shady, restful trees.

94.

JUDICIAL MURDER.—The two greatest judicial murders * in the world's history are, to speak without exaggeration, concealed and well-concealed suicide. In both cases a man *willed* to die, and in both cases he let his breast be pierced by the sword in the hand of human injustice.

95.

"LOVE."—The finest artistic conception wherein Christianity had the advantage over other religious

---

* This, of course, refers to Jesus and Socrates.—TR.

systems lay in one word—Love. Hence it became
the *lyric* religion (whereas in its two other creations
Semitism bestowed heroico-epical religions upon
the world). In the word "love" there is so much
meaning, so much that stimulates and appeals to
memory and hope, that even the meanest intelligence and the coldest heart feel some glimmering
of its sense. The cleverest woman and the lowest
man think of the comparatively unselfish moments
of their whole life, even if with them Eros never
soared high : and the vast number of beings who
miss love from their parents or children or sweet-
hearts, especially those whose sexual instincts have
been refined away, have found their heart's desire
in Christianity.

96.

THE FULFILMENT OF CHRISTIANITY. — In
Christianity there is also an Epicurean trend of
thought, starting from the idea that God can only
demand of man, his creation and his image, what it
is possible for man to fulfil, and accordingly that
Christian virtue and perfection are attainable and
often attained. Now, for instance, the belief in loving
one's enemies—even if it is only a belief or fancy,
and by no means a psychological reality (a real
love)—gives unalloyed happiness, so long as it is
genuinely believed. (As to the reason of this,
psychologist and Christian might well differ.)
Hence earthly life, through the belief, I mean the
fancy, that it satisfies not only the injunction to
love our enemies, but all the other injunctions of
Christianity, and that it has really assimilated

and embodied in itself the Divine perfection according to the command, " Be perfect as your Father in heaven is perfect," might actually become a holy life. Thus error can make Christ's promise come true.

97.

OF THE FUTURE OF CHRISTIANITY.—We may be allowed to form a conjecture as to the disappearance of Christianity and as to the places where it will be the slowest to retreat, if we consider where and for what reasons Protestantism spread with such startling rapidity. As is well known, Protestantism promised to do far more cheaply all that the old Church did, without costly masses, pilgrimages, and priestly pomp and circumstance. It spread particularly among the Northern nations, which were not so deeply rooted as those of the South in the old Church's symbolism and love of ritual. In the South the more powerful pagan religion survived in Christianity, whereas in the North Christianity meant an opposition to and a break with the old-time creed, and hence was from the first more thoughtful and less sensual, but for that very reason, in times of peril, more fanatical and more obstinate. If from the standpoint of *thought* we succeed in uprooting Christianity, we can at once know the point where it will begin to disappear—the very point at which it will be most stubborn in defence. In other places it will bend but not break, lose its leaves but burst into leaf afresh, because the senses, and not thought, have gone over to its side. But it is the senses

that maintain the belief that with all its expensive
outlay the Church is more cheaply and conveniently
managed than under the stern conditions of work
and wages. Yet what does one hold leisure (or
semi-idleness) to be worth, when once one has become accustomed to it? The senses plead against
a dechristianised world, saying that there would
be too much work to do in it and an insufficient
supply of leisure. They take the part of magic—
that is, they let God work himself (*oremus nos, Deus
laboret*).

98.

THEATRICALITY AND HONESTY OF UN-
BELIEVERS.—There is no book that contains in
such abundance or expresses so faithfully all that
man occasionally finds salutary—ecstatic inward
happiness, ready for sacrifice or death in the belief
in and contemplation of *his* truth—as the book
that tells of Christ. From that book a clever man
may learn all the means whereby a book can be
made into a world-book, a vade-mecum for all, and
especially that master-means of representing everything as discovered, nothing as future and uncertain.
All influential books try to leave the same impression, as if the widest intellectual horizon were circumscribed here and as if about the sun that shines
here every constellation visible at present or in the
future must revolve.—Must not then all purely
scientific books be poor in influence on the same
grounds as such books are rich in influence? Is
not the book fated to live humble and among
humble folk, in order to be crucified in the end
and never resurrected? In relation to what the

religious inform us of their "knowledge" and their
"holy spirit," are not all upright men of science
"poor in spirit"?   Can any religion demand more
self-denial and draw the selfish out of themselves
more inexorably than science?—This and similar
things we may say, in any case with a certain
theatricality, when we have to defend ourselves
against believers, for it is impossible to conduct a
defence without a certain amount of theatricality.
But between ourselves our language must be more
honest, and we employ a freedom that those believers are not even allowed, in their own interests,
to understand.   Away, then, with the monastic
cowl of self-denial, with the appearance of humility!
Much more and much better—so rings our truth!
If science were not linked with the pleasure of
knowledge, the utility of the thing known, what
should we care for science?   If a little faith, love,
and hope did not lead our souls to knowledge,
what would attract us to science?   And if in science
the ego means nothing, still the inventive, happy
ego, every upright and industrious ego, means a
great deal in the republic of the men of science.
The homage of those who pay homage, the joy of
those whom we wish well or honour, in some cases
glory and a fair share of immortality, is the personal
reward for every suppression of personality: to say
nothing here of meaner views and rewards, although
it is just on this account that the majority have sworn
and always continue to swear fidelity to the laws of
the republic and of science.   If we had not remained
in some degree unscientific, what would science
matter to us?   Taking everything together and

speaking in plain language: "To a purely knowing
being knowledge would be indifferent."—Not the
quality but the quantity of faith and devoutness
distinguishes us from the pious, the believers.   We
are content with less.   But should one of them cry
out to us: "Be content and show yourselves contented!" we could easily answer: "As a matter
of fact, we do not belong to the most discontented
class. But you, if your faith makes you happy,
show yourselves to be happy. Your faces have
always done more harm to your faith than our
reasons!   If that glad message of your Bible were
written in your faces, you would not need to demand belief in the authority of that book in such
stiff-necked fashion. Your words, your actions
should continually make the Bible superfluous—in
fact, through you a new Bible should continually
come into being. As it is, your apologia for
Christianity is rooted in your unchristianity, and
with your defence you write your own condemna-
tion. If you, however, should wish to emerge from
your dissatisfaction with Christianity, you should
ponder over the experience of two thousand years,
which, clothed in the modest form of a question,
may be voiced as follows: "If Christ really intended to redeem the world, may he not be said
to have failed?"

99.

THE POET AS GUIDE TO THE FUTURE.—All
the surplus poetical force that still exists in modern
humanity, but is not used under our conditions of
life, should (without any deduction) be devoted to

a definite goal—not to depicting the present nor to reviving and summarising the past, but to pointing the way to the future. Nor should this be so done as if the poet, like an imaginative political economist, had to anticipate a more favourable national and social state of things and picture their realisation. Rather will he, just as the earlier poets portrayed the images of the Gods, portray the fair images of men. He will divine those cases where, in the midst of our modern world and reality (which will not be shirked or repudiated in the usual poetic fashion), a great, noble soul is still possible, where it may be embodied in harmonious, equable conditions, where it may become permanent, visible, and representative of a type, and so, by the stimulus to imitation and envy, help to create the future. The poems of such a poet would be distinguished by appearing secluded and protected from the heated atmosphere of the passions. The irremediable failure, the shattering of all the strings of the human instrument, the scornful laughter and gnashing of teeth, and all tragedy and comedy in the usual old sense, would appear by the side of this new art as mere archaic lumber, a blurring of the outlines of the world-picture. Strength, kindness, gentleness, purity, and an unsought, innate moderation in the personalities and their action: a levelled soil, giving rest and pleasure to the foot: a shining heaven mirrored in faces and events: science and art welded into a new unity: the mind living together with her sister, the soul, without arrogance or jealousy, and enticing from contrasts the grace of seriousness, not the impatience of discord—all this would be the general environment, the background on which the delicate differences of the embodied ideals would make the real picture, that of ever-growing human majesty.   Many roads to this poetry of the future start from Goethe, but the quest needs good pathfinders and above all a far greater strength than is possessed by modern poets, who unscrupulously represent the half-animal and the immaturity and intemperance that are mistaken by them for power and naturalness.

100.

THE MUSE AS PENTHESILEA.*—"Better to rot than to be a woman without charm."   When once the Muse thinks thus, the end of her art is again at hand.   But it can be a tragic and also a comic finale.

101.

THE CIRCUITOUS PATH TO THE BEAUTIFUL.— If the beautiful is to be identified with that which gives pleasure—and thus sang the Muses once— the useful is often the necessary circuitous path to the beautiful, and has a perfect right to spurn the short-sighted censure of men who live for the moment, who will not wait, and who think that they can reach all good things without ever taking a circuitous path.

102.

AN EXCUSE FOR MANY A TRANSGRESSION.—The ceaseless desire to create, the eternal looking out-

* Queen of the Amazons, slain by Achilles in the Trojan War.—TR.

ward of the artist, hinders him from becoming better and more beautiful as a personality : unless his craving for glory be great enough to compel him to exhibit in his relations with other men a growth corresponding to the growing beauty and greatness of his works. In any case he has but a limited measure of strength, and how could the proportion of strength that he spends on himself be of any benefit to his work—or *vice versa* ?

103.

SATISFYING THE BEST PEOPLE.—If we have satisfied the best people of our time with our art, it is a sign that we shall not satisfy the best people of the succeeding period. We have indeed " lived for all time," and the applause of the best people ensures our fame.*

104.

OF ONE SUBSTANCE.—If we are of one substance with a book or a work of art, we think in our heart of hearts that it must be excellent, and are offended if others find it ugly, over-spiced, or pretentious.

105.

SPEECH AND EMOTION.—That speech is not given to us to communicate our emotions may be seen from the fact that all simple men are ashamed to seek for words to express their deeper feelings. These

---

* From Schiller, *Wallenstein's Lager* : " Wer den Besten seiner Zeit genug gethan, der hat gelebt für alle Zeiten " (" He that has satisfied the best men of his time has lived for all time ").

feelings are expressed only in actions, and even here such men blush if others seem to divine their motives. After all, among poets, to whom God generally denies this shame, the more noble are more mono-syllabic in the language of emotion, and evince a certain constraint : whereas the real poets of emotion are for the most part shameless in practical life.

106.

A MISTAKE ABOUT A PRIVATION.—He that has not for a long time been completely weaned from an art, and is still always at home in it, has no idea how small a privation it is to live without that art.

107.

THREE-QUARTER STRENGTH.—A work that is meant to give an impression of health should be produced with three-quarters, at the most, of the strength of its creator. If he has gone to his farthest limit, the work excites the observer and disconcerts him by its tension. All good things have some-thing lazy about them and lie like cows in the meadow.

108.

REFUSING TO HAVE HUNGER AS A GUEST.—As refined fare serves a hungry man as well as and no better than coarser food, the more pretentious artist will not dream of inviting the hungry man to his meal.

109.

LIVING WITHOUT ART AND WINE.—It is with works of art as with wine—it is better if one can do without both and keep to water, and if from the inner fire and inner sweetness of the soul the water spontaneously changes again into wine.

110.

THE PIRATE-GENIUS.—The pirate-genius in art, who even knows how to deceive subtle minds, arises when some one unscrupulously and from youth upwards regards all good things, that are not protected by law, as the property of a particular person, as his legitimate spoil. Now all the good things of past ages and masters lie free around us, hedged about and protected by the reverential awe of the few who know them. To these few our robber-genius, by the force of his impudence, bids defiance and accumulates for himself a wealth that once more calls forth homage and awe.

111.

TO THE POETS OF GREAT TOWNS.—In the gardens of modern poetry it will clearly be observed that the sewers of great towns are too near. With the fragrance of flowers is mingled something that betrays abomination and putrescence. With pain I ask : " Must you poets always request wit and dirt to stand godfather, when an innocent and beautiful sensation has to be christened by you ? Are you obliged to dress your noble goddess in a hood of devilry and caricature ? But whence this necessity, this obligation ? " The reason is—because you live too near the sewers.

112.

OF THE SALT OF SPEECH.—No one has ever explained why the Greek writers, having at command such an unparalleled wealth and power of language, made so sparing a use of their resources that every post-classical Greek book appears by comparison crude, over-coloured, and extravagant. It is said that towards the North Polar ice and in the hottest countries salt is becoming less and less used, whereas on the other hand the dwellers on the plains and by the coast in the more temperate zones use salt in great abundance. Is it possible that the Greeks from a twofold reason—because their intellect was colder and clearer but their fundamental passionate nature far more tropical than ours—did not need salt and spice to the same extent that we do?

113.

THE FREEST WRITER.—In a book for free spirits one cannot avoid mention of Laurence Sterne, the man whom Goethe honoured as the freest spirit of his century. May he be satisfied with the honour of being called the freest writer of all times, in comparison with whom all others appear stiff, square-toed, intolerant, and downright boorish! In his case we should not speak of the clear and rounded but of "the endless melody"—if by this phrase we arrive at a name for an artistic style in which the definite form is continually broken, thrust aside and transferred to the realm of the indefinite, so that it signifies one and the other at the same time. Sterne is the great master of *double entendre*, this phrase being naturally used in a far wider sense than is commonly done when one applies it to sexual relations. We may give up for lost the reader who always wants to know exactly what Sterne thinks about a matter, and whether he be making a serious or a smiling face (for he can do both with one wrinkling of his features; he can be and even wishes to be right and wrong at the same moment, to interweave profundity and farce). His digressions are at once continuations and further developments of the story, his maxims contain a satire on all that is sententious, his dislike of seriousness is bound up with a disposition to take no matter merely externally and on the surface. So in the proper reader he arouses a feeling of uncertainty whether he be walking, lying, or standing, a feeling most closely akin to that of floating in the air. He, the most versatile of writers, communicates something of this versatility to his reader. Yes, Sterne unexpectedly changes the parts, and is often as much reader as author, his book being like a play within a play, a theatre audience before another theatre audience. We must surrender at discretion to the mood of Sterne, although we can always expect it to be gracious. It is strangely instructive to see how so great a writer as Diderot has affected this *double entendre* of Sterne's — to be equally ambiguous throughout is just the Sternian super-humour. Did Diderot imitate, admire, ridicule, or parody Sterne in his *Jacques le Fataliste*? One cannot be exactly certain, and this uncertainty was perhaps intended by the author. This very doubt makes the French unjust to the work of one of their first masters, one

who need not be ashamed of comparison with any
of the ancients or moderns. For humour (and
especially for this humorous attitude towards
humour itself) the French are too serious. Is it
necessary to add that of all great authors Sterne is
the worst model, in fact the inimitable author, and
that even Diderot had to pay for his daring? What
the worthy Frenchmen and before them some
Greeks and Romans aimed at and attained in prose
is the very opposite of what Sterne aims at and
attains. He raises himself as a masterly exception
above all that artists in writing demand of themselves—propriety, reserve, character, steadfastness
of purpose, comprehensiveness, perspicuity, good
deportment in gait and feature. Unfortunately
Sterne the man seems to have been only too closely
related to Sterne the writer. His squirrel-soul
sprang with insatiable unrest from branch to
branch; he knew what lies between sublimity and
rascality; he had sat on every seat, always with un-
abashed watery eyes and mobile play of feature.
He was—if language does not revolt from such a
combination—of a hard-hearted kindness, and in
the midst of the joys of a grotesque and even corrupt imagination he showed the bashful grace of
innocence. Such a carnal and spiritual hermaphro-
ditism, such untrammelled wit penetrating into
every vein and muscle, was perhaps never possessed
by any other man.

114.

A CHOICE REALITY.—Just as the good prose
writer only takes words that belong to the language
of daily intercourse, though not by a long way all

its words—whence arises a choice style—so the good poet of the future will only represent the real and turn his eyes away from all fantastic, superstitious, half-voiced, forgotten stories, to which earlier poets devoted their powers.   Only reality, though by a long way not every reality—but a choice reality.

115.

DEGENERATE SPECIES OF ART.—Side by side with the genuine species of art, those of great repose and great movement, there are degenerate species —weary, blasé art and excited art.   Both would have their weakness taken for strength and wish to be confounded with the genuine species.

116.

A HERO IMPOSSIBLE FROM LACK OF COLOUR.— The typical poets and artists of our age like to compose their pictures upon a background of shimmering red, green, grey, and gold, on the background of nervous sensuality—a condition well understood by the children of this century.   The drawback comes when we do *not* look at these pictures with the eyes of our century.   Then we see that the great figures painted by these artists have something flickering, tremulous, and dizzy about them, and accordingly we do not ascribe to them heroic deeds, but at best mock-heroic, swaggering *mis*deeds.

117.

OVERLADEN STYLE.—The overladen style is a consequence of the impoverishment of the organis-

ing force together with a lavish stock of expedients
and intentions.   At the beginnings of art the very
reverse conditions sometimes appear.

118.

PULCHRUM EST PAUCORUM HOMINUM.—History
and experience tell us that the significant grotesque-
ness that mysteriously excites the imagination and
carries one beyond everyday reality, is older and
grows more luxuriantly than the beautiful and reverence for the beautiful in art: and that it begins
to flourish exceedingly when the sense for beauty
is on the wane.   For the vast majority of mankind
this grotesque seems to be a higher need than the
beautiful, presumably because it contains a coarser
narcotic.

119.

ORIGINS OF TASTE IN WORKS OF ART.—If we
consider the primary germs of the artistic sense, and
ask ourselves what are the various kinds of joy
produced by the firstlings of art—as, for example,
among savage tribes—we find first of all the joy
of understanding what another means.   Art in this
case is a sort of conundrum, which causes its solver
pleasure in his own quick and keen perceptions.—
Then the roughest works of art remind us of the
pleasant things we have actually experienced, and
so give joy—as, for example, when the artist alludes
to a chase, a victory, a wedding.—Again, the repre-
sentation may cause us to feel excited, touched, inflamed, as for instance in the glorification of revenge

and danger. Here the enjoyment lies in the excitement itself, in the victory over tedium.—The memory, too, of unpleasant things, so far as they have been overcome or make us appear interesting to the listener as subjects for art (as when the singer describes the mishaps of a daring seaman), can inspire great joy, the credit for which is given to art.—A more subtle variety is the joy that arises at the sight of all that is regular and symmetrical in lines, points, and rhythms. For by a certain analogy is awakened the feeling for all that is orderly and regular in life, which one has to thank alone for all well-being. So in the cult of symmetry we unconsciously do homage to rule and proportion as the source of our previous happiness, and the joy in this case is a kind of hymn of thanksgiving. Only when a certain satiety of the last-mentioned joy arises does a more subtle feeling step in, that enjoyment might even lie in a violation of the symmetrical and regular. This feeling, for example, impels us to seek reason in apparent unreason, and the sort of æsthetic riddle-guessing that results is in a way the higher species of the first-named artistic joy.—He who pursues this speculation still further will know what kind of hypotheses for the explanation of æsthetic phenomena are hereby fundamentally rejected.

120.

NOT TOO NEAR.—It is a disadvantage for good thoughts when they follow too closely on one another, for they hide the view from each other.

That is why great artists and writers have made an abundant use of the mediocre.

121.

ROUGHNESS AND WEAKNESS.—Artists of all periods have made the discovery that in roughness lies a certain strength, and that not every one can be rough who wants to be : also that many varieties of weakness have a powerful effect on the emotions. From this source are derived many artistic substitutes, which not even the greatest and most conscientious artists can abstain from using.

122.

GOOD MEMORY.—Many a man fails to become a thinker for the sole reason that his memory is too good.

123.

AROUSING INSTEAD OF APPEASING HUNGER.— Great artists fancy that they have taken full possession of a soul. In reality, and often to their painful disappointment, that soul has only been made more capacious and insatiable, so that a dozen greater artists could plunge into its depths without filling it up.

124.

ARTISTS' ANXIETY.—The anxiety lest people may not believe that their figures are *alive* can mislead many artists of declining taste to portray these figures so that they appear as if mad. From the same anxiety, on the other hand, Greek artists of the earliest ages gave even dead and sorely wounded men that smile which they knew as the most vivid sign of life—careless of the actual forms bestowed by nature on life at its last gasp.

125.

THE CIRCLE MUST BE COMPLETED.—He who follows a philosophy or a genre of art to the end of its career and beyond, understands from inner experience why the masters and disciples who come after have so often turned, with a depreciatory gesture, into a new groove. The circle must be described—but the individual, even the greatest, sits firm on his point of the circumference, with an inexorable look of obstinacy, as if the circle ought never to be completed.

126.

THE OLDER ART AND THE SOUL OF THE PRESENT.—Since every art becomes more and more adapted to the expression of spiritual states, of the more lively, delicate, energetic, and passionate states, the later masters, spoilt by these means of expression, do not feel at their ease in the presence of the old-time works of art. They feel as if the ancients had merely been lacking in the means of making their souls speak clearly, also perhaps in some necessary technical preliminaries. They think that they must render some assistance in this quarter, for they believe in the similarity or even unity of all souls. In truth, however, measure, symmetry, a

contempt for graciousness and charm, an unconscious severity and morning chilliness, an evasion
of passion, as if passion meant the death of art—
such are the constituents of sentiment and morality
in all old masters, who selected and arranged their
means of expression not at random but in a necessary connection with their morality. Knowing this,
are we to deny those that come after the right to
animate the older works with their soul? No, for
these works can only survive through our giving
them our soul, and our blood alone enables them
to speak to *us*. The real "historic" discourse would
talk ghostly speech to ghosts. We honour the great
artists less by that barren timidity that allows every
word, every note to remain intact than by energetic
endeavours to aid them continually to a new life.—
True, if Beethoven were suddenly to come to life
and hear one of his works performed with that
modern animation and nervous refinement that bring
glory to our masters of execution, he would probably
be silent for a long while, uncertain whether he should
raise his hand to curse or to bless, but perhaps say
at last : " Well, well ! That is neither I nor not-I, but
a third thing—it seems to me, too, something right,
if not just *the* right thing. But you must know yourselves what to do, as in any case it is you who have
to listen. As our Schiller says, ' the living man is
right.' So have it your own way, and let me go
down again."

127.

AGAINST THE DISPARAGERS OF BREVITY.—A
brief dictum may be the fruit and harvest of long

reflection. The reader, however, who is a novice in this field and has never considered the case in point, sees something embryonic in all brief dicta, not without a reproachful hint to the author, requesting him not to serve up such raw and ill-prepared food.

128.

AGAINST THE SHORT-SIGHTED.—Do you think it is piece-work because it is (and must be) offered you in pieces?

129.

READERS OF APHORISMS.—The worst readers of aphorisms are the friends of the author, if they make a point of referring the general to the particular instance to which the aphorism owes its origin. This namby-pamby attitude brings all the author's trouble to naught, and instead of a philosophic lesson and a philosophic frame of mind, they deservedly gain nothing but the satisfaction of a vulgar curiosity.

130.

READERS' INSULTS.—The reader offers a two-fold insult to the author by praising his second book at the expense of his first (or *vice versa*) and by expecting the author to be grateful to him on that account.

131.

THE EXCITING ELEMENT IN THE HISTORY OF ART.—We fall into a state of terrible tension when we follow the history of an art—as, for example, that of Greek oratory—and, passing from master to master, observe their increasing precautions to obey the old and the new laws and all these self-imposed limitations. We see that the bow *must* snap, and that the so-called "loose" composition, with the wonderful means of expression smothered and concealed (in this particular case the florid style of Asianism), was once necessary and almost *beneficial.*

132.

TO THE GREAT IN ART.—That enthusiasm for some object which you, O great man, introduce into this world causes the intelligence of the many to be stunted. The knowledge of this fact spells humiliation. But the enthusiast wears his hump with pride and pleasure, and you have the consolation of feeling that you have increased the world's happiness.

133.

CONSCIENCELESS ÆSTHETES.—The real fanatics of an artistic school are perhaps those utterly inartistic natures that are not even grounded in the elements of artistic study and creation, but are impressed with the strongest of all the elementary influences of an art. For them there is no æsthetic conscience—hence nothing to hold them back from fanaticism.

134.

HOW THE SOUL SHOULD BE MOVED BY THE NEW MUSIC.—The artistic purpose followed by the new music, in what is now forcibly but none too lucidly termed " endless melody," can be understood by going into the sea, gradually losing one's firm tread on the bottom, and finally surrendering unconditionally to the fluid element. One has to *swim*. In the previous, older music one was forced, with delicate or stately or impassioned movement, to *dance*. The measure necessary for dancing, the observance of a distinct balance of time and force in the soul of the hearer, imposed a continual self-control. Through the counteraction of the cooler draught of air which came from this caution and the warmer breath of musical enthusiasm, that music exercised its spell.—Richard Wagner aimed at a different excitation of the soul, allied, as above said, to swimming and floating. This is perhaps the most essential of his innovations. His famous method, originating from this aim and adapted to it—the " endless melody "—strives to break and sometimes even to despise all mathematical equilibrium of time and force. He is only too rich in the invention of such effects, which sound to the old school like rhythmic paradoxes and blasphemies. He dreads petrifaction, crystallisation, the development of music into the architectural. He accordingly sets up a three-time rhythm in opposition to the double-time, not infrequently introduces five-time and seven-time, immediately repeats a phrase, but with a prolation, so that its time is again doubled and trebled. From an easy-going imitation of such art may arise a great danger to music, for by the side of the superabundance of rhythmic emotion demoralisation and decadence lurk in ambush. The danger will become very great if such music comes to associate itself more and more closely with a quite naturalistic art of acting and pantomime, trained and dominated by no higher plastic models ; an art that knows no measure in itself and can impart no measure to the kindred element, the all-too-womanish nature of music.

135.

POET AND REALITY.—The Muse of the poet who is not in love with reality will not be reality, and will bear him children with hollow eyes and all too tender bones.

136.

MEANS AND END.—In art the end does not justify the means, but holy means can justify the end.

137.

THE WORST READERS.—The worst readers are those who act like plundering soldiers. They take out some things that they might use, cover the rest with filth and confusion, and blaspheme about the whole.

138.

SIGNS OF A GOOD WRITER.—Good writers have two things in common: they prefer being understood to being admired, and they do not write for the critical and over-shrewd reader.

139.

THE MIXED SPECIES.—The mixed species in art bear witness to their authors' distrust of their own strength. They seek auxiliary powers, advocates, hiding-places—such is the case with the poet who calls in philosophy, the musician who calls in the drama, and the thinker who calls in rhetoric to his aid.

140.

SHUTTING ONE'S MOUTH.—When his book opens its mouth, the author must shut his.

141.

BADGES OF RANK.—All poets and men of letters who are in love with the superlative want to do more than they can.

142.

COLD BOOKS.—The deep thinker reckons on readers who feel with him the happiness that lies in deep thinking. Hence a book that looks cold and sober, if seen in the right light, may seem bathed in the sunshine of spiritual cheerfulness and become a genuine soul-comforter.

143.

A KNACK OF THE SLOW-WITTED.—The slow-witted thinker generally allies himself with loquacity and ceremoniousness. By the former he thinks he is gaining mobility and fluency, by the latter he gives his peculiarity the appearance of being a result of free will and artistic purpose, with a view to dignity, which needs slow movement.

144.

*LE STYLE BAROQUE.**—He who as thinker and writer is not born or trained to dialectic and the consecutive arrangement of ideas, will unconsciously turn to the rhetoric and dramatic forms. For, after all, his object is to make himself understood and to carry the day by force, and he is indifferent whether, as shepherd, he honestly guides to himself the hearts of his fellow-men, or, as robber, he captures them by surprise. This is true of the plastic arts as of music: where the feeling of insufficient dialectic or a deficiency in expression or narration, together with an urgent, over-powerful impulse to form, gives birth to that species of style known as "baroque." Only the ill-educated and the arrogant will at once find a depreciatory force in this word. The baroque style always arises at the time of decay of a great art, when the demands of art in classical expression have become too great. It is a natural phenomenon which will be observed with melancholy—for it is a forerunner of the night—but at the same time with admiration for its peculiar compensatory arts of expression and narration. To this style belongs already a choice of material and subjects of the highest dramatic tension, at which the heart trembles even when there is no art, because heaven and hell are all too near the emotions: then, the oratory of strong passion and gestures, of ugly sublimity, of great

---

* In German *Barockstil, i.e.* the degenerate post-Renaissance style in art and literature, which spread from Italy in the seventeenth century.—TR.

masses, in fact of absolute quantity *per se* (as is shown in Michael Angelo, the father or grandfather of the Italian baroque stylists): the lights of dusk, illumination and conflagration playing upon those strongly moulded forms: ever-new ventures in means and aims, strongly underscored by artists for artists, while the layman must fancy he sees an unconscious overflowing of all the horns of plenty of an original nature-art: all these characteristics that constitute the greatness of that style are neither possible nor permitted in the earlier ante-classical and classical periods of a branch of art. Such luxuries hang long on the tree like forbidden fruit. Just now, when music is passing into this last phase, we may learn to know the phenomenon of the baroque style in peculiar splendour, and, by comparison, find much that is instructive for earlier ages. For from Greek times onward there has often been a baroque style, in poetry, oratory, prose writing, sculpture, and, as is well known, in architecture. This style, though wanting in the highest nobility,—the nobility of an innocent, unconscious, triumphant perfection,—has nevertheless given pleasure to many of the best and most serious minds of their time. Hence, as aforesaid, it is presumptuous to depreciate it without reserve, however happy we may feel because our taste for it has not made us insensible to the purer and greater style.

145.

THE VALUE OF HONEST BOOKS.—Honest books make the reader honest, at least by exciting his hatred and aversion, which otherwise cunning cleverness knows so well how to conceal. Against a book, however, we let ourselves go, however restrained we máy be in our relations with men.

146.

HOW ART MAKES PARTISANS.—Individual fine passages, an exciting general tenor, a moving and absorbing finale—so much of a work of art is accessible even to most laymen. In an art period when it is desired to win over the great majority of the laymen to the side of the artists and to make a party perhaps for the very preservation of art, the creative artist will do well to offer nothing more than the above. Then he will not be a squanderer of his strength, in spheres where no one is grateful to him. For to perform the remaining functions, the imitation of Nature in her organic development and growth, would in that case be like sowing seeds in water.

147.

BECOMING GREAT TO THE DETRIMENT OF HISTORY.—Every later master who leads the taste of art-lovers into his channel unconsciously gives rise to a selection and revaluation of the older masters and their works. Whatever in them is conformable and akin to him, and anticipates and foreshadows him, appears henceforth as the only important element in them and their works—a fruit in which a great error usually lies hidden like a worm.

148.

HOW AN EPOCH BECOMES LURED TO ART.—If we teach people by all the enchantments of artists and thinkers to feel reverence for their defects, their intellectual poverty, their absurd infatuations and passions (as it is quite possible to do); if we show them only the lofty side of crime and folly, only the touching and appealing element in weakness and flabbiness and blind devotion (that too has often enough been done):—we have employed the means for inspiring even an unphilosophical and inartistic age with an ecstatic love of philosophy and art (especially of thinkers and artists as personalities) and, in the worst case, perhaps with the only means of defending the existence of such tender and fragile beings.

149.

CRITICISM AND JOY.—Criticism, one-sided and unjust as well as intelligent criticism, gives so much pleasure to him who exercises it that the world is indebted to every work and every action that inspires much criticism and many critics. For criticism draws after it a glittering train of joyousness, wit, self-admiration, pride, instruction, designs of improvement.—The God of joy created the bad and the mediocre for the same reason that he created the good.

150.

BEYOND HIS LIMITS.—When an artist wants to be more than an artist—for example, the moral awakener of his people—he at last falls in love, as a punishment, with a monster of moral substance. The Muse laughs, for, though a kind-hearted Goddess, she can also be malignant from jealousy. Milton and Klopstock are cases in point.

151.

A GLASS EYE.—The tendency of a talent towards moral subjects, characters, motives, towards the "beautiful soul" of the work of art, is often only a glass eye put on by the artist who lacks a beautiful soul. It may result, though rarely, that his eye finally becomes living Nature, if indeed it be Nature with a somewhat troubled look. But the ordinary result is that the whole world thinks it sees Nature where there is only cold glass.

152.

WRITING AND DESIRE FOR VICTORY.—Writing should always indicate a victory, indeed a conquest of oneself which must be communicated to others for their behoof. There are, however, dyspeptic authors who only write when they cannot digest something, or when something has remained stuck in their teeth. Through their anger they try unconsciously to disgust the reader too, and to exercise violence upon him—that is, they desire victory, but victory over others.

153.

A GOOD BOOK NEEDS TIME.—Every good book tastes bitter when it first comes out, for it has the defect of newness. Moreover, it suffers damage from its living author, if he is well known and much talked about. For all the world is accustomed to confuse the author with his work. Whatever of profundity, sweetness, and brilliance the work may contain must be developed as the years go by, under the care of growing, then old, and lastly traditional reverence. Many hours must pass, many a spider must have woven its web about the book. A book is made better by good readers and clearer by good opponents.

154.

EXTRAVAGANCE AS AN ARTISTIC MEANS.— Artists well understand the idea of using extravagance as an artistic means in order to convey an impression of wealth. This is one of those innocent wiles of soul-seduction that the artist must know, for in his world, which has only appearance in view, the means to appearance need not necessarily be genuine.

155.

THE HIDDEN BARREL-ORGAN.—Genius, by virtue of its more ample drapery, knows better than talent how to hide its barrel-organ. Yet after all ˙ it too can only play its seven old pieces over and over again.

156.

THE NAME ON THE TITLE-PAGE.—It is now a matter of custom and almost of duty for the author's name to appear on the book, and this is a main cause of the fact that books have so little influence. If they are good, they are worth more than the personalities of their authors, of which they are the quintessences. But as soon as the author makes himself known on the title-page, the quintessence, from the reader's point of view, becomes diluted with the personal, the most personal element, and the aim of the book is frustrated.   It is the ambition of the intellect no longer to appear individual.

157.

THE MOST CUTTING CRITICISM.—We make the most cutting criticism of a man or a book when we indicate his or its ideal.

158.

LITTLE OR NO LOVE.—Every good book is written for a particular reader and men of his stamp, and for that very reason is looked upon unfavourably by all other readers, by the vast majority.   Its reputation accordingly rests on a narrow basis and must be built up by degrees.—The mediocre and bad book is mediocre and bad because it seeks to please, and does please, a great number.

159.

MUSIC AND DISEASE.—The danger of the new music lies in the fact that it puts the cup of rapture and exaltation to the lips so invitingly, and with such a show of moral ecstasy, that even the noble and temperate man always drinks a drop too much. This minimum of intemperance, constantly repeated, can in the end bring about a deeper convulsion and destruction of mental health than any coarse excess could do.   Hence nothing remains but some day to fly from the grotto of the nymph, and through perils and billowy seas to forge one's way to the smoke of Ithaca and the embraces of a simpler and more human spouse.

160.

ADVANTAGE FOR OPPONENTS.—A book full of intellect communicates something thereof even to its opponents.

161.

YOUTH AND CRITICISM.—To criticise a book means, for the young, not to let oneself be touched by a single productive thought therefrom, and to protect one's skin with hands and feet. The youngster lives in opposition to all novelty that he cannot love in the lump, in a position of self-defence, and in this connection he commits, as often as he can, a superfluous sin.

162.

EFFECT OF QUANTITY.—The greatest paradox in the history of poetic art lies in this : that in all that constitutes the greatness of the old poets a man may be a barbarian, faulty and deformed from top to toe, and still remain the greatest of poets. This is the case with Shakespeare, who, as compared with Sophocles, is like a mine of immeasurable wealth in gold, lead, and rubble, whereas Sophocles is not merely gold, but gold in its noblest form, one that almost makes us forget the money-value of the metal. But quantity in its highest intensity has the same effect as quality. That is a good thing for Shakespeare.

163.

ALL BEGINNING IS DANGEROUS.—The Poet can choose whether to raise emotion from one grade to another, and so finally to exalt it to a great height —or to try a surprise attack, and from the start to pull the bell-rope with might and main.   Both processes have their danger—in the first case his hearer may run away from him through boredom, in the second through terror.

164.

IN FAVOUR OF CRITICS.—Insects sting, not from malice, but because they too want to live.   It is the same with our critics—they desire our blood, not our pain.

165.

SUCCESS OF APHORISMS.—The inexperienced, when an aphorism at once illuminates their minds with its naked truth, always think that it is old and well known.   They look askance at the author, as if he had wanted to steal the common property of all, whereas they enjoy highly spiced half-truths, and give the author to understand as much.   He knows how to appreciate the hint, and easily guesses thereby where he has succeeded and failed.

166.

THE DESIRE FOR VICTORY. — An artist who exceeds the limit of his strength in all that he undertakes will end by carrying the multitude along with him through the spectacle of violent wrestling that he affords.   Success is not always the accompaniment only of victory, but also of the desire for victory.

167.

SIBI SCRIBERE.—The sensible author writes for no other posterity than his own—that is, for his age—so as to be able even then to take pleasure in himself.

168.

PRAISE OF THE APHORISM.—A good aphorism is too hard for the tooth of time, and is not worn away by all the centuries, although it serves as food for every epoch.   Hence it is the greatest paradox in literature, the imperishable in the midst of change, the nourishment which always remains highly valued, as salt does, and never becomes stupid like salt.

169.

THE ART-NEED OF THE SECOND ORDER.—The people may have something of what can be called art-need, but it is small, and can be cheaply satisfied.   On the whole, the remnant of art (it must be honestly confessed) suffices for this need.   Let us consider, for example, the kind of melodies and songs in which the most vigorous, unspoiled, and true-hearted classes of the population find genuine delight; let us live among shepherds, cowherds, peasants, huntsmen, soldiers, and sailors, and give ourselves the answer.   And in the country town, just in the houses that are the homes of inherited civic virtue, is it not the worst music at present produced

that is loved and, one might say, cherished ? He who
speaks of deeper needs and unsatisfied yearnings
for art among the people, as it is, is a crank or an impostor. Be honest ! Only in exceptional men is there
now an art-need in the highest sense—because art
is once more on the down-grade, and human powers
and hopes are for the time being directed to other
matters.—Apart from this, outside the populace,
there exists indeed, in the higher and highest strata
of society, a broader and more comprehensive art-
need, but *of the second order.*   Here there is a sort
of artistic commune, which possibly means to be
sincere. But let us look at the elements ! They
are in general the more refined malcontents, who
attain no genuine pleasure in themselves; the cultured, who have not become free enough to dispense
with the consolations of religion, and yet do not
find its incense sufficiently fragrant; the half-aristo-
cratic, who are too weak to combat by a heroic
conversion or renunciation the one fundamental
error of their lives or the pernicious bent of their
characters ; the highly gifted, who think themselves
too dignified to be of service by modest activity,
and are too lazy for real, self-sacrificing work ; girls
who cannot create for themselves a satisfactory
sphere of duties ; women who have tied themselves
by a light-hearted or nefarious marriage, and know
that they are not tied securely enough ; scholars,
physicians, merchants, officials who specialised too
early and never gave their lives a free enough scope
—who do their work efficiently, it is true, but with a
worm gnawing at their hearts ; finally, all imperfect
artists—these are nowadays the true needers of art !

What do they really desire from art? Art is to drive away hours and moments of discomfort, boredom, half-bad conscience, and, if possible, transform the faults of their lives and characters into faults of world-destiny. Very different were the Greeks, who realised in their art the outflow and overflow of their own sense of well-being and health, and loved to see their perfection once more from a standpoint outside themselves. They were led to art by delight in themselves; our contemporaries—by disgust of themselves.

170.

THE GERMANS IN THE THEATRE.—The real theatrical talent of the Germans was Kotzebue. He and his Germans, those of higher as well as those of middle-class society, were necessarily associated, and his contemporaries should have said of him in all seriousness, "in him we live and move and have our being." Here was nothing—no constraint, pretence, or half-enjoyment : what he could and would do was understood. Yes, until now the honest theatrical success on the German stage has been in the hands of the shamefaced or unashamed heirs of Kotzebue's methods and influence—that is, as far as comedy still flourishes at all. The result is that much of the Germanism of that age, sometimes far off from the great towns, still survives. Good-natured ; incontinent in small pleasures; always ready for tears ; with the desire, in the theatre at any rate, to be able to get rid of their innate sobriety and strict attention to duty and exercise; a smiling, nay, a laughing indulgence; confusing goodness and sym-

pathy and welding them into one, as is the essential
characteristic of German sentimentality; exceedingly happy at a noble, magnanimous action; for
the rest, submissive towards superiors, envious of
each other, and yet in their heart of hearts thoroughly self-satisfied—such were they and such was
he.—The second dramatic talent was Schiller. He
discovered a class of hearers which had hitherto
never been taken into consideration: among the
callow German youth of both sexes. His poetry
responded to their higher, nobler, more violent if
more confused emotions, their delight in the jingle
of moral words (a delight that begins to disappear
when we reach the thirties). Thus he won for himself, by virtue of the passionateness and partisanship
of the young, a success which gradually reacted with
advantage upon those of riper years. Generally
speaking, Schiller rejuvenated the Germans. Goethe
stood and still stands above the Germans in every
respect. To them he will never belong. How could
a nation in well-being and well-wishing come up to
the intellectuality of Goethe? Beethoven composed
and Schopenhauer philosophised above the heads
of the Germans, and it was above their heads, in
the same way, that Goethe wrote his *Tasso*, his
Iphigenie. He was followed by a small company
of highly cultured persons, who were educated by
antiquity, life, and travel, and had grown out of
German ways of thought. He himself did not
wish it to be otherwise.—When the Romantics set
up their well-conceived Goethe cult; when their
amazing skill in appreciation was passed on to the
disciples of Hegel, the real educators of the Germans

of this century; when the awakening national ambition turned out advantageous to the fame of the
German poets ; when the real standard of the nation,
as to whether it could honestly find enjoyment in
anything, became inexorably subordinated to the
judgment of individuals and to that national ambition,—that is, when people began to enjoy by
compulsion,—then arose that false, spurious German
culture which was ashamed of Kotzebue; which
brought Sophocles, Calderon, and even the Second
Part of Goethe's *Faust* on the stage; and which,
on account of its foul tongue and congested stomach,
no longer knows now what it likes and what it finds
tedious.—Happy are those who have taste, even if
it be a bad taste !   Only by this characteristic can
one be wise as well as happy.   Hence the Greeks,
who were very refined in such matters, designated
the sage by a word that means " man of taste," and
called wisdom, artistic as well as scientific, " taste "
(*sophia*).

171.

MUSIC AS A LATE-COMER IN EVERY CULTURE.
—Among all the arts that are accustomed to grow
on a definite culture-soil and under definite social
and political conditions, music is the last plant to
come up, arising in the autumn and fading-season
of the culture to which it belongs.   At the same
time, the first signs and harbingers of a new spring
are usually already noticeable, and sometimes music,
like the language of a forgotten age, rings out into
a new, astonished world, and comes too late.   In the
art of the Dutch and Flemish musicians the soul

of the Christian middle ages at last found its fullest
tone: their sound-architecture is the posthumous
but legitimate and equal sister of Gothic.   Not until
Handel's music was heard the note of the best in
the soul of Luther and his kin, the great Judæo-
heroical impulse that created the whole Reformation movement.   Mozart first expressed in golden
melody the age of Louis XIV. and the art of Racine
and Claude Lorrain.   The eighteenth century—that
century of rhapsody, of broken ideals and transitory
happiness—only sang itself out in the music of Beethoven and Rossini.   A lover of sentimental similes
might say that all really important music was a
swan-song.—Music is, in fact, not a universal language
for all time, as is so often said in its praise, but re-
sponds exactly to a particular period and warmth
of emotion which involves a quite definite, individual
culture, determined by time and place, as its inner
law.   The music of Palestrina would be quite unintelligible to a Greek; and again, what would the
music of Rossini convey to Palestrina?—It may be
that our most modern German music, with all its pre-
eminence and desire of pre-eminence, will soon be
no longer understood.   For this music sprang from
a culture that is undergoing a rapid decay, from the
soil of that epoch of reaction and restoration in
which a certain Catholicism of feeling, as well as a
delight in all indigenous, national, primitive manners, burst into bloom and scattered a blended per-
fume over Europe.   These two emotional tendencies,
adopted in their greatest strength and carried to
their farthest limits, found final expression in the
music of Wagner.   Wagner's predilection for the old

native sagas, his free idealisation of their unfamiliar
gods and heroes,—who are really sovereign beasts
of prey with occasional fits of thoughtfulness, magnanimity, and boredom,—his re-animation of those
figures, to which he gave in addition the mediæval
Christian thirst for ecstatic sensuality and spiritual-
isation—all this Wagnerian give-and-take with regard to materials, souls, figures, and words—would
clearly express the spirit of his music, if it could not,
like all music, speak quite unambiguously of itself.
This spirit wages the last campaign of reaction
against the spirit of illumination which passed into
this century from the last, and also against the super-
national ideas of French revolutionary romanticism
and of English and American insipidity in the
reconstruction of state and society.—But is it not
evident that the spheres of thought and emotion
apparently suppressed by Wagner and his school
have long since acquired fresh strength, and that
his late musical protest against them generally rings
into ears that prefer to hear different and opposite
notes; so that one day that high and wonderful
art will suddenly become unintelligible and will be
covered by the spider's web of oblivion?—In considering this state of affairs we must not let ourselves be led astray by those transitory fluctuations
which arise like a reaction within a reaction, as a
temporary sinking of the mountainous wave in the
midst of the general upheaval. Thus, this decade of
national war, ultramontane martyrdom, and socialistic unrest may, in its remoter after-effect, even aid
the Wagnerian art to acquire a sudden halo, without guaranteeing that it " has a future " or that it

has *the* future.   It is in the very nature of music
that the fruits of its great culture-vintage should
lose their taste and wither earlier than the fruits of
the plastic arts or those that grow on the tree of
knowledge.   Among all the products of the human
artistic sense ideas are the most solid and lasting.

172.

THE POET NO LONGER A TEACHER.—Strange
as it may sound to our time, there were once poets
and artists whose soul was above the passions with
their delights and convulsions, and who therefore
took their pleasure in purer materials, worthier men,
more delicate complications and dénouements.   If
the artists of our day for the most part unfetter the
will, and so are under certain circumstances for that
very reason emancipators of life, those were tamers of
the will, enchanters of animals, creators of men.   In
fact, they moulded, re-moulded, and new-moulded
life, whereas the fame of poets of our day lies in
unharnessing, unchaining, and shattering.—The ancient Greeks demanded of the poet that he should
be the teacher of grown men.   How ashamed the
poet would be now if this demand were made of
him !   He is not even a good student of himself,
and so never himself becomes a good poem or a fine
picture.   Under the most favourable circumstances
he remains the shy, attractive ruin of a temple, but
at the same time a cavern of cravings, overgrown
like a ruin with flowers, nettles, and poisonous weeds,
inhabited and haunted by snakes, worms, spiders,
and birds ; an object for sad reflection as to why the
noblest and most precious must grow up at once

like a ruin, without the past and future of perfection.

173.

LOOKING FORWARD AND BACKWARD.—An art like that which streams out of Homer, Sophocles, Theocritus, Calderon, Racine, Goethe, as the superabundance of a wise and harmonious conduct of life —that is the true art, at which we grasp when we have ourselves become wiser and more harmonious. It is not that barbaric, if ever so delightful, outpouring of hot and highly coloured things from an undisciplined, chaotic soul, which is what we understood by "art" in our youth. It is obvious from the nature of the case that for certain periods of life an art of overstrain, excitement, antipathy to the orderly, monotonous, simple, logical, is an inevitable need, to which artists must respond, lest the soul of such periods should unburden itself in other ways, through all kinds of disorder and impropriety. Hence youths as they generally are, full, fermenting, tortured above all things by boredom, and women who lack work that fully occupies their soul, require that art of delightful disorder. All the more violently on that account are they inflamed with a desire for satisfaction without change, happiness without stupor and intoxication.

174.

AGAINST THE ART OF WORKS OF ART.—Art is above all and first of all meant to embellish life, to make us ourselves endurable and if possible agreeable in the eyes of others. With this task in view,

art moderates us and holds us in restraint, creates
forms of intercourse, binds over the uneducated to
laws of decency, cleanliness, politeness, well-timed
speech and silence. Hence art must conceal or
transfigure everything that is ugly—the painful,
terrible, and disgusting elements which in spite of
every effort will always break out afresh in accordance with the very origin of human nature. Art
has to perform this duty especially in regard to the
passions and spiritual agonies and anxieties, and to
cause the significant factor to shine through unavoidable or unconquerable ugliness. To this great, super-
great task the so-called art proper, that of works of
art, is a mere accessary. A man who feels within
himself a surplus of such powers of embellishment,
concealment, and transfiguration will finally seek
to unburden himself of this surplus in works of art.
The same holds good, under special circumstances,
of a whole nation.—But as a rule we nowadays begin
art at the end, hang on to its tail, and think that
works of art constitute art proper, and that life
should be improved and transformed by this means
—fools that we are! If we begin a dinner with
dessert, and try sweet after sweet, small wonder that
we ruin our digestions and even our appetites for
the good, hearty, nourishing meal to which art invites us!

175.

CONTINUED EXISTENCE OF ART.—Why, really,
does a creative art nowadays continue to exist? Because the majority who have hours of leisure (and
such an art is for them only) think that they cannot

fill up their time without music, theatres and picture-galleries, novels and poetry. Granted that one could keep them from this indulgence, either they would strive less eagerly for leisure, and the invidious sight of the rich would be less common (a great gain for the stability of society), or they would have leisure, but would learn to reflect on what can be learnt and unlearnt: on their work, for instance, their associations, the pleasure they could bestow. All the world, with the exception of the artist, would in both cases reap the advantage.—Certainly, there are many vigorous, sensible readers who could take objection to this. Still, it must be said on behalf of the coarse and malignant that the author himself is concerned with this protest, and that there is in his book much to be read that is not actually written down therein.

176.

THE MOUTHPIECE OF THE GODS.—The poet expresses the universal higher opinions of the nation, he is its mouthpiece and flute; but by virtue of metre and all other artistic means he so expresses them that the nation regards them as something quite new and wonderful, and believes in all seriousness that he is the mouthpiece of the Gods. Yes, under the clouds of creation the poet himself forgets whence he derives all his intellectual wisdom—from father and mother, from teachers and books of all kinds, from the street and particularly from the priest. He is deceived by his own art, and really believes, in a naïve period, that a God is speaking through him, that he is creating in a

state of religious inspiration.   As a matter of fact,
he is only saying what he has learnt, a medley of
popular wisdom and popular foolishness.   Hence,
so far as a poet is really *vox populi* he is held to be
vox dei.

177.

WHAT ALL ART WANTS TO DO AND CANNOT.—
The last and hardest task of the artist is the presentment of what remains the same, reposes in
itself, is lofty and simple and free from the bizarre.
Hence the noblest forms of moral perfection are
rejected as inartistic by weaker artists, because the
sight of these fruits is too painful for their ambition.
The fruit gleams at them from the topmost branches
of art, but they lack the ladder, the courage, the
grip to venture so high.   In himself a Phidias is
quite possible as a poet, but, if modern strength be
taken into consideration, almost solely in the sense
that to God nothing is impossible.   The desire for
a poetical Claude Lorrain is already an immodesty
at present, however earnestly one man's heart may
yearn for such a consummation.—The presentment
of the highest man, the most simple and at the same
time the most complete, has hitherto been beyond
the scope of all artists.   Perhaps, however, the
Greeks, in the ideal of Athene, saw farther than
any men did before or after their time.

178.

ART AND RESTORATION.—The retrograde movements in history, the so-called periods of restoration, which try to revive intellectual and social

conditions that existed before those immediately preceding,—and seem really to succeed in giving them a brief resurrection, — have the charm of sentimental recollection, ardent longing for what is almost lost, hasty embracing of a transitory happiness. It is on account of this strange trend towards seriousness that in such transient and almost dreamy periods art and poetry find a natural soil, just as the tenderest and rarest plants grow on mountain-slopes of steep declivity.—Thus many a good artist is unwittingly impelled to a "restoration" way of thinking in politics and society, for which, on his own account, he prepares a quiet little corner and garden. Here he collects about himself the human remains of the historical epoch that appeals to him, and plays his lyre to many who are dead, half-dead, and weary to death, perhaps with the above-mentioned result of a brief resurrection.

179.

HAPPINESS OF THE AGE.—In two respects our age is to be accounted happy. With respect to the *past*, we enjoy all cultures and their productions, and nurture ourselves on the noblest blood of all periods. We stand sufficiently near to the magic of the forces from whose womb these periods are born to be able in passing to submit to their spell with pleasure and terror; whereas earlier cultures could only enjoy themselves, and never looked beyond themselves, but were rather overarched by a bell of broader or narrower dome, through which indeed light streamed down to them, but which their gaze could not pierce. With respect to the *future*,

there opens out to us for the first time a mighty,
comprehensive vista of human and economic purposes engirdling the whole inhabited globe.   At
the same time, we feel conscious of a power ourselves to take this new task in hand without presumption, without requiring supernatural aids.   Yes,
whatever the result of our enterprise, however much
we may have overestimated our strength, at any
rate we need render account to no one but ourselves, and mankind can henceforth begin to do
with itself what it will.—There are, it is true,
peculiar human bees, who only know how to suck
the bitterest and worst elements from the chalice
of every flower.   It is true that all flowers contain
something that is not honey, but these bees may
be allowed to feel in their own way about the
happiness of our time, and continue to build up
their hive of discomfort.

180.

A VISION.—Hours of instruction and meditation
for adults, even the most mature, and such institutions visited without compulsion but in accordance
with the moral injunction of the whole community ;
the churches as the meeting-places most worthy and
rich in memories for the purpose ; at the same time
daily festivals in honour of the reason that is attained and attainable by man ; a newer and fuller
budding and blooming of the ideal of the teacher,
in which the clergyman, the artist and the physician,
the man of science and the sage are blended, and
their individual virtues should come to the fore as

a collective virtue in their teaching itself, in their discourses, in their method—this is my ever-recurring vision, of which I firmly believe that it has raised a corner of the veil of the future.

181.

EDUCATION A DISTORTION.—The extraordinary haphazardness of the whole system of education, which leads every adult to say nowadays that his sole educator was chance, and the weathercock-nature of educational methods and aims, may be explained as follows. The oldest and the newest culture-powers, as in a turbulent mass-meeting, would rather be heard than understood, and wish to prove at all costs by their outcries and clamourings that they still exist or already exist. The poor teachers and educators are first dazed by this senseless noise, then become silent and finally apathetic, allowing anything to be done to them just as they in their turn allow anything to be done to their pupils. They are not trained themselves, so how are they to train others? They are themselves no straight-growing, vigorous, succulent trees, and he who wishes to attach himself to them must wind and bend himself and finally become distorted and deformed as they.

182.

PHILOSOPHERS AND ARTISTS OF THE AGE.— Rhapsody and frigidity, burning desires and waning of the heart's glow—this wretched medley is to be found in the picture of the highest European society of the present day. There the artist thinks that he is achieving a great deal when through his art he lights the torch of the heart as well as the torch of desire. The philosopher has the same notion, when in the chilliness of his heart, which he has in common with his age, he cools hot desires in himself and his following by his world-denying judgments.

183.

NOT TO BE A SOLDIER OF CULTURE WITHOUT NECESSITY.—At last people are learning what it costs us so dear not to know in our youth—that we must first do superior actions and secondly seek the superior wherever and under whatever names it is to be found ; that we must at once go out of the way of all badness and mediocrity *without fighting it* ; and that even doubt as to the excellence of a thing (such as quickly arises in one of practised taste) should rank as an argument against it and a reason for completely avoiding it. We must not shrink from the danger of occasionally making a mistake and confounding the less accessible good with the bad and imperfect. Only he who can do nothing better should attack the world's evils as the soldier of culture. But those who should support culture and spread its teachings ruin themselves if they go about armed, and by precautions, nightwatches, and bad dreams turn the peace of their domestic and artistic life into sinister unrest.

184.

HOW NATURAL HISTORY SHOULD BE EX-POUNDED.—Natural history, like the history of the

war and victory of moral and intellectual forces
in the campaign against anxiety, self-delusion, laziness, superstition, folly, should be so expounded
that every reader or listener may be continually
aroused to strive after mental and physical health
and soundness, after the feeling of joy, and be
awakened to the desire to be the heir and continu-
ator of mankind, to an ever nobler adventurous impulse.   Hitherto natural history has not found its
true language, because the inventive and eloquent
artists—who are needed for this purpose—never
rid themselves of a secret mistrust of it, and above
all never wish to learn from it a thorough lesson.
Nevertheless it must be conceded to the English
that their scientific manuals for the lower strata
of the people have made admirable strides towards
that ideal.   But then such books are written by
their foremost men of learning, full, complete, and
inspiring natures, and not, as among us, by mediocre
investigators.

185.

GENIUS IN HUMANITY.—If genius, according to
Schopenhauer's observation, lies in the coherent
and vivid recollection of our own experience, a
striving towards genius in humanity collectively
might be deduced from the striving towards knowledge of the whole historic past—which is beginning to mark off the modern age more and more
as compared with earlier ages and has for the first
time broken down the barriers between nature and
spirit, men and animals, morality and physics.   A
perfectly conceived history would be cosmic self-
consciousness.

186.

THE CULT OF CULTURE.—On great minds is bestowed the terrifying all-too-human of their natures, their blindnesses, deformities, and extravagances, so that their more powerful, easily all-too-powerful influence may be continually held within bounds through the distrust aroused by such qualities. For the sum-total of all that humanity needs for its continued existence is so comprehensive, and demands powers so diverse and so numerous, that for every one-sided predilection, whether in science or politics or art or commerce, to which such natures would persuade us, mankind as a whole has to pay a heavy price. It has always been a great disaster to culture when human beings are worshipped. In this sense we may understand the precept of Mosaic law which forbids us to have any other gods but God.—Side by side with the cult of genius and violence we must always place, as its complement and remedy, the cult of culture. This cult can find an intelligent appreciation even for the material, the inferior, the mean, the misunderstood, the weak, the imperfect, the one-sided, the incomplete, the untrue, the apparent, even the wicked and horrible, and can grant them the concession that *all this is necessary*. For the continued harmony of all things human, attained by amazing toil and strokes of luck, and just as much the work of Cyclopes and ants as of geniuses, shall never be lost. How, indeed, could we dispense with that deep, universal, and often uncanny bass, without which, after all, melody cannot be melody?

187.

THE ANTIQUE WORLD AND PLEASURE.—The man of the antique world understood better how to rejoice, we understand better how to grieve less. They continually found new motives for feeling happy, for celebrating festivals, being inventive with all their wealth of shrewdness and reflection. We, on the other hand, concentrate our intellect rather on the solving of problems which have in view painlessness and the removal of sources of discomfort. With regard to suffering existence, the ancients sought to forget or in some way to convert the sensation into a pleasant one, thus trying to supply palliatives. We attack the causes of suffering, and on the whole prefer to use prophylactics.— Perhaps we are only building upon a foundation whereon a later age will once more set up the temple of joy.

188.

THE MUSES AS LIARS.—"We know how to tell many lies," so sang the Muses once, when they revealed themselves to Hesiod.—The conception of the artist as deceiver, once grasped, leads to important discoveries.

189.

HOW PARADOXICAL HOMER CAN BE.—Is there anything more desperate, more horrible, more incredible, shining over human destiny like a winter sun, than that idea of Homer's:

" So the decree of the Gods willed it, and doomed man to perish, that it might be a matter for song even to distant generations " ?

In other words, we suffer and perish so that poets may not lack material, and this is the dispensation of those very Gods of Homer who seem much concerned about the joyousness of generations to come, but very little about us men of the present. To think that such ideas should ever have entered the head of a Greek !

190.

SUPPLEMENTARY JUSTIFICATION OF EXISTENCE.—Many ideas have come into the world as errors and fancies but have turned out truths, because men have afterwards given them a genuine basis to rest upon.

191.

PRO AND CON NECESSARY.—He who has not realised that every great man must not only be encouraged but also, for the sake of the common welfare, opposed, is certainly still a great child—or himself a great man.

192.

INJUSTICE OF GENIUS.—Genius is most unjust towards geniuses, if they be contemporary. Either it thinks it has no need of them and considers them superfluous (for it can do without them), or their influence crosses the path of its electric current, in which case it even calls them pernicious.

193.

THE SADDEST DESTINY OF A PROPHET.—He has worked twenty years to convince his contemporaries, and succeeds at last, but in the meantime his adversaries have also succeeded—he is no longer convinced of himself.

194.

THREE THINKERS LIKE ONE SPIDER.—In every philosophical school three thinkers follow one another in this relation: the first produces from himself sap and seed, the second draws it out in threads and spins a cunning web, the third waits in this web for the victims who are caught in it—and tries to live upon this philosophy.

195.

FROM ASSOCIATION WITH AUTHORS.—It is as bad a habit to go about with an author grasping him by the nose as grasping him by the horn (and every author has his horn).

196.

A TEAM OF TWO.—Vagueness of thought and outbursts of sentimentality are as often wedded to the reckless desire to have one's own way by hook or by crook, to make oneself alone of any consequence, as a genuinely helpful, gracious, and kindly spirit is wedded to the impulse towards clearness and purity of thought and towards emotional moderation and self-restraint.

197.

BINDING AND SEPARATING FORCES.—Surely it is in the heads of men that there arises the force that binds them—an understanding of their common interest or the reverse; and in their hearts the force that separates them—a blind choosing and groping in love and hate, a devotion to one at the expense of all, and a consequent contempt for the common utility.

198.

MARKSMEN AND THINKERS.—There are curious marksmen who miss their mark, but leave the shooting-gallery with secret pride in the fact that their bullet at any rate flew very far (beyond the mark, it is true), or that it did not hit the mark but hit something else. There are thinkers of the same stamp.

199.

ATTACK FROM TWO SIDES.—We act as enemies towards an intellectual tendency or movement when we are superior to it and disapprove of its aim, or when its aim is too high and unrecognisable to our eye—in other words, when it is superior to us. So the same party may be attacked from two sides, from above and from below. Not infrequently the assailants, from common hatred, form an alliance which is more repulsive than all that they hate.

200.

ORIGINAL.—Original minds are distinguished not by being the first to see a new thing, but by seeing the old, well-known thing, which is seen and over-looked by every one, as something new. The first discoverer is usually that quite ordinary and un-intellectual visionary—chance.

201.

ERROR OF PHILOSOPHERS.—The philosopher believes that the value of his philosophy lies in the whole, in the structure. Posterity finds it in the stone with which he built and with which, from that time forth, men will build oftener and better—in other words, in the fact that the structure may be destroyed and yet have value as material.

202.

WIT.—Wit is the epitaph of an emotion.

203.

THE MOMENT BEFORE SOLUTION.—In science it occurs every day and every hour that a man, im-mediately before the solution, remains stuck, being convinced that his efforts have been entirely in vain —like one who, in untying a noose, hesitates at the moment when it is nearest to coming loose, because at that very moment it looks most like a knot. .

204.

AMONG THE VISIONARIES. — The thoughtful man, and he who is sure of his intelligence, may profitably consort with visionaries for a decade and abandon himself in their torrid zone to a moderate insanity. He will thus have travelled a good part of the road towards that cosmopolitánism of the intellect which can say without presumption, " Nothing intellectual is alien to me."

205.

KEEN AIR.—The best and healthiest element in science as amid the mountains is the keen air that plays about it.—Intellectual molly-coddles (such as artists) dread and abuse science on account of this atmosphere.

206.

WHY SAVANTS ARE NOBLER THAN ARTISTS. —Science requires nobler natures than does poetry; natures that are more simple, less ambitious, more restrained, calmer, that think less of posthumous fame and can bury themselves in studies which, in the eye of the many, scarcely seem worthy of such a sacrifice of personality. There is another loss of which they are conscious. The nature of their occupation, its continual exaction of the greatest sobriety, weakens their will; the fire is not kept up so vigorously as on the hearths of poetic minds. As such, they often lose their strength and prime earlier than artists do—and, as has been said, they are aware of their danger. Under all circumstances they seem less gifted because they shine less, and thus they will always be rated below their value.

207.

HOW FAR PIETY OBSCURES.—In later centuries the great man is credited with all the great qualities and virtues of his century. Thus all that is best is continually obscured by piety, which treats the picture as a sacred one, to be surrounded with all manner of votive offerings. In the end the picture is completely veiled and covered by the offerings, and thenceforth is more an object of faith than of contemplation.

208.

STANDING ON ONE'S HEAD.—If we make truth stand on its head, we generally fail to notice that our own head, too, is not in its right position.

209.

ORIGIN AND UTILITY OF FASHION.—The obvious satisfaction of the individual with his own form excites imitation and gradually creates the form of the many—that is, fashion. The many desire, and indeed attain, that same comforting satisfaction with their own form. Consider how many reasons every man has for anxiety and shy self-concealment, and how, on this account, three-fourths of his energy and goodwill is crippled and may become unproductive! So we must be very grateful to fashion for unfettering that three-fourths and communicating self-confidence and the power of cheerful compromise to those who feel themselves bound to each other by its law. Even foolish laws give freedom and calm of the spirit, so long as many persons have submitted to their sway.

210.

LOOSENERS OF TONGUES.—The value of many men and books rests solely on their faculty for compelling all to speak out the most hidden and intimate things. They are looseners of tongues and crowbars to open the most stubborn teeth. Many events and misdeeds which are apparently only sent as a curse to mankind possess this value and utility.

211.

INTELLECTUAL FREEDOM OF DOMICILE.*—Who of us could dare to call himself a "free spirit" if he could not render homage after his fashion, by taking on his own shoulders a portion of that burden of public dislike and abuse, to men to whom this name is attached as a reproach? We might as well call ourselves in all seriousness "spirits free of domicile" (*Freizügig*) (and without that arrogant or high-spirited defiance) because we feel the impulse to freedom (*Zug zur Freiheit*) as the strongest instinct of our minds and, in contrast to fixed and limited minds, practically see our ideal in an intellectual nomadism—to use a modest and almost depreciatory expression.

---

* The original word, *Freizügig*, means, in the modern German Empire, possessing the free right of migration, without pecuniary burdens or other restrictions, from one German state to another. The play on words in *Zug zur Freiheit* ("impulse to freedom") is untranslateable.—TR.

212.

YES, THE FAVOUR OF THE MUSES!—What Homer says on this point goes right to our heart, so true, so terrible is it:

" The Muse loved him with all her heart and gave him good and evil, for she took away his eyes and vouchsafed him sweet song."

This is an endless text for thinking men: she gives good and evil, that is *her* manner of loving with all her heart and soul! And each man will interpret specially for himself why we poets and thinkers have to give up our eyes in her service.*

213.

AGAINST THE CULTIVATION OF MUSIC.—The artistic training of the eye from childhood upwards by means of drawing, painting, landscape-sketching, figures, scenes, involves an estimable gain in life, making the eyesight keen, calm, and enduring in the observation of men and circumstances. No similar secondary advantage arises from the artistic cultivation of the ear, whence public schools will generally do well to give the art of the eye a preference over that of the ear.

214.

THE DISCOVERERS OF TRIVIALITIES.—Subtle minds, from which nothing is farther than trivialities, often discover a triviality after taking all manner of

---

* Nietzsche seems to allude to his own case, for he ultimately contracted a myopia which bordered on blindness. —TR.

circuitous routes and mountain paths, and, to the astonishment of the non-subtle, rejoice exceedingly.

215.

MORALS OF SAVANTS.—A regular and rapid advance in the sciences is only possible when the individual is compelled to be not so distrustful as to test every calculation and assertion of others, in fields which are remote from his own. A necessary condition, however, is that every man should have competitors in his own sphere, who are extremely distrustful and keep a sharp eye upon him. From this juxtaposition of "not too distrustful" and "extremely distrustful" arises sincerity in the republic of learning.

216.

REASONS FOR STERILITY.—There are highly gifted minds which are always sterile only because, from temperamental weakness, they are too impatient to wait for their pregnancy.

217

THE PERVERTED WORLD OF TEARS. — The manifold discomforts which the demands of higher culture cause to man finally pervert his nature to such an extent that he usually keeps himself stoical and unbending. Thus he has tears in reserve only for rare occasions of happiness, so that many must weep even at the enjoyment of painlessness—only when happy does his heart still beat.

218.

THE GREEKS AS INTERPRETERS.—When we speak of the Greeks we unwittingly speak of to-day and yesterday; their universally known history is a blank mirror, always reflecting something that is not in the mirror itself. We enjoy the freedom of speaking about them in order to have the right of being silent about others—so that these Greeks themselves may whisper something in the ear of the reflective reader. Thus the Greeks facilitate to modern men the communication of much that is debatable and hard to communicate.

219.

OF THE ACQUIRED CHARACTER OF THE GREEKS. —We are easily led astray by the renowned Greek clearness, transparency, simplicity, and order, by their crystal-like naturalness and crystal-like art, into believing that all these gifts were bestowed on the Greeks—for instance, that they could not but write well, as Lichtenberg expressed it on one occasion. Yet no statement could be more hasty and more untenable. The history of prose from Gorgias to Demosthenes shows a course of toiling and wrestling towards light from the obscure, overloaded, and tasteless, reminding one of the labour of heroes who had to construct the first roads through forest and bog. The dialogue of tragedy was the real achievement of the dramatist, owing to its uncommon clearness and precision, whereas the national tendency was to riot in symbolism and innuendo, a tendency expressly fostered by the great choral lyric.   Similarly it was the achievement of Homer to liberate the Greeks from Asiatic pomp and gloom, and to have attained the clearness of architecture in details great and small.   Nor was it by any means thought easy to say anything in a pure and illuminating style.   How else should we account for the great admiration for the epigram of Simonides, which shows itself so simple, with no gilded points or arabesques of wit, but says all that it has to say plainly and with the calm of the sun, not with the straining after effect of the lightning.   Since the struggle towards light from an almost native twilight is Greek, a thrill of jubilation runs through the people when they hear a laconic sentence, the language of elegy or the maxims of the Seven Wise Men.   Hence they were so fond of giving precepts in verse, a practice that we find objectionable.   This was the true Apolline task of the Hellenic spirit, with the aim of rising superior to the perils of metre and the obscurity which is otherwise characteristic of poetry. Simplicity, flexibility, and sobriety were wrestled for and not given by nature to this people.   The danger of a relapse into Asianism constantly hovered over the Greeks, and really overtook them from time to time like a murky, overflowing tide of mystical impulses, primitive savagery and darkness.   We see them plunge in; we see Europe, as it were, flooded, washed away—for Europe was very small then ; but they always emerge once more to the light, good swimmers and divers that they are, those fellow-countrymen of Odysseus.

220.

THE PAGAN CHARACTERISTIC.—Perhaps there is nothing more astonishing to the observer of the Greek world than to discover that the Greeks from time to time held festivals, as it were, for all their passions and evil tendencies alike, and in fact even established a kind of series of festivals, by order of the State, for their "all-too-human." This is the pagan characteristic of their world, which Christianity has never understood and never can understand, and has always combated and despised.—They accepted this all-too-human as unavoidable, and preferred, instead of railing at it, to give it a kind of secondary right by grafting it on to the usages of society and religion. All in man that has power they called divine, and wrote it on the walls of their heaven. They do not deny this natural instinct that expresses itself in evil characteristics, but regulate and limit it to definite cults and days, so as to turn those turbulent streams into as harmless a course as possible, after devising sufficient precautionary measures. That is the root of all the moral broad-mindedness of antiquity. To the wicked, the dubious, the backward, the animal element, as to the barbaric, pre-Hellenic and Asiatic, which still lived in the depths of Greek nature, they allowed a moderate outflow, and did not strive to destroy it utterly. The whole system was under the domain of the State, which was built up not on individuals or castes, but on common human qualities. In the structure of the State the Greeks show that wonderful sense for typical facts which later on enabled them to become investigators of Nature, historians, geographers, and philosophers. It was not a limited moral law of priests or castes, which had to decide about the constitution of the State and State worship, but the most comprehensive view of the reality of all that is human. Whence do the Greeks derive this freedom, this sense of reality? Perhaps from Homer and the poets who preceded him. For just those poets whose nature is generally not the most wise or just possess, in compensation, that delight in reality and activity of every kind, and prefer not to deny even evil. It suffices for them if evil moderates itself, does not kill or inwardly poison everything—in other words, they have similar ideas to those of the founders of Greek constitutions, and were their teachers and forerunners.

221.

EXCEPTIONAL GREEKS.—In Greece, deep, thorough, serious minds were the exception. The national instinct tended rather to regard the serious and thorough as a kind of grimace. To borrow forms from a foreign source, not to create but to transform into the fairest shapes—that is Greek. To imitate, not for utility but for artistic illusion, ever and anon to gain the mastery over forced seriousness, to arrange, beautify, simplify—that is the continual task from Homer to the Sophists of the third and fourth centuries of our era, who are all outward show, pompous speech, declamatory gestures, and address themselves to shallow souls that care only for appearance, sound, and effect. And now let us estimate the greatness of those exceptional Greeks, who created science! Whoever tells of them, tells the most heroic story of the human mind!

222.

SIMPLICITY NOT THE FIRST NOR THE LAST THING IN POINT OF TIME.—In the history of religious ideas many errors about development and false gradations are made in matters which in reality are not consecutive outgrowths but contemporary yet separate phenomena. In particular, simplicity has still far too much the reputation of being the oldest, the initial thing. Much that is human arises by subtraction and division, and not merely by doubling, addition, and unification.—For instance, men still believe in a gradual development of the idea of God from those unwieldy stones and blocks of wood up to the highest forms of anthropomorphism. Yet the fact is that so long as divinity was attributed to and felt in trees, logs of wood, stones, and beasts, people shrank from humanising their forms as from an act of godlessness. First of all, poets, apart from all considerations of cult and the ban of religious shame, have had to make the inner imagination of man accustomed and compliant to this notion. Wherever more pious periods and phases of thought gained the upper hand, this liberating influence of poets fell into the background, and sanctity remained, after as before, on the side of the monstrous, uncanny, quite peculiarly inhuman. And then, much of what the inner imagination ventures to picture to itself would exert a painful influence if externally and corporeally represented. The inner eye is far bolder and more shameless than the outer (whence the well-known difficulty and, to some extent, impossibility, of

working epic material into dramatic form). The
religious imagination for a long time entirely refuses
to believe in the identity of God with an image:
the image is meant to fix the *numen* of the Deity,
actually and specifically, although in a mysterious
and not altogether intelligible way. The oldest
image of the Gods is meant to shelter and at the
same time to hide* the God—to indicate him but not
to expose him to view. No Greek really looked upon
his Apollo as a pointed pillar of wood, his Eros as
a lump of stone. These were symbols, which were
intended to inspire dread of the manifestation of the
God. It was the same with those blocks of wood
out of which individual limbs, generally in excessive
number, were fashioned with the scantiest of carv-
ing—as, for instance, a Laconian Apollo with four
hands and four ears. In the incomplete, symbolical,
or excessive lies a terrible sanctity, which is meant
to prevent us from thinking of anything human or
similar to humanity. It is not an embryonic stage
of art in which such things are made—as if they
were not *able* to speak more plainly and portray
more sensibly in the age when such images were
honoured! Rather, men are afraid of just one thing
—direct speaking out. Just as the cella hides and
conceals in a mysterious twilight, yet not completely,
the holy of holies, the real *numen* of the Deity; just
as, again, the peripteric temple hides the cella, pro-
tecting it from indiscreet eyes as with a screen and
a veil, yet not completely—so it is with the image of
the Deity, and at the same time the concealment of

---

* The play on *bergen* (shelter) and *verbergen* (hide) is untranslateable.—TR.

the Deity.—Only when outside the cult, in the profane world of athletic contest, the joy in the victor had risen so high that the ripples thus started reacted upon the lake of religious emotion, was the statue of the victor set up before the temple. Then the pious pilgrim had to accustom his eye and his soul, whether he would or no, to the inevitable sight of human beauty and super-strength, so that the worship of men and Gods melted into each other from physical and spiritual contact. Then too for the first time the fear of really humanising the figures of the Gods is lost, and the mighty arena for great plastic art is opened—even now with the limitation that wherever there is to be adoration the primitive form and ugliness are carefully preserved and copied. But the Hellene, as he dedicates and makes offerings, may now with religious sanction indulge in his delight in making God become a man.

223.

WHITHER WE MUST TRAVEL.—Immediate self-observation is not enough, by a long way, to enable us to learn to know ourselves. We need history, for the past continues to flow through us in a hundred channels. We ourselves are, after all, nothing but our own sensation at every moment of this continued flow. Even here, when we wish to step down into the stream of our apparently most peculiar and personal development, Heraclitus' aphorism, "You cannot step twice into the same river," holds good.— This is a piece of wisdom which has, indeed, gradually become trite, but nevertheless has remained as

strong and true as it ever was.   It is the same with
the saying that, in order to understand history, we
must scrutinise the living remains of historical
periods ; that we must travel, as old Herodotus travelled, to other nations, especially to those so-called
savage or half-savage races in regions where man
has doffed or not yet donned European garb.   For
they are ancient and firmly established steps of
culture on which we can stand.   There is, however,
a more subtle art and aim in travelling, which does
not always necessitate our passing from place to
place and going thousands of miles away.   Very
probably the last three centuries, in all their colourings and refractions of culture, survive even in our
vicinity, only they have to be discovered.   In some
families, or even in individuals, the strata are still
superimposed on each other, beautifully and per-
ceptibly ; in other places there are dispersions and
displacements of the structure which are harder to
understand.   Certainly in remote districts, in less
known mountain valleys, circumscribed communities have been able more easily to maintain an admirable pattern of a far older sentiment, a pattern
that must here be investigated.   On the other hand,
it is improbable that such discoveries will be made
in Berlin, where man comes into the world washed-
out and sapless.   He who after long practice of this
art of travel has become a hundred-eyed Argus will
accompany his Io—I mean his ego—everywhere, and
in Egypt and Greece, Byzantium and Rome, France
and Germany, in the age of wandering or settled
races, in Renaissance or Reformation, at home and
abroad, in sea, forest, plant, and mountain, will again

light upon the travel-adventure of this ever-growing, ever-altered ego.—Thus self-knowledge becomes universal knowledge as regards the entire past, and, by another chain of observation, which can only be indicated here, self-direction and self-training in the freest and most far-seeing spirits might become universal direction as regards all future humanity.

224.

BALM AND POISON.—We cannot ponder too deeply on this fact : Christianity is the religion of antiquity grown old ; it presupposes degenerate old culture-stocks, and on them it had, and still has, power to work like balm. There are periods when ears and eyes are full of slime, so that they can no longer hear the voice of reason and philosophy or see the wisdom that walks in bodily shape, whether it bears the name of Epictetus or of Epicurus. Then, perhaps, the erection of the martyr's cross and the " trumpet of the last judgment " may have the effect of still inspiring such races to end their lives decently. If we think of Juvenal's Rome, of that poisonous toad with the eyes of Venus, we understand what it means to make the sign of the Cross before the world, we honour the silent Christian community and are grateful for its having stifled the Greco-Roman Empire. If, indeed, most men were then born in spiritual slavery, with the sensuality of old men, what a pleasure to meet beings who were more soul than body, and who seemed to realise the Greek idea of the shades of the under-world—shy, scurrying, chirping, kindly creatures, with a rever-

sion on the "better life," and therefore so unassum-
ing, so secretly scornful, so proudly patient !—This
Christianity, as the evening chime of the *good* antiquity, with cracked, weary and yet melodious bell,
is balm in the ears even to one who only now tra-
verses those centuries historically.   What must it
have been to those men themselves !—To young and
fresh barbarian nations, on the other hand, Christianity is a poison.   For to implant the teaching of
sinfulness and damnation in the heroic, childlike,
and animal soul of the old Germans is nothing but
poisoning. An enormous chemical fermentation and
decomposition, a medley of sentiments and judgments, a rank growth of adventurous legend, and
hence in the long run a fundamental weakening of
such barbarian peoples, was the inevitable result.
True, without this weakening what should we have
left of Greek culture, of the whole cultured past of
the human race ?   For the barbarians untouched by
Christianity knew very well how to make a clean
sweep of old cultures, as was only too clearly shown
by the heathen conquerors of Romanised Britain.
Thus Christianity, against its will, was compelled to
aid in making "the antique world" immortal.—There
remains, however, a counter-question and the possibility of a counter-reckoning. Without this weakening through the poisoning referred to, would any of
those fresh stocks—the Germans, for instance—have
been in a position gradually to find by themselves a
higher, a peculiar, a new culture, of which the most
distant conception would therefore have been lost
to humanity ?—In this, as in every case, we do not
know, Christianly speaking, whether God owes the

devil or the devil God more thanks for everything having turned out as it has.

225.

FAITH MAKES HOLY AND CONDEMNS. — A Christian who happened upon forbidden paths of thought might well ask himself on some occasion whether it is really necessary that there should be a God, side by side with a representative Lamb, if faith in the existence of these beings suffices to produce the same influences? If they do exist after all, are they not superfluous beings? For all that is given by the Christian religion to the human soul, all that is beneficent, consoling, and edifying, just as much as all that depresses and crushes, emanates from that faith and not from the objects of that faith. It is here as in another well-known case—there were indeed no witches, but the terrible effects of the belief in witches were the same as if they really had existed. For all occasions where the Christian awaits the immediate intervention of a God, though in vain (for there is no God), his religion is inventive enough to find subterfuges and reasons for tranquillity. In so far Christianity is an ingenious religion.—Faith, indeed, has up to the present not been able to move real mountains, although I do not know who assumed that it could. But it can put mountains where there are none.

226.

THE TRAGI-COMEDY OF REGENSBURG.—Here and there we see with terrible clearness the harlequinade of Fortune, how she fastens the rope, on

which she wills that succeeding centuries should
dance, on to a few days, one place, the condition
and opinions of one brain.   Thus the fate of modern
German history lies in the days of that disputation
at Regensburg : the peaceful settlement of ecclesi-
astical and moral affairs, without religious wars or a
counter-reformation, and also the unity of the German nation, seemed assured : the deep, gentle spirit of
Contarini hovered for one moment over the theologi-
cal squabble, victorious, as representative of the riper
Italian piety, reflecting the morning glory of intellectual freedom.   But Luther's hard head, full of
suspicions and strange misgivings, showed resistance.   Because justification by grace appeared to
him *his* greatest motto and discovery, he did not
believe the phrase in the mouth of Italians ; whereas, in point of fact, as is well known, they had
invented it much earlier and spread it throughout
Italy in deep silence.   In this apparent agreement
Luther saw the tricks of the devil, and hindered the
work of peace as well as he could, thereby advancing to a great extent the aims of the Empire's foes.
—And now, in order to have a still stronger idea of
the dreadful farcicality of it all, let us add that none
of the principles about which men then disputed in
Regensburg—neither that of original sin, nor that of
redemption by proxy, nor that of justification by
faith—is in any way true or even has any connection
with truth : that they are now all recognised as incapable of being discussed.   Yet on this account
the world was set on fire—that is to say, by opinions
which correspond to no things or realities ; whereas
as regards purely philological questions—as, for in-

stance, that of the sacramental words in the Eucharist
—discussion at any rate is permitted, because in this
case the truth can be said. But " where nothing is,
even truth has lost her right." *—Lastly, it only remains to be said that it is true these principles give
rise to sources of power so mighty that without them
all the mills of the modern world could not be driven
with such force. And it is primarily a matter of
force, only secondarily of truth (and perhaps not
even secondarily)—is it not so, my dear up-to-date
friends ?

227.

GOETHE'S ERRORS.—Goethe is a signal exception among great artists in that he did not live
within the limited confines of his real capacity, as if
that must be the essential, the distinctive, the unconditional, and the last thing in him and for all the
world. Twice he intended to possess something
higher than he really possessed—and went astray
in the second half of his life, where he seems quite
convinced that he is one of the great scientific discoverers and illuminators. So too in the first half
of his life he demanded of himself something higher
than the poetic art seemed to him—and here already
he made a mistake. That nature wished to make
him a plastic artist,—*this* was his inwardly glowing
and scorching secret, which finally drove him to
Italy, that he might give vent to his mania in this
direction and make to it every possible sacrifice.
At last, shrewd as he was, and honestly averse to

---

* Allusion to German proverb : " Where there is nothing,
the Emperor has lost his rights."—TR.

any mental perversion in himself, he discovered that
a tricksy elf of desire had attracted him to the belief
in this calling, and that he must free himself of the
greatest passion of his heart and bid it farewell. The
painful conviction, tearing and gnawing at his vitals,
that it was necessary to bid farewell, finds full expression in the character of Tasso. Over Tasso,
that Werther intensified, hovers the premonition of
something worse than death, as when one says:
" Now it is over, after this farewell: how shall I go
on living without going mad ? "   These two fundamental errors of his life gave Goethe, in face of a
purely literary attitude towards poetry (the only
attitude then known to the world), such an unem-
barrassed and apparently almost arbitrary position.
Not to speak of the period when Schiller (poor
Schiller, who had no time himself and left no time
to others) drove away his shy dread of poetry, his
fear of all literary life and craftsmanship, Goethe
appears like a Greek who now and then visits his
beloved, doubting whether she be not a Goddess
to whom he can give no proper name.   In all his
poetry one notices the inspiring neighbourhood of
plastic art and Nature.   The features of these figures
that floated before him—and perhaps he always
thought he was on the track of the metamorphoses
of one Goddess—became, without his will or knowledge, the features of all the children of his art.
Without the extravagances of error he would not
have been Goethe—that is, the only German artist
in writing who has not yet become out of date—just
because he desired as little to be a writer as a German
by vocation.

228.

TRAVELLERS AND THEIR GRADES. — Among travellers we may distinguish five grades. The first and lowest grade is of those who travel and are seen—they become really travelled and are, as it were, blind. Next come those who really see the world. The third class experience the results of their seeing. The fourth weave their experience into their life and carry it with them henceforth. Lastly, there are some men of the highest strength who, as soon as they have returned home, must finally and necessarily work out in their lives and productions all the things seen that they have experienced and incorporated in themselves.—Like these five species of travellers, all mankind goes through the whole pilgrimage of life, the lowest as purely passive, the highest as those who act and live out their lives without keeping back any residue of inner experiences.

229.

IN CLIMBING HIGHER.—So soon as we climb higher than those who hitherto admired us, we appear to them as sunken and fallen. For they imagined that under all circumstances they were on the heights in our company (maybe also through our agency).

230.

MEASURE AND MODERATION.—Of two quite lofty things, measure and moderation, it is best never to speak. A few know their force and significance,

from the mysterious paths of inner experiences
and conversions: they honour in them something
quite godlike, and are afraid to speak aloud.   All
the rest hardly listen when they are spoken about,
and think the subjects under discussion are tedium
and mediocrity.   We must perhaps except those
who have once heard a warning note from that
realm but have stopped their ears against the sound.
The recollection of it makes them angry and ex-
asperated.

231.

HUMANITY OF FRIENDSHIP AND COMRADE-
SHIP.—" If thou wilt take the left hand, then I will
go to the right," * that feeling is the hall-mark of
humanity in intimate intercourse, and without that
feeling every friendship, every band of apostles or
disciples, sooner or later becomes a fraud.

232.

THE PROFOUND.—Men of profound thought appear to themselves in intercourse with others like
comedians, for in order to be understood they must
always simulate superficiality.

233.

FOR THE SCORNERS OF " HERD-HUMANITY."—
He who regards human beings as a herd, and flies
from them as fast as he can, will certainly be caught
up by them and gored upon their horns.

---

* Genesis xiii. 9.—TR.

234.

THE MAIN TRANSGRESSION AGAINST THE VAIN.—In society, he who gives another an opportunity of favourably setting forth his knowledge, sentiments, and experience sets himself above him. Unless he is felt by the other to be a superior being without limitation, he is guilty of an attack upon his vanity, while what he aimed at was the gratification of the other man's vanity.

235.

DISAPPOINTMENT.—When a long life of action distinguished by speeches and writings gives publicity to a man's personality, personal intercourse with him is generally disappointing on two grounds. Firstly, one expects too much from a brief period of intercourse (namely, all that the thousand and one opportunities of life can alone bring out). Secondly, no recognised person gives himself the trouble to woo recognition in individual cases. He is too careless, and we are at too high a tension.

236.

TWO SOURCES OF KINDNESS.—To treat all men with equal good-humour, and to be kind without distinction of persons, may arise as much from a profound contempt for mankind as from an ingrained love of humanity.

237.

THE WANDERER IN THE MOUNTAINS TO HIMSELF.—There are certain signs that you have gone

farther and higher.   There is a freer, wider prospect
before you, the air blows cooler yet milder in your
face (you have unlearned the folly of confounding
mildness with warmth), your gait is more firm and
vigorous, courage and discretion have waxed together.   On all these grounds your journey may
now be more lonely and in any case more perilous
than heretofore, if indeed not to the extent believed by those who from the misty valley see you,
the roamer, striding on the mountains.

238.

WITH THE EXCEPTION OF OUR NEIGHBOUR.
—I admit that my head is set wrong on my neck
only, for every other man, as is well known, knows
better than I what I should do or leave alone.
The only one who cannot help me is myself, poor
beggar!   Are we not all like statues on which false
heads have been placed?   Eh, dear neighbour?—
Ah no; you, just you, are the exception!

239.

CAUTION.—We must either not go about at all
with people who are lacking in the reverence for
personalities, or inexorably fetter them beforehand
with the manacles of convention.

240.

THE WISH TO APPEAR VAIN.—In conversation
with strangers or little-known acquaintances, to
express only selected thoughts, to speak of one's
famous acquaintances, and important experiences

and travels, is a sign that one is not proud, or at least would not like to appear proud. Vanity is the polite mask of pride.

241.

GOOD FRIENDSHIP.—A good friendship arises when the one man deeply respects the other, more even than himself; loves him also, though not so much as himself; and finally, to facilitate intercourse, knows how to add the delicate bloom and veneer of intimacy, but at the same time wisely refrains from a true, real intimacy, from the confounding of *meum* and *tuum*.

242.

FRIENDS AS GHOSTS.—If we change ourselves vitally, our friends, who have not changed, become ghosts of our own past: their voice sounds shadowy and dreadful to us, as if we heard our own voice speaking, but younger, harder, less mellow.

243.

ONE|EYE AND TWO GLANCES.—The same people whose eyes naturally plead for favours and indulgences are accustomed, from their frequent humiliations and cravings for revenge, to assume a shameless glance as well.

244.

THE HAZE OF DISTANCE.—A child throughout life—that sounds very touching, but is only the verdict from the distance. Seen and known close at hand, he is always called "puerile throughout life."

245.

ADVANTAGE AND DISADVANTAGE IN THE SAME MISUNDERSTANDING. — The mute perplexity of the subtle brain is usually understood by the non-subtle as a silent superiority, and is much dreaded whereas the perception of perplexity would produce good will.

246.

THE SAGE GIVING HIMSELF OUT TO BE A FOOL.—The philanthropy of the sage sometimes makes him decide to pretend to be excited, enraged, or delighted, so that he may not hurt his surroundings by the coldness and rationality of his true nature.

247.

FORCING ONESELF TO ATTENTION.—So soon as we note that any one in intercourse and conversation with us has to force himself to attention, we have adequate evidence that he loves us not, or loves us no longer.

248.

THE WAY TO A CHRISTIAN VIRTUE.—Learning from one's enemies is the best way to love them, for it inspires us with a grateful mood towards them.

249.

STRATAGEM OF THE IMPORTUNATE.—The importunate man gives us gold coins as change for our convention coins, and thereby tries to force us afterwards to treat our convention as an oversight and him as an exception.

250.

REASON FOR DISLIKE.—We become hostile to many an artist or writer, not because we notice in the end that he has duped us, but because he did not find more subtle means necessary to entrap us.

251.

IN PARTING. — Not by the way one soul approaches another, but by the way it separates, do I recognise its relationship and homogeneity with the other.

252.

SILENTIUM.—We must not speak about our friends, or we renounce the sentiment of friendship.

253.

IMPOLITENESS.—Impoliteness is often the sign of a clumsy modesty, which when taken by surprise loses its head and would fain hide the fact by means of rudeness.

254.

HONESTY'S MISCALCULATION.—Our newest acquaintances are sometimes the first to learn what we have hitherto kept dark. We have the foolish notion that our proof of confidence is the strongest fetter wherewith to hold them fast. But *they* do not know enough about us to feel so strongly the sacrifice involved in our speaking out, and betray our secrets to others without any idea of betrayal. Hereby we possibly lose our old friends.

255.

IN THE ANTE-CHAMBER OF FAVOUR.—All men whom we let stand long in the ante-chamber of our favour get into a state of fermentation or become bitter.

256.

WARNING TO THE DESPISED.—When we have sunk unmistakably in the estimation of mankind we should cling tooth and nail to modesty in inter-course, or we shall betray to others that we have sunk in our own estimation as well. Cynicism in intercourse is a sign that a man, when alone, treats himself too as a dog.

257.

IGNORANCE OFTEN ENNOBLES.—With regard to the respect of those who pay respect, it is an ad-vantage ostensibly not to understand certain things. Ignorance, too, confers privileges.

258.

THE OPPONENT OF GRACE.—The impatient and arrogant man does not care for grace, feeling it to be a corporeal, visible reproach against himself. For grace is heartfelt toleration in movement and gesture.

259.

ON SEEING AGAIN.—When old friends see each other again after a long separation, it often happens that they affect an interest in matters to which they have long since become indifferent. Sometimes both remark this, but dare not raise the veil—from a mournful doubt. Hence arise conversations as in the realm of the dead.

260.

MAKING FRIENDS ONLY WITH THE INDUSTRIOUS.—The man of leisure is dangerous to his friends, for, having nothing to do, he talks of what his friends are doing or not doing, interferes, and finally makes himself a nuisance. The clever man will only make friends with the industrious.

261.

ONE WEAPON TWICE AS MUCH AS TWO.—It is an unequal combat when one man defends his cause with head and heart, the other with head alone. The first has sun and wind against him, as it were, and his two weapons interfere with each other: he loses the prize—in the eyes of truth. True, the victory of the second, with his one weapon, is seldom a victory after the hearts of all the other spectators, and makes him unpopular.

262.

DEPTH AND TROUBLED WATERS.—The public easily confounds him who fishes in troubled waters with him who pumps up from the depths.

263.

DEMONSTRATING ONE'S VANITY TO FRIEND AND FOE.—Many a man, from vanity, maltreats even his friends, when in the presence of witnesses to whom he wishes to make his own preponderance clear. Others exaggerate the merits of their enemies, in order to point proudly to the fact that they are worthy of such foes.

264.

COOLING OFF.—The over-heating of the heart is generally allied with illness of the head and judgment. He who is concerned for a time with the health of his head must know what he has to cool, careless of the future of his heart. For if we are capable at all of giving warmth, we are sure to become warm again and then have our summer.

265.

MINGLED FEELINGS.—Towards science women and self-seeking artists entertain a feeling that is composed of envy and sentimentality.

266.

WHERE DANGER IS GREATEST. — We seldom break our leg so long as life continues a toilsome upward climb. The danger comes when we begin to take things easily and choose the convenient paths.

267.

NOT TOO EARLY.—We must beware of becoming sharp too early, or we shall also become thin too early.

268.

JOY IN REFRACTORINESS. — The good teacher knows cases where he is proud that his pupil remains true to himself in opposition to him—at times when the youth must not understand the man or would be harmed by understanding him.

269.

THE EXPERIMENT OF HONESTY.—Young men, who wish to be more honest than they have been, seek as victim some one acknowledged to be honest, attacking him first with an attempt to reach his height by abuse—with the underlying notion that this first experiment at any rate is void of danger. For just such a one has no right to chastise the impudence of the honest man.

270.

THE ETERNAL CHILD.—We think, short-sighted that we are, that fairy-tales and games belong to childhood. As if at any age we should care to live without fairy-tales and games! Our words and sentiments are indeed different, but the essential fact remains the same, as is proved by the child himself looking on games as his work and fairy-tales as his truth. The shortness of life ought to preserve us from a pedantic distinction between the different ages—as if every age brought something new—and a poet ought one day to portray a man of two hundred, who really lives without fairy-tales and games.

271.

EVERY PHILOSOPHY IS THE PHILOSOPHY OF A PERIOD OF LIFE.—The period of life in which a philosopher finds his teaching is manifested by his teaching; he cannot avoid that, however elevated above time and hour he may feel himself. Thus, Schopenhauer's philosophy remains a mirror of his hot and melancholy youth—it is no mode of thought for older men. Plato's philosophy reminds one of the middle thirties, when a warm and a cold current generally rush together, so that spray and delicate clouds and, under favourable circumstances and glimpses of sunshine, enchanting rainbow-pictures result.

272.

OF THE INTELLECT OF WOMEN.—The intellectual strength of a woman is best proved by the fact that she offers her own intellect as a sacrifice out of love for a man and his intellect, and that nevertheless in the new domain, which was previously foreign to her nature, a second intellect at once arises as an aftergrowth, to which the man's mind impels her.

273.

RAISING AND LOWERING IN THE SEXUAL DOMAIN. — The storm of desire will sometimes carry a man up to a height where all desire is silenced, where he really loves and lives in a better state of being rather than in a better state of choice. On the other hand, a good woman, from true love, often climbs down to desire, and lowers herself in her own eyes. The latter action in particular is one of the most pathetic sensations which the idea of a good marriage can involve.

274.

MAN PROMISES, WOMAN FULFILS.—By woman Nature shows how far she has hitherto achieved her task of fashioning humanity, by man she shows what she has had to overcome and what she still proposes to do for humanity.—The most perfect woman of every age is the holiday-task of the Creator on every seventh day of culture, the re-creation of the artist from his work.

275.

TRANSPLANTING.—If we have spent our intellect in order to gain mastery over the intemperance of the passions, the sad result often follows that we transfer the intemperance to the intellect, and from that time forth are extravagant in thought and desire of knowledge.

276.

LAUGHTER AS TREACHERY.—How and when a woman laughs is a sign of her culture, but in the ring of laughter her nature reveals itself, and in highly cultured women perhaps even the last insoluble residue of their nature. Hence the psychologist will say with Horace, though from different reasons: " Ridete puellae."

277.

FROM THE YOUTHFUL SOUL.—Youths varyingly show devotion and impudence towards the same person, because at bottom they only despise or admire themselves in that other person, and between the two feelings but stagger to and fro in themselves, so long as they have not found in experience the measure of their will and ability.

278.

FOR THE AMELIORATION OF THE WORLD.—If we forbade the discontented, the sullen, and the atrabilious to propagate, we might transform the world into a garden of happiness.—This aphorism belongs to a practical philosophy for the female sex.

279.

NOT TO DISTRUST YOUR EMOTIONS. — The feminine phrase "Do not distrust your emotions" does not mean much more than "Eat what tastes good to you." This may also, especially for moderate natures, be a good everyday rule. But other natures must live according to another maxim: "You must eat not only with your mouth but also with your brain, in order that the greediness of your mouth may not prove your undoing."

280.

A CRUEL FANCY OF LOVE.—Every great love involves the cruel thought of killing the object of love, so that it may be removed once for all from the mischievous play of change. For love is more afraid of change than of destruction.

281.

DOORS.—In everything that is learnt or experienced, the child, just like the man, sees doors;

but for the former they are places to go *to*, for the latter to go *through*.

282.

SYMPATHETIC WOMEN. — The sympathy of women, which is talkative, takes the sick-bed to market.

283.

EARLY MERIT.—He who acquires merit early in life tends to forget all reverence for age and old people, and accordingly, greatly to his disadvantage, excludes himself from the society of the mature, those who confer maturity. Thus in spite of his early merit he remains green, importunate, and boyish longer than others.

284.

SOULS ALL OF A PIECE.—Women and artists think that where we do not contradict them we cannot. Reverence on ten counts and silent disapproval on ten others appears to them an impossible combination, because their souls are all of a piece.

285.

YOUNG TALENTS.—With respect to young talents we must strictly follow Goethe's maxim, that we should often avoid harming error in order to avoid harming truth. Their condition is like the diseases of pregnancy, and involves strange appetites. These appetites should be satisfied and humoured as far as possible, for the sake of the fruit they may be expected to produce. It is true that, as nurse of these

remarkable invalids, one must learn the difficult
art of voluntary self-abasement.

286.

DISGUST WITH TRUTH.—Women are so constituted that all truth (in relation to men, love, children, society, aim of life) disgusts them—and that
they try to be revenged on every one who opens
their eyes.

287.

THE SOURCE OF GREAT LOVE.—Whence arises
the sudden passion of a man for a woman, a passion
so deep, so vital? Least of all from sensuality only:
but when a man finds weakness, need of help, and
high spirits united in the same creature, he suffers
a sort of overflowing of soul, and is touched and
offended at the same moment. At this point arises
the source of great love.

288.

CLEANLINESS.—In the child, the sense for cleanliness should be fanned into a passion, and then
later on he will raise himself, in ever new phases,
to almost every virtue, and will finally appear, in
compensation for all talent, as a shining cloud of
purity, temperance, gentleness, and character, happy
in himself and spreading happiness around.

289.

OF VAIN OLD MEN.—Profundity of thought
belongs to youth, clarity of thought to old age.

When, in spite of this, old men sometimes speak and write in the manner of the profound, they do so from vanity, imagining that they thereby assume the charm of juvenility, enthusiasm, growth, apprehensiveness, hopefulness.

290.

ENJOYMENT OF NOVELTY.—Men use a new lesson or experience later on as a ploughshare or perhaps also as a weapon, women at once make it into an ornament.

291.

HOW BOTH SEXES BEHAVE WHEN IN THE RIGHT. —If it is conceded to a woman that she is right, she cannot deny herself the triumph of setting her heel on the neck of the vanquished ; she must taste her victory to the full. On the other hand, man towards man in such a case is ashamed of being right. But then man is accustomed to victory ; with woman it is an exception.

292.

ABNEGATION IN THE WILL TO BEAUTY.—In order to become beautiful, a woman must not desire to be considered pretty. That is to say, in ninety-nine out of a hundred cases where she could please she must scorn and put aside all thoughts of pleasing. Only then can she ever reap the delight of him whose soul's portal is wide enough to admit the great.

293.

UNINTELLIGIBLE, UNENDURABLE. — A youth cannot understand that an old man has also had his delights, his dawns of feeling, his changings and soarings of thought. It offends him to think that such things have existed before. But it makes him very bitter to hear that, to become fruitful, he must lose those buds and dispense with their fragrance.

294.

THE PARTY WITH THE AIR OF MARTYRDOM.— Every party that can assume an air of martyrdom wins good-natured souls over to its side and thereby itself acquires an air of good nature—greatly to its advantage.

295.

ASSERTIONS SURER THAN ARGUMENTS.—An assertion has, with the majority of men at any rate, more effect than an argument, for arguments provoke mistrust. Hence demagogues seek to strengthen the arguments of their party by assertions.

296.

THE BEST CONCEALERS.—All regularly successful men are profoundly cunning in making their faults and weaknesses look like manifestations of strength. This proves that they must know their defects uncommonly well.

297.

FROM TIME TO TIME.—He sat in the city gateway and said to one who passed through that this was the city gate. The latter replied that this was true, but that one must not be too much in the right if one expected to be thanked for it. "Oh," answered the other, "I don't want thanks, but from time to time it is very pleasant not merely to be in the right but to remain in the right."

298.

VIRTUE WAS NOT INVENTED BY THE GERMANS. —Goethe's nobleness and freedom from envy, Beethoven's fine hermitical resignation, Mozart's cheerfulness and grace of heart, Handel's unbending manliness and freedom under the law, Bach's confident and luminous inner life, such as does not even need to renounce glamour and success—are these qualities peculiarly German?—If they are not, they at least prove to what goal Germans should strive and to what they can attain.

299.

PIA FRAUS OR SOMETHING ELSE.—I hope I am mistaken, but I think that in Germany of to-day a twofold sort of hypocrisy is set up as the duty of the moment for every one. From imperial-political misgivings Germanism is demanded, and from social apprehensions Christianity—but both only in words and gestures, and particularly in ability to keep silent. It is the veneer that nowadays costs so much and is paid for so highly; and for the benefit of the spectators the face of the nation assumes German and Christian wrinkles.

300.

HOW FAR EVEN IN THE GOOD THE HALF MAY BE MORE THAN THE WHOLE.—In all things that

are constructed to last and demand the service of
many hands, much that is less good must be made
a rule, although the organiser knows what is better
and harder very well.   He will calculate that there
will never be a lack of persons who *can* correspond
to the rule, and he knows that the middling good is
the rule.—The youth seldom sees this point, and as
an innovator thinks how marvellously he is in the
right and how strange is the blindness of others.

301.

THE PARTISAN.—The true partisan learns nothing more, he only experiences and judges.   It is
significant that Solon, who was never a partisan but
pursued his aims above and apart from parties or
even against them, was the father of that simple
phrase wherein lies the secret of the health and
vitality of Athens: "I grow old, but I am always
learning."

302.

WHAT IS GERMAN ACCORDING TO GOETHE.—
They are really intolerable people of whom one
cannot even accept the good, who have freedom of
disposition but do not remark that they are lacking
in freedom of taste and spirit.   Yet just this, according to Goethe's well-weighed judgment, is German.—
His voice and his example indicate that the German
should be more than a German if he wishes to be
useful or even endurable to other nations—and
which direction his striving should take, in order
that he may rise above and beyond himself.

303.

WHEN IT IS NECESSARY TO REMAIN STATION-
ARY.—When the masses begin to rage, and reason
is under a cloud, it is a good thing, if the health of
one's soul is not quite assured, to go under a door-
way and look out to see what the weather is like.

304.

THE REVOLUTION-SPIRIT AND THE POSSES-
SION-SPIRIT.—The only remedy against Socialism
that still lies in your power is to avoid provoking
Socialism—in other words, to live in moderation and
contentment, to prevent as far as possible all lavish
display, and to aid the State as far as possible in its
taxing of all superfluities and luxuries. You do not
like this remedy? Then, you rich bourgeois who
call yourselves "Liberals," confess that it is your own
inclination that you find so terrible and menacing
in Socialists, but allow to prevail in yourselves as
unavoidable, as if with you it were something
different. As you are constituted, if you had not
your fortune and the cares of maintaining it, this
bent of yours would make Socialists of you. Possession alone differentiates you from them. If you
wish to conquer the assailants of your prosperity,
you must first conquer yourselves.—And if that
prosperity only meant well-being, it would not be
so external and provocative of envy; it would be
more generous, more benevolent, more compensatory,
more helpful. But the spurious, histrionic element in
your pleasures, which lie more in the feeling of contrast (because others have them not, and feel envious)

than in feelings of realised and heightened power—
your houses, dresses, carriages, shops, the demands
of your palates and your tables, your noisy operatic
and musical enthusiasm ; lastly your women, formed
and fashioned but of base metal, gilded but without the ring of gold, chosen by you for show and
considering themselves meant for show—these are
the things that spread the poison of that national
disease, which seizes the masses ever more and more
as a Socialistic heart-itch, but has its origin and
breeding-place in you.   Who shall now arrest this
epidemic ?

305.

PARTY TACTICS.—When a party observes that a
previous member has changed from an unqualified
to a qualified adherent, it endures it so ill that
it irritates and mortifies him in every possible way
with the object of forcing him to a decisive break
and making him an opponent.   For the party sus-
pects that the intention of finding a relative value
in its faith, a value which admits of pro and con, of
weighing and discarding, is more dangerous than
downright opposition.

306.

FOR THE STRENGTHENING OF PARTIES.—Whoever wishes to strengthen a party internally should
give it an opportunity of being forcibly treated
with obvious injustice.   The party thus acquires a
capital of good conscience, which hitherto it perhaps
lacked.

307.

TO PROVIDE FOR ONE'S PAST.—As men after all only respect the old-established and slowly developed, he who would survive after his death must not only provide for posterity but still more for the past. Hence tyrants of every sort (including tyrannical artists and politicians) like to do violence to history, so that history may seem a preparation and a ladder up to them.

308.

PARTY WRITERS.—The beating of drums, which delights young writers who serve a party, sounds to him who does not belong to the party like a rattling of chains, and excites sympathy rather than admiration.

309.

TAKING SIDES AGAINST OURSELVES. — Our followers never forgive us for taking sides against ourselves, for we seem in their eyes not only to be spurning their love but to be exposing them to the charge of lack of intelligence.

310.

DANGER IN WEALTH.—Only a man of intellect should hold property : otherwise property is dangerous to the community. For the owner, not knowing how to make use of the leisure which his possessions might secure to him, will continue to strive after more property. This strife will be his occupation, his strategy in the war with ennui. So in the end real wealth is produced from the moderate property that would be enough for an intellectual man. Such wealth, then, is the glittering outcrop of intellectual dependence and poverty, but it looks quite different from what its humble origin might lead one to expect, because it can mask itself with culture and art—it can, in fact, purchase the mask. Hence it excites envy in the poor and uncultured—who at bottom always envy culture and see no mask in the mask— and gradually paves the way for a social revolution. For a gilded coarseness and a histrionic blowing of trumpets in the pretended enjoyment of culture inspires that class with the thought, " It is only a matter of money," whereas it is indeed to some extent a matter of money, but far more of intellect.

311.

JOY IN COMMANDING AND OBEYING. — Commanding is a joy, like obeying; the former when it has not yet become a habit, the latter just when it has become a habit. Old servants under new masters advance each other mutually in giving pleasure.

312.

AMBITION FOR A FORLORN HOPE.—There is an ambition for a forlorn hope which forces a party to place itself at the post of extreme danger.

313.

WHEN ASSES ARE NEEDED.—We shall not move the crowd to cry " Hosanna ! " until we have ridden into the city upon an ass.

314.

PARTY USAGE.—Every party attempts to represent the important elements that have sprung up outside it as unimportant, and if it does not succeed, it attacks those elements the more bitterly, the more excellent they are.

315.

BECOMING EMPTY.—Of him who abandons himself to the course of events, a smaller and smaller residue is continually left, Great politicians may therefore become quite empty men, although they were once full and rich.

316.

WELCOME ENEMIES. — The Socialistic movements are nowadays becoming more and more agreeable rather than terrifying to the dynastic governments, because by these movements they are provided with a right and a weapon for making exceptional rules, and can thus attack their real bogies, democrats and anti-dynasts.—Towards all that such governments professedly detest they feel a secret cordiality and inclination. But they are compelled to draw the veil over their soul.

317.

POSSESSION POSSESSES.—Only up to a certain point does possession make men feel freer and more independent ; one step farther, and possession becomes lord, the possessor a slave. The latter must

sacrifice his time, his thoughts to the former, and
feels himself compelled to an intercourse, nailed to
a spot, incorporated with the State—perhaps quite
in conflict with his real and essential needs.

318.

OF THE MASTERY OF THEM THAT KNOW.—It
is easy, ridiculously easy, to set up a model for the
choice of a legislative body.   First of all the honest
and reliable men of the nation, who at the same
time are masters and experts in some one branch,
have to become prominent by mutual scenting-out
and recognition.   From these, by a narrower process
of selection, the learned and expert of the first rank
in each individual branch must again be chosen, also
by mutual recognition and guarantee.   If the legislative body be composed of these, it will finally be
necessary, in each individual case, that only the
voices and judgments of the most specialised experts should decide; the honesty of all the rest
should have become so great that it is simply a
matter of decency to leave the voting also in the
hands of these men.   The result would be that
the law, in the strictest sense, would emanate from
the intelligence of the most intelligent.—As things
now are, voting is done by parties, and at every
division there must be hundreds of uneasy con-
sciences among the ill-taught, the incapable of judgment, among those who merely repeat, imitate, and
go with the tide.   Nothing lowers the dignity of
a new law so much as this inherent shamefaced
feeling of insincerity that necessarily results at every

party division. But, as has been said, it is easy,
ridiculously easy, to set up such a model : no power
on earth is at present strong enough to realise such
an ideal—unless the belief in the highest utility of
knowledge, and of those that know, at last dawns
even upon the most hostile minds and is preferred
to the prevalent belief in majorities. In the sense
of such a future may our watchword be: " More
reverence for them that know, and down with all
parties ! "

319.

OF THE " NATION OF THINKERS " (OR OF BAD
THINKING).—The vague, vacillating, premonitory,
elementary, intuitive elements—to choose obscure
names for obscure things—that are attributed to the
German nature would be, if they really still existed,
a proof that our culture has remained several stages
behind and is still surrounded by the spell and
atmosphere of the Middle Ages.—It is true that in
this backwardness there are certain advantages : by
these qualities the Germans (if, as has been said
before, they still possess them) would possess the
capacity, which other nations have now lost, for
doing certain things and particularly for understanding certain things. Much undoubtedly is lost
if the lack of sense—which is just the common
factor in all those qualities—is lost. Here too, however, there are no losses without the highest compensatory gains, so that no reason is left for
lamenting, granting that we do not, like children,
and gourmands, wish to enjoy at once the fruits of
all seasons of the year.

320.

CARRYING COALS TO NEWCASTLE.—The governments of the great States have two instruments for
keeping the people dependent, in fear and obedience:
a coarser, the army, and a more refined, the school.
With the aid of the former they win over to their
side the ambition of the higher strata and the
strength of the lower, so far as both are characteristic of active and energetic men of moderate or
inferior gifts.   With the aid of the latter they win
over gifted poverty, especially the intellectually pretentious semi-poverty of the middle classes.   Above
all, they make teachers of all grades into an intellectual court looking unconsciously "towards the
heights."   By putting obstacle after obstacle in the
way of private schools and the wholly distasteful
individual tuition they secure the disposal of a
considerable number of educational posts, towards
which numerous hungry and submissive eyes are
turned to an extent five times as great as can ever
be satisfied.   These posts, however, must support
the holder but meagrely, so that he maintains a
feverish thirst for promotion and becomes still more
closely attached to the views of the government.
For it is always more advantageous to foster
moderate discontent than contentment, the mother
of courage, the grandmother of free thought and
exuberance.   By means of this physically and
mentally bridled body of teachers, the youth of the
country is as far as possible raised to a certain level
of culture that is useful to the State and arranged
on a suitable sliding-scale.   Above all, the immature

and ambitious minds of all classes are almost imperceptibly imbued with the idea that only a career which is recognised and hall-marked by the State can lead immediately to social distinction. The effect of this belief in government examinations and titles goes so far that even men who have remained independent and have risen by trade or handicraft still feel a pang of discontent in their hearts until their position too is marked and acknowledged by a gracious bestowal of rank and orders from above—until one becomes a " somebody."   Finally the State connects all these hundreds of offices and posts in its hands with the obligation of being trained and hall-marked in these State schools if one ever wishes to enter this charmed circle.   Honour in society, daily bread, the possibility of a family, protection from above, the feeling of community in a common culture—all this forms a network of hopes into which every young man walks : how should he feel the slightest breath of mistrust ?   In the end, perhaps, the obligation of being a soldier for one year has become with every one, after the lapse of a few generations, an unreflecting habit, an understood thing, with an eye to which we construct the plan of our lives quite early.   Then the State can venture on the master-stroke of weaving together school and army, talent, ambition and strength by means of common advantages—that is, by attracting the more highly gifted on favourable terms to the army and inspiring them with the military spirit of joyful obedience ; so that finally, perhaps, they become attached permanently to the flag and endow it by their talents with an ever new and more brilliant

lustre. Then nothing more is wanted but an opportunity for great wars. These are provided from
professional reasons (and so in all innocence) by
diplomats, aided by newspapers and Stock Ex-
changes. For "the nation," as a nation of soldiers,
need never be supplied with a good conscience in
war—it has one already.

321.

THE PRESS.—If we consider how even to-day all
great political transactions glide upon the stage
secretly and stealthily ; how they are hidden by
unimportant events, and seem small when close at
hand ; how they only show their far-reaching effect,
and leave the soil still quaking, long after they have
taken place ;—what significance can we attach to
the Press in its present position, with its daily expenditure of lung-power in order to bawl, to deafen,
to excite, to terrify ? Is it anything more than an
everlasting false alarm, which tries to lead our ears
and our wits into a false direction ?

322.

AFTER A GREAT EVENT.—A nation and a man
whose soul has come to light through some great
event generally feel the immediate need of some
act of childishness or coarseness, as much from
shame as for purposes of recreation.

323.

TO BE A GOOD GERMAN MEANS TO DE-GER-
MANISE ONESELF.— National differences consist,

far more than has hitherto been observed, only in
the differences of various grades of culture, and are
only to a very small extent permanent (nor even
that in a strict sense).   For this reason all arguments
based on national character are so little binding on
one who aims at the alteration of convictions—in
other words, at culture.   If, for instance, we consider
all that has already been German, we shall improve
upon the hypothetical question, "What is German?"
by the counter-question, "What is *now* German?"
and every good German will answer it practically,
by overcoming his German characteristics.   For
when a nation advances and grows, it bursts the
girdle previously given to it by its national outlook.
When it remains stationary or declines, its soul is
surrounded by a fresh girdle, and the crust, as it
becomes harder and harder, builds a prison around,
with walls growing ever higher.   Hence if a nation
has much that is firmly established, this is a sign
that it wishes to petrify and would like to become
nothing but a monument.   This happened, from a
definite date, in the case of Egypt.   So he who is
well-disposed towards the Germans may for his part
consider how he may more and more grow out of
what is German.   The tendency to be un-German
has therefore always been a mark of efficient members of our nation.

324.

FOREIGNISMS.—A foreigner who travelled in Germany found favour or the reverse by certain assertions of his, according to the districts in which he
stayed.   All intelligent Suabians, he used to say,

are coquettish.—The other Suabians still believed
that Uhland was a poet and Goethe immoral.—The
best about German novels now in vogue was that
one need not read them, for one knew already what
they contained.—The native of Berlin seemed more
good-humoured than the South German, for he was
all too fond of mocking, and so could endure
mockery himself, which the South German could
not.—The intellect of the Germans was kept down
by their beer and their newspapers: he recommended them tea and pamphlets, of course as a
cure.—He advised us to contemplate the different
nations of worn-out Europe and see how well each
displayed some particular quality of old age, to the
delight of those who sit before the great spectacle:
how the French successfully represent the cleverness and amiability of old age, the English the
experience and reserve, the Italians the innocence
and candour.   Can the other masks of old age be
wanting?   Where is the proud old man, the dom-
ineering old man, the covetous old man?—The
most dangerous region in Germany was Saxony and
Thuringia: nowhere else was there more mental
nimbleness, more knowledge of men, side by side
with freedom of thought; and all this was so
modestly veiled by the ugly dialect and the zealous
officiousness of the inhabitants that one hardly
noticed that one here had to deal with the intellectual drill-sergeants of Germany, her teachers for
good or evil.—The arrogance of the North Germans
was kept in check by their tendency to obey, that
of the South Germans by their tendency—to make
themselves comfortable.—It appeared to him that

in their women German men possessed awkward but self-opinionated housewives, who belauded themselves so perseveringly that they had almost persuaded the world, and at any rate their husbands, of their peculiarly German housewifely virtue.— When the conversation turned on Germany's home and foreign policy, he used to say (he called it "betray the secret") that Germany's greatest statesman did not believe in great statesmen.—The future of Germany he found menaced and menacing, for Germans had forgotten how to enjoy themselves (an art that the Italians understood so well), but, by the great games of chance called wars and dynastic revolutions, had accustomed themselves to emotionalism, and consequently would one day have an *émeute*. For that is the strongest emotion that a nation can procure for itself.—The German Socialist was all the more dangerous because impelled by no definite necessity : his trouble lay in not knowing what he wanted ; so, even if he attained many of his objects, he would still pine away from desire in the midst of delights, just like Faust, but presumably like a very vulgar Faust. "For the Faust-Devil," he finally exclaimed, "by whom cultured Germans were so much plagued, was exorcised by Bismarck ; but now the Devil has entered into the swine,* and is worse than ever ! "

325.

OPINIONS.—Most men are nothing and count for nothing until they have arrayed themselves in

---

* Luke viii. 33.—TR.

universal convictions and public opinions. This is
in accordance with the tailors' philosophy, "The
apparel makes the man." Of exceptional men,
however, it must be said, "The wearer primarily
makes the apparel." Here opinions cease to be
public, and become something else than masks,
ornament, and disguise.

326.

TWO KINDS OF SOBRIETY.—In order not to confound the sobriety arising from mental exhaustion
with that arising from moderation, one must remark
that the former is peevish, the latter cheerful.

327.

DEBASEMENT OF JOY.—To call a thing good not
a day longer than it appears to us good, and above
all not a day earlier—that is the only way to keep
joy pure. Otherwise, joy all too easily becomes in-
sipid and rotten to the taste, and counts, for whole
strata of the people, among the adulterated food-
stuffs.

328.

THE SCAPEGOAT OF VIRTUE.—When a man
does his very best, those who mean well towards
him, but are not capable of appreciating him,
speedily seek a scapegoat to immolate, thinking it
is the scapegoat of sin—but it is the scapegoat of
virtue.

329.

SOVEREIGNTY.—To honour and acknowledge
even the bad, when it *pleases* one, and to have no

conception of how one could be ashamed of being pleased thereat, is the mark of sovereignty in things great and small.

330.

INFLUENCE A PHANTOM, NOT A REALITY.— The man of mark gradually learns that so far as he has influence he is a phantom in other brains, and perhaps he falls into a state of subtle vexation of soul, in which he asks himself whether he must not maintain this phantom of himself for the benefit of his fellow-men.

331.

GIVING AND TAKING.—When one takes away (or anticipates) the smallest thing that another possesses, the latter is blind to the fact that he has been given something greater, nay, even the greatest thing.

332.

GOOD PLOUGHLAND.—All rejection and negation betoken a deficiency in fertility. If we were good ploughland, we should allow nothing to be unused or lost, and in every thing, event, or person we should welcome manure, rain, or sunshine.

333.

INTERCOURSE AS AN ENJOYMENT.—If a man renounces the world and intentionally lives in solitude, he may come to regard intercourse with others, which he enjoys but seldom, as a special delicacy.

334

TO KNOW HOW TO SUFFER IN PUBLIC.—We must advertise our misfortunes and from time to time heave audible sighs and show visible marks of impatience. For if we could let others see how assured and happy we are in spite of pain and privation, how envious and ill-tempered they would become at the sight !—But we must take care not to corrupt our fellow-men; besides, if they knew the truth, they would levy a heavy toll upon us. At any rate our public misfortune is our private advantage.

335.

WARMTH ON THE HEIGHTS.—On the heights it is warmer than people in the valleys suppose, especially in winter. The thinker recognises the full import of this simile.

336.

TO WILL THE GOOD AND BE CAPABLE OF THE BEAUTIFUL.—It is not enough to practise the good one must have willed it, and, as the poet says, include the Godhead in our will. But the beautiful we must not will, we must be capable of it, in innocence and blindness, without any psychical curiosity. He that lights his lantern to find perfect men should remember the token by which to know them. They are the men who always act for the sake of the good and in so doing always attain to the beautiful without thinking of the beautiful. Many better and nobler men, from impotence or from want of beauty in their souls, remain unrefreshing and ugly to behold, with all their good will and good works. They rebuff and injure even virtue through the repulsive garb in which their bad taste arrays her.

337.

DANGER OF RENUNCIATION.—We must beware of basing our lives on too narrow a foundation of appetite. For if we renounce all the joys involved in positions, honours, associations, revels, creature comforts, and arts, a day may come when we perceive that this repudiation has led us not to wisdom but to satiety of life.

338.

FINAL OPINION ON OPINIONS. — Either we should hide our opinions or hide ourselves behind our opinions. Whoever does otherwise, does not know the way of the world, or belongs to the order of pious fire-eaters.

339.

"*GAUDEAMUS IGITUR.*"—Joy must contain edifying and healing forces for the moral nature of man. Otherwise, how comes it that our soul, as soon as it basks in the sunshine of joy, unconsciously vows to itself, " I will be good !" " I will become perfect ! " and is at once seized by a premonition of perfection that is like a shudder of religious awe ?

340.

TO ONE WHO IS PRAISED.—So long as you are praised, believe that you are not yet on your own course but on that of another.

341.

LOVING THE MASTER.—The apprentice and the master love the master in different ways.

342.

ALL-TOO-BEAUTIFUL AND HUMAN.—" Nature is too beautiful for thee, poor mortal," one often feels. But now and then, at a profound contemplation of all that is human, in its fulness, vigour, tenderness, and complexity, I have felt as if I must say, in all humility, " Man also is too beautiful for the contemplation of man!" Nor did I mean the moral man alone, but every one.

343.

REAL AND PERSONAL ESTATE.—When life has treated us in true robber fashion, and has taken away all that it could of honour, joys, connections, health, and property of every kind, we perhaps discover in the end, after the first shock, that we are richer than before. For now we know for the first time what is so peculiarly ours that no robber hand can touch it, and perhaps, after all the plunder and devastation, we come forward with the airs of a mighty real estate owner.

344.

INVOLUNTARILY IDEALISED.—The most painful feeling that exists is finding out that we are always taken for something higher than we really are. For we must thereby confess to ourselves, " There is in you some element of fraud—your speech, your expression, your bearing, your eye, your dealings; and this deceitful something is as necessary as your usual honesty, but constantly destroys its effect and its value.

345.

IDEALIST AND LIAR.—We must not let ourselves be tyrannised even by that finest faculty of idealising things : otherwise, truth will one day part company from us with the insulting remark : " Thou arch-liar, what have I to do with thee?"

346.

BEING MISUNDERSTOOD.—When one is misunderstood generally, it is impossible to remove a particular misunderstanding. This point must be recognised, to save superfluous expenditure of energy in self-defence.

347.

THE WATER-DRINKER SPEAKS.—Go on drinking your wine, which has refreshed you all your life —what affair is it of yours if I have to be a water-drinker? Are not wine and water peaceable, brotherly elements, that can live side by side without mutual recriminations?

348.

FROM CANNIBAL COUNTRY.—In solitude the lonely man is eaten up by himself, among crowds by the many. Choose which you prefer.

349.

THE FREEZING-POINT OF THE WILL.—"Some time the hour will come at last, the hour that will envelop you in the golden cloud of painlessness; when the soul enjoys its own weariness and, happy in patient playing with patience, resembles the waves of a lake, which on a quiet summer day, in the reflection of a many-hued evening sky, sip and sip at the shore and again are hushed—without end, without purpose, without satiety, without need—all calm rejoicing in change, all ebb and flow of Nature's pulse." Such is the feeling and talk of all invalids, but if they attain that hour, a brief period of enjoyment is followed by ennui. But this is the thawing-wind of the frozen will, which awakes, stirs, and once more begets desire upon desire.—Desire is a sign of convalescence or recovery.

350.

THE DISCLAIMED IDEAL. — It happens sometimes by an exception that a man only reaches the highest when he disclaims his ideal. For this ideal previously drove him onward too violently, so that in the middle of the track he regularly got out of breath and had to rest.

351.

A TREACHEROUS INCLINATION.—It should be regarded as a sign of an envious but aspiring man, when he feels himself attracted by the thought that with regard to the eminent there is but one salvation —love.

352.

STAIRCASE HAPPINESS.—Just as the wit of many men does not keep pace with opportunity (so that opportunity has already passed through the door while wit still waits on the staircase outside), so others have a kind of staircase happiness, which walks too slowly to keep pace with swift-footed Time. The best that it can enjoy of an experience, of a whole span of life, falls to its share long afterwards, often only as a weak, spicy fragrance, giving rise to longing and sadness—as if " it might have been possible "—some time or other—to drink one's fill of this element : but now it is too late.

353.

WORMS.—The fact that an intellect contains a few worms does not detract from its ripeness.

354.

THE SEAT OF VICTORY.—A good seat on horseback robs an opponent of his courage, the spectator of his heart—why attack such a man ? Sit like one who has been victorious !

355.

DANGER IN ADMIRATION.—From excessive admiration for the virtues of others one can lose the sense of one's own, and finally, through lack of practice, lose these virtues themselves, without retaining the alien virtues as compensation.

356.

USES OF SICKLINESS.—He who is often ill not only has a far greater pleasure in health, on account of his so often getting well, but acquires a very keen sense of what is healthy or sickly in actions and achievements, both his own and others'. Thus, for example, it is just the writers of uncertain health—among whom, unfortunately, nearly all great writers must be classed—who are wont to have a far more even and assured tone of health in their writings, because they are better versed than are the physically robust in the philosophy of psychical health and convalescence and in their teachers—morning, sunshine, forest, and fountain.

357.

DISLOYALTY A CONDITION OF MASTERY.—It cannot be helped—every master has but one pupil, and *he* becomes disloyal to him, for he also is destined for mastery.

358.

NEVER IN VAIN.—In the mountains of truth you never climb in vain. Either you already reach a higher point to-day, or you exercise your strength in order to be able to climb higher to-morrow.

359.

THROUGH GREY WINDOW-PANES.—Is what you see through this window of the world so beautiful that you do not wish to look through any other window—ay, and even try to prevent others from so doing?

360.

A SIGN OF RADICAL CHANGES. — When we dream of persons long forgotten or dead, it is a sign that we have suffered radical changes, and that the soil on which we live has been completely undermined. The dead rise again, and our antiquity becomes modernity.

361.

MEDICINE OF THE SOUL.—To lie still and think little is the cheapest medicine for all diseases of the soul, and, with the aid of good-will, becomes pleasanter every hour that it is used.

362.

INTELLECTUAL ORDER OF PRECEDENCE.—You rank far below others when you try to establish the exception and they the rule.

363.

THE FATALIST. — You must believe in fate—science can compel you thereto. All that develops in you out of that belief—cowardice, devotion or loftiness, and uprightness—bears witness to the soil in which the grain was sown, but not to the grain itself, for from that seed anything and everything can grow.

364.

THE REASON FOR MUCH FRETFULNESS.—He that prefers the beautiful to the useful in life will undoubtedly, like children who prefer sweetmeats to bread, destroy his digestion and acquire a very fretful outlook on the world.

365.

EXCESS AS A REMEDY.—We can make our own talent once more acceptable to ourselves by honouring and enjoying the opposite talent for some time to excess.—Using excess as a remedy is one of the more refined devices in the art of life.

366.

"WILL A SELF."—Active, successful natures act, not according to the maxim, "Know thyself," but as if always confronted with the command, "Will a self, so you will become a self."—Fate seems always to have left them a choice. Inactive, contemplative natures, on the other hand, reflect on how they have chosen their self "once for all" at their entry into life.

367.

TO LIVE AS FAR AS POSSIBLE WITHOUT A FOLLOWING.—How small is the importance of followers we first grasp when we have ceased to be the followers of our followers.

368.

OBSCURING ONESELF.—We must understand how to obscure ourselves in order to get rid of the gnat-swarms of pestering admirers.

369.

ENNUI.—There is an ennui of the most subtle and cultured brains, to which the best that the world can offer has become stale. Accustomed to eat ever more and more recherché fare and to feel disgust at coarser diet, they are in danger of dying of hunger. For the very best exists but in small quantities, and has sometimes become inaccessible or hard as stone, so that even good teeth can no longer bite it.

370.

THE DANGER IN ADMIRATION.—The admiration of a quality or of an art may be so strong as to deter us from aspiring to possess that quality or art.

371.

WHAT IS REQUIRED OF ART.—One man wants to enjoy himself by means of art, another for a time to get out of or above himself.—To meet both requirements there exists a twofold species of artists.

372.

SECESSIONS.—Whoever secedes from us offends not us, perhaps, but certainly our adherents.

373.

AFTER DEATH.—It is only long after the death of a man that we find it inconceivable that he should be missed—in the case of really great men, only after decades. Those who are honest usually think when any one dies that he is not much missed, and that the pompous funeral oration is a piece of hypocrisy. Necessity first teaches the necessariness of an individual, and the proper epitaph is a belated sigh.

374.

LEAVING IN HADES. — We must leave many things in the Hades of half-conscious feeling, and not try to release them from their shadow-existence, or else they will become, as thoughts and words, our demoniacal tyrants, with cruel lust after our blood.

375.

NEAR TO BEGGARY.—Even the richest intellect sometimes mislays the key to the room in which his hoarded treasures repose. He is then like the poorest of the poor, who must beg to get a living.

376.

CHAIN-THINKERS.—To him who has thought a great deal, every new thought that he hears or reads at once assumes the form of a chain.

377.

PITY.—In the gilded sheath of pity is sometimes hidden the dagger of envy.

378.

WHAT IS GENIUS?—To aspire to a lofty aim and to will the means to that aim.

379.

VANITY OF COMBATANTS.—He who has no hope of victory in a combat, or who is obviously worsted, is all the more desirous that his style of fighting should be admired.

380.

THE PHILOSOPHIC LIFE MISINTERPRETED.—At the moment when one is beginning to take philosophy seriously, the whole world fancies that one is doing the reverse.

381.

IMITATION.—By imitation, the bad gains, the good loses credit—especially in art.

382.

FINAL TEACHING OF HISTORY.—"Oh that I had but lived in those times!" is the exclamation of foolish and frivolous men. At every period of history that we seriously review, even if it be the most belauded era of the past, we shall rather cry out at the end, "Anything but a return to that! The spirit of that age would oppress you with the weight of a hundred atmospheres, the good and beautiful in it you would not enjoy, its evil you could not digest." Depend upon it, posterity will pass the same verdict on our own epoch, and say that it was unbearable, that life under such conditions was intolerable. "And yet every one can endure his own times?" Yes, because the spirit of his age not only lies *upon* him but is *in* him.   The spirit of the age offers resistance to itself and can bear itself.

383.

GREATNESS AS A MASK.—By greatness in our comportment we embitter our foes; by envy that we do not conceal we almost reconcile them to us.   For envy levels and makes equal; it is an unconscious, plaintive variety of modesty.—It may be indeed that here and there, for the sake of the above-named advantage, envy has been assumed as a mask by those who are not envious.   Certainly, however, greatness in comportment is often used as the mask of envy by ambitious men who would rather suffer drawbacks and embitter their foes than let it be seen that they place them on an equal footing with themselves.

384.

UNPARDONABLE.—You gave him an opportunity of displaying the greatness of his character, and he did not make use of the opportunity.   He will never forgive you for that.

385.

CONTRASTS.—The most senile thought ever conceived about men lies in the famous saying, " The ego is always hateful," the most childish in the still more famous saying, " Love thy neighbour as thyself."—With the one knowledge of men has ceased, with the other it has not yet begun.

386.

A DEFECTIVE EAR.—"We still belong to the mob so long as we always shift the blame on to others; we are on the track of wisdom when we always make ourselves alone responsible; but the wise man finds no one to blame, neither himself nor others."—Who said that? Epictetus, eighteen hundred years ago.—The world has heard but forgotten the saying.—No, the world has not heard and not forgotten it: everything is not forgotten. But we had not the necessary ear, the ear of Epictetus.— So he whispered it into his own ear?—Even so: wisdom is the whispering of the sage to himself in the crowded market-place.

387.

A DEFECT OF STANDPOINT, NOT OF VISION.— We always stand a few paces too near ourselves and a few paces too far from our neighbour. Hence we judge him too much in the lump, and ourselves too much by individual, occasional, insignificant features and circumstances.

388.

IGNORANCE ABOUT WEAPONS.—How little we care whether another knows a subject or not!— whereas he perhaps sweats blood at the bare idea that he may be considered ignorant on the point. Yes, there are exquisite fools, who always go about with a quiverful of mighty, excommunicatory utterances, ready to shoot down any one who shows freely that there are matters in which their judgment is not taken into acccount.

389.

AT THE DRINKING-TABLE OF EXPERIENCE.—
People whose innate moderation leads them to
drink but the half of every glass, will not admit
that everything in the world has its lees and sedi-
ment.

390.

SINGING-BIRDS.—The followers of a great man
often put their own eyes out, so that they may be
the better able to sing his praise.

391.

BEYOND OUR KEN.—The good generally displeases us when it is beyond our ken.

392.

RULE AS MOTHER OR AS CHILD.—There is one
condition that gives birth to rules, another to which
rules give birth.

393.

COMEDY.—We sometimes earn honour or love
for actions and achievements which we have long
since sloughed as the snake sloughs his skin. We
are hereby easily seduced into becoming the comic
actors of our own past, and into throwing the old
skin once more about our shoulders—and that not
merely from vanity, but from good-will towards our
admirers.

394.

A MISTAKE OF BIOGRAPHERS.—The small force
that is required to launch a boat into the stream

must not be confounded with the force of the stream that carries the boat along. Yet this mistake is made in nearly all biographies.

395.

NOT BUYING TOO DEAR.—The things that we buy too dear we generally turn to bad use, because we have no love for them but only a painful recollection. Thus they involve a twofold drawback.

396.

THE PHILOSOPHY THAT SOCIETY ALWAYS NEEDS.—The pillars of the social structure rest upon the fundamental fact that every one cheerfully contemplates all that he is, does, and attempts, his sickness or health, his poverty or affluence, his honour or insignificance, and says to himself, " After all, I would not change places with any one!"—Whoever wishes to add a stone to the social structure should always try to implant in mankind this cheerful philosophy of contentment and refusal to change places.

397.

THE MARK OF A NOBLE SOUL.—A noble soul is not that which is capable of the highest flights, but that which rises little and falls little, living always in a free and bright atmosphere and altitude

398.

GREATNESS AND ITS CONTEMPLATOR.—The noblest effect of greatness is that it gives the contemplator a power of vision that magnifies and embellishes.

399.

BEING SATISFIED. — We show that we have attained maturity of understanding when we no longer go where rare flowers lurk under the thorniest hedges of knowledge, but are satisfied with gardens, forests, meadows, and ploughlands, remembering that life is too short for the rare and uncommon.

400.

ADVANTAGE IN PRIVATION.—He who always lives in the warmth and fulness of the heart, and, as it were, in the summer air of the soul, cannot form an idea of that fearful delight which seizes more wintry natures, who for once in a way are kissed by the rays of love and the milder breath of a sunny February day.

401.

RECIPE FOR THE SUFFERER. — You find the burden of life too heavy?   Then you must increase the burden of your life.   When the sufferer finally thirsts after and seeks the river of Lethe, then he must become a *hero* to be certain of finding it.

402.

THE JUDGE.—He who has seen another's ideal becomes his inexorable judge, and as it were his evil conscience.

403.

THE UTILITY OF GREAT RENUNCIATION.—The useful thing about great renunciation is that it invests us with that youthful pride through which we can thenceforth easily demand of ourselves small renunciations.

404.

HOW DUTY ACQUIRES A GLAMOUR.—You can change a brazen duty into gold in the eyes of all by always performing something more than you have promised.

405.

PRAYER TO MANKIND.—"Forgive us our virtues" —so should we pray to mankind.

406.

THEY THAT CREATE AND THEY THAT ENJOY. —Every one who enjoys thinks that the principal thing to the tree is the fruit, but in point of fact the principal thing to it is the seed.—Herein lies the difference between them that create and them that enjoy.

407.

THE GLORY OF ALL GREAT MEN.—What is the use of genius if it does not invest him who contemplates and reveres it with such freedom and loftiness of feeling that he no longer has need of genius? —To make themselves superfluous is the glory of all great men.

408.

THE JOURNEY TO HADES.—I too have been in the underworld, even as Odysseus, and I shall often be there again. Not sheep alone have I sacrificed,

that I might be able to converse with a few dead
souls, but not even my own blood have I spared.
There were four pairs who responded to me in my
sacrifice: Epicurus and Montaigne, Goethe and
Spinoza, Plato and Rousseau, Pascal and Schopenhauer. With them I have to come to terms. When
I have long wandered alone, I will let them prove
me right or wrong; to them will I listen, if they
prove each other right or wrong. In all that I say,
conclude, or think out for myself and others, I
fasten my eyes on those eight and see their eyes
fastened on mine.—May the living forgive me if I
look upon them at times as shadows, so pale and
fretful, so restless and, alas! so eager for life. Those
eight, on the other hand, seem to me so living that
I feel as if even now, after their death, they could
never become weary of life. But eternal vigour of
life is the important point: what matters "eternal
life," or indeed life at all?

PART II.

THE WANDERER AND HIS SHADOW.

THE WANDERER AND HIS SHADOW.

The Shadow: It is so long since I heard you speak that I should like to give you an opportunity of talking.

The Wanderer: I hear a voice—where? whose? I almost fancied that 1 heard myself speaking, but with a voice yet weaker than my own.

The Shadow (after a pause): Are you not glad to have an opportunity of speaking?

The Wanderer: By God and everything else in which I disbelieve, it is my shadow that speaks. I hear it, but I do not believe it.

The Shadow: Let us assume that it exists, and think no more about it. In another hour all will be over.

The Wanderer: That is just what I thought when in a forest near Pisa I saw first two and then five camels.

The Shadow: It is all the better if we are both equally forbearing towards each other when for once our reason is silent. Thus we shall avoid losing our tempers in conversation, and shall not at once apply mutual thumb-screws in the event of any word sounding for once unintelligible to us. If one does not know exactly how to answer, it is enough to

say *something*. Those are the reasonable terms on
which I hold conversation with any person.   During
a long talk the wisest of men becomes a fool once
and a simpleton thrice.

The Wanderer: Your moderation is not flatter-
ing to those to whom you confess it.

The Shadow: Am I, then, to flatter?

The Wanderer: I thought a man's shadow was
his vanity.   Surely vanity would never say, " Am
I, then, to flatter?"

The Shadow: Nor does human vanity, so far as
I am acquainted with it, ask, as I have done twice,
whether it may speak.   It simply speaks.

The Wanderer: Now I see for the first time how
rude I am to you, my beloved shadow.   I have not
said a word of my supreme *delight* in hearing and
not merely seeing you.   You must know that I love
shadows even as I love light.   For the existence of
beauty of face, clearness of speech, kindliness and
firmness of character, the shadow is as necessary
as the light.   They are not opponents—rather do
they hold each other's hands like good friends ; and
when the light vanishes, the shadow glides after it.

The Shadow: Yes, and I hate the same thing
that you hate—night.   I love men because they are
votaries of life.   I rejoice in the gleam of their eyes
when they recognise and discover, they who never
weary of recognising and discovering.   That
shadow which all things cast when the sunshine
of knowledge falls upon them—that shadow too
am I.

The Wanderer: I think I understand you, although you have expressed yourself in somewhat

shadowy terms. You are right. Good friends give to each other here and there, as a sign of mutual understanding, an obscure phrase which to any third party is meant to be a riddle. And we are good friends, you and I. So enough of preambles! Some few hundred questions oppress my soul, and the time for you to answer them is perchance but short. Let us see how we may come to an understanding as quickly and peaceably as possible.

The Shadow: But shadows are more shy than men. You will not reveal to any man the manner of our conversation?

The Wanderer: *The manner* of our conversation? Heaven preserve me from wire-drawn, literary dialogues! If Plato had found less pleasure in spinning them out, his readers would have found more pleasure in Plato. A dialogue that in real life is a source of delight, when turned into writing and read, is a picture with nothing but false perspectives. Everything is too long or too short.—Yet perhaps I may reveal the *points on which* we have come to an understanding?

The Shadow: With that I am content. For every one will only recognise your views once more, and no one will think of the shadow.

The Wanderer: Perhaps you are wrong, my friend! Hitherto they have observed in my views more of the shadow than of me.

The Shadow: More of the shadow than of the light? Is that possible?

The Wanderer: Be serious, dear fool! My very first question demands seriousness.

*   *   *   *   *   *

I.

OF THE TREE OF KNOWLEDGE.—Probability, but no truth; the semblance of freedom, but no freedom—these are the two fruits by virtue of which the tree of knowledge cannot be confounded with the tree of life.

2.

THE WORLD'S REASON.—That the world is *not* the abstract essence of an eternal reasonableness is sufficiently proved by the fact that that *bit of the world* which we know—I mean our human reason—is none too reasonable. And if *this* is not eternally and wholly wise and reasonable, the rest of the world will not be so either. Here the conclusion *a minori ad majus, a parte ad totum* holds good, and that with decisive force.

3.

"IN THE BEGINNING WAS."—To glorify the origin—that is the metaphysical after-shoot which sprouts again at the contemplation of history, and absolutely makes us imagine that *in the beginning* of things lies all that is most valuable and essential.

4.

STANDARD FOR THE VALUE OF TRUTH.—The difficulty of climbing mountains is no gauge of their height. Yet in the case of science it is different!— we are told by certain persons who wish to be considered "the initiated,"—the difficulty in finding truth is to determine the value of truth!   This insane morality originates in the idea that "truths" are really nothing more than gymnastic appliances, with which we have to exercise ourselves until we are thoroughly tired.   It is a morality for the athletes and gymnasts of the intellect.

5.

USE OF WORDS AND REALITY.—There exists a simulated contempt for all the things that mankind actually holds most important, for all everyday matters.   For instance, we say "we only eat to live" —an abominable *lie*, like that which speaks of the procreation of children as the real purpose of all sexual pleasure.   Conversely, the reverence for "the most important things" is hardly ever quite genuine. The priests and metaphysicians have indeed accustomed us to a hypocritically exaggerated *use of words* regarding these matters, but they have not altered the feeling that these most important things are not so important as those despised "everyday matters."   A fatal consequence of this twofold hypocrisy is that we never make these everyday matters (such as eating, housing, clothes, and intercourse) the object of a constant unprejudiced and *universal* reflection and revision, but, as such a process appears degrading, we divert from them our serious intellectual and artistic side.   Hence in such matters habit and frivolity win an easy victory over the thoughtless, especially over inexperienced youth. On the other hand, our continual transgressions of the simplest laws of body and mind reduce us all, young and old, to a disgraceful state of dependence and servitude — I mean to that fundamentally superfluous dependence upon physicians, teachers and clergymen, whose dead-weight still lies heavy upon the whole of society.

6.

EARTHLY INFIRMITIES AND THEIR MAIN CAUSE. —If we look about us, we are always coming across men who have eaten eggs all their lives without observing that the oblong-shaped taste the best; who do not know that a thunder-storm is beneficial to the stomach ; that perfumes are most fragrant in cold, clear air; that our sense of taste varies in different parts of our mouths ; that every meal at which we talk well or listen well does harm to the digestion. If we are not satisfied with these examples of defective powers of observation, we shall concede all the more readily that the everyday matters are very imperfectly seen and rarely observed by the majority.   Is this a matter of indifference?—Let us remember, after all, that from this defect are derived *nearly all the bodily and spiritual infirmities* of the individual.   Ignorance of what is good and bad for us, in the arrangement of our mode of life, the division of our day, the selection of our friends and the time we devote to them, in business and leisure, commanding and obeying, our feeling for nature and for art, our eating, sleeping, and meditation ; ignorance and lack of keen perceptions *in the smallest and most ordinary details*—this it is that makes the world " a vale of tears " for so many.   Let us not say that here

as everywhere the fault lies with human *unreason*.
Of reason there is enough and to spare, but it is
wrongly directed and *artificially diverted* from these
little intimate things.   Priests and teachers, and the
sublime ambition of all idealists, coarser and subtler,
din it even into the child's ears that the means of
serving mankind at large depend upon altogether
different *things*—upon the salvation of the soul, the
service of the State, the advancement of science, or
even upon social position and property; whereas the
needs of the individual, his requirements great and
small during the twenty-four hours of the day, are
quite paltry or indifferent.—Even Socrates attacked
with all his might this arrogant neglect of the human
for the benefit of humanity, and loved to indicate by
a quotation from Homer the true sphere and conception of all anxiety and reflection: " All that really
matters," he said, "is the good and evil hap I find
at home."

7.

TWO MEANS OF CONSOLATION.—Epicurus, the
soul-comforter of later antiquity, said, with that marvellous insight which to this very day is so rarely to
be found, that for the calming of the spirit the solution of the final and ultimate theoretical problems is
by no means necessary.   Hence, instead of raising a
barren and remote discussion of the final question,
whether the Gods existed, it sufficed him to say to
those who were tormented by "fear of the Gods":
" If there are Gods, they do not concern themselves
with us."   The latter position is far stronger and

more favourable, for, by conceding a few points to the
other, one makes him readier to listen and to take
to heart. But as soon as he sets about proving the
opposite (that the Gods do concern themselves with
us), into what thorny jungles of error must the poor
man fall, quite of his own accord, and without any
cunning on the part of his interlocutor! The latter
must only have enough subtlety and humanity to
conceal his sympathy with this tragedy. Finally, the
other comes to feel disgust—the strongest argument
against any proposition—disgust with his own hypothesis. He becomes cold, and goes away in the same
frame of mind as the pure atheist who says, " What
do the Gods matter to me? The devil take them!"—
In other cases, especially when a half-physical, half-
moral assumption had cast a gloom over his spirit,
Epicurus did not refute the assumption. He agreed
that it might be true, but that there was *a second
assumption* to explain the same phenomenon, and
that it could perhaps be maintained in other ways.
The plurality of hypotheses (for example, that concerning the origin of conscientious scruples) suffices
even in our time to remove from the soul the shadows
that arise so easily from pondering over a hypothesis
which is isolated, merely visible, and hence overvalued
a hundredfold.—Thus whoever wishes to console the
unfortunate, the criminal, the hypochondriac, the
dying, may call to mind the two soothing suggestions
of Epicurus, which can be applied to a great number
of problems. In their simplest form they would run :
firstly, granted the thing is so, it does not concern
us ; secondly, the thing may be so, but it may also
be otherwise.

8.

IN THE NIGHT.—So soon as night begins to fall our sensations concerning everyday matters are altered.   There is the wind, prowling as if on forbidden paths, whispering as if in search of something, fretting because he cannot find it.   There is the lamplight, with its dim red glow, its weary look, unwillingly fighting against night, a sullen slave to wakeful man.   There are the breathings of the sleeper, with their terrible rhythm, to which an ever-recurring care seems to blow the trumpet-melody—we do not hear it, but when the sleeper's bosom heaves we feel our heart-strings tighten ; and when the breath sinks and almost dies away into a deathly stillness, we say to ourselves, "Rest awhile, poor troubled spirit !"   All living creatures bear so great a burden that we wish them an eternal rest ; night invites to death.—If human beings were deprived of the sun and resisted night by means of moonlight and oil-lamps, what a philosophy would cast its veil over them !   We already see only too plainly how a shadow is thrown over the spiritual and intellectual nature of man by that moiety of darkness and sunlessness that envelops life.

9.

ORIGIN OF THE DOCTRINE OF FREE WILL.—Necessity sways one man in the shape of his passions, another as a habit of hearing and obeying, a third as a logical conscience, a fourth as a caprice and a mischievous delight in evasions.   These four,

however, seek the freedom of their will at the very
point where they are most securely fettered. It is
as if the silkworm sought freedom of will in spinning.
What is the reason? Clearly this, that every one
thinks himself most free where his vitality is strongest; hence, as I have said, now in passion, now in
duty, now in knowledge, now in caprice. A man unconsciously imagines that where he is strong, where
he feels most thoroughly alive, the element of his
freedom must lie. He thinks of dependence and
apathy, independence and vivacity as forming inevitable pairs.—Thus an experience that a man
has undergone in the social and political sphere is
wrongly transferred to the ultimate metaphysical
sphere. There the strong man is also the free man,
there the vivid feeling of joy and sorrow, the high
hopes, the keen desires, the powerful hates are the
attributes of the ruling, independent natures, while
the thrall and the slave live in a state of dazed
oppression.—The doctrine of free will is an invention
of the ruling classes.

10.

ABSENCE OF FEELING OF NEW CHAINS.—So
long as we do not feel that we are in some way dependent, we consider ourselves independent—a false
conclusion that shows how proud man is, how eager
for dominion. For he hereby assumes that he would
always be sure to observe and recognise dependence
so soon as he suffered it, the preliminary hypothesis
being that he generally lives in independence, and
that, should he lose that independence for once in a
way, he would immediately detect a contrary sensa-

tion.—Suppose, however, the reverse to be true—
that he is always living in a complex state of dependence, but thinks himself free where, through long
habit, he no longer feels the weight of the chain?
He only suffers from new chains, and "free will"
really means nothing more than an absence of feeling of new chains.

II.

FREEDOM OF THE WILL AND THE ISOLATION OF
FACTS.—Our ordinary inaccurate observation takes
a group of phenomena as one and calls them a fact.
Between this fact and another we imagine a vacuum,
we isolate each fact.   In reality, however, the sum
of our actions and cognitions is no series of facts
and intervening vacua, but a continuous stream.
Now the belief in free will is incompatible with the
idea of a continuous, uniform, undivided, indivisible
flow.   This belief presupposes that every single
action is isolated and indivisible; it is an atomic
theory as regards volition and cognition.—We misunderstand facts as we misunderstand characters,
speaking of similar characters and similar facts,
whereas both are non-existent.   Further, we bestow
praise and blame only on this false hypothesis, that
there are similar facts, that a graduated order of
species of facts exists, corresponding to a graduated
order of values.   Thus we isolate not only the single
fact, but the groups of apparently equal facts (good,
evil, compassionate, envious actions, and so forth).
In both cases we are wrong.—The word and the
concept are the most obvious reason for our belief
in this isolation of groups of actions.   We do not

merely thereby designate the things ; the thought at
the back of our minds is that by the word and the
concept we can grasp the essence of the actions.
We are still constantly led astray by words and
actions, and are induced to think of things as simpler
than they are, as separate, indivisible, existing in
the absolute.   Language contains a hidden philosophical mythology, which, however careful we may
be, breaks out afresh at every moment.   The belief
in free will—that is to say, in similar facts and isolated facts—finds in language its continual apostle
and advocate.

12.

THE FUNDAMENTAL ERRORS.—A man cannot
feel any psychical pleasure or pain unless he is
swayed by one of two illusions.   Either he believes
in the identity of certain facts, certain sensations,
and in that case finds spiritual pleasure and pain
in comparing present with past conditions and in
noting their similarity or difference (as is invariably
the case with recollection); or he believes in the
freedom of the will, perhaps when he reflects, " I
ought not to have done this," " This might have
turned out differently," and from these reflections
likewise he derives pleasure and pain.   Without
the errors that are rife in every psychical pain and
pleasure, humanity would never have developed.
For the root idea of humanity is that man is free in a
world of bondage—man, the eternal wonder-worker,
whether his deeds be good or evil—man, the amazing exception, the super-beast, the quasi-God, the
mind of creation, the indispensable, the key-word

to the cosmic riddle, the mighty lord of nature and despiser of nature, the creature that calls *its* history "the history of the world"! *Vanitas vanitatum homo.*

13.

REPETITION.—It is an excellent thing to express a thing consecutively in two ways, and thus provide it with a right and a left foot. Truth can stand indeed on one leg, but with two she will walk and complete her journey.

14.

MAN AS THE COMIC ACTOR OF THE WORLD.— It would require beings more intellectual than men to relish to the full the humorous side of man's view of himself as the goal of all existence and of his serious pronouncement that he is satisfied only with the prospect of fulfilling a world-mission. If a God created the world, he created man to be his ape, as a perpetual source of amusement in the midst of his rather tedious eternities. The music of the spheres surrounding the world would then presumably be the mocking laughter of all the other creatures around mankind. God in his boredom uses pain for the tickling of his favourite animal, in order to enjoy his proudly tragic gestures and expressions of suffering, and, in general, the intellectual inventiveness of the vainest of his creatures—as inventor of this inventor. For he who invented man as a joke had more intellect and more joy in intellect than has man.—Even here, where our human nature is willing to humble itself, our vanity again plays us a trick, in that we men should like in this vanity at least to be quite marvellous and incomparable. Our uniqueness in the world! Oh, what an improbable thing it is! Astronomers, who occasionally acquire a horizon outside our world, give us to understand that the drop of life on the earth is without significance for the total character of the mighty ocean of birth and decay; that countless stars present conditions for the generation of life similar to those of the earth—and yet these are but a handful in comparison with the endless number that have never known, or have long been cured, of the eruption of life; that life on each of these stars, measured by the period of its existence, has been but an instant, a flicker, with long, long intervals afterwards—and thus in no way the aim and final purpose of their existence. Possibly the ant in the forest is quite as firmly convinced that it is the aim and purpose of the existence of the forest, as we are convinced in our imaginations (almost unconsciously) that the destruction of mankind involves the destruction of the world. It is even modesty on our part to go no farther than this, and not to arrange a universal twilight of the world and the Gods as the funeral ceremony of the last man. Even to the eye of the most unbiassed astronomer a lifeless world can scarcely appear otherwise than as a shining and swinging star wherein man lies buried.

15.

THE MODESTY OF MAN.—How little pleasure is enough for the majority to make them feel that life is good! How modest is man!

16.

WHERE INDIFFERENCE IS NECESSARY.—Nothing would be more perverse than to wait for the truths that science will finally establish concerning the first and last things, and until then to think (and especially to believe) in the traditional way, as one is so often advised to do. The impulse that bids us seek nothing but *certainties* in this domain is a religious offshoot, nothing better—a hidden and only apparently sceptical variety of the " metaphysical need," the underlying idea being that for a long time no view of these ultimate certainties will be obtainable, and that until then the " believer" has the right not to trouble himself about the whole subject. We have no need of these certainties about the farthermost horizons in order to live a full and efficient human life, any more than the ant needs them in order to be a good ant. Rather must we ascertain the origin of that troublesome significance that we have attached to these things for so long. For this we require the history of ethical and religious sentiments, since it is only under the influence of such sentiments that these most acute problems of knowledge have become so weighty and terrifying. Into the outermost regions to which the mental eye can penetrate (without ever penetrating *into* them), we have smuggled such concepts as guilt and punishment (everlasting punishment, too !). The darker those regions, the more careless we have been. For ages men have let their imaginations run riot where they

could establish nothing, and have induced posterity
to accept these fantasies as something serious and
true, with this abominable lie as their final trump-
card : that faith is worth more than knowledge.
What we need now in regard to these ultimate things
is not knowledge as against faith, but indifference
as against faith and pretended knowledge in these
matters !—Everything must lie nearer to us than
what has hitherto been preached to us as the most
important thing, I mean the questions : " What end
does man serve ? " " What is his fate after death ? "
" How does he make his peace with God ? " and all
the rest of that bag of tricks.   The problems of the
dogmatic philosophers, be they idealists, materialists,
or realists, concern us as little as do these religious
questions.   They all have the same object in view
—to force us to a decision in matters where neither
faith nor knowledge is needed.   It is better even
for the most ardent lover of knowledge that the
territory open to investigation and to reason should
be encircled by a belt of fog-laden, treacherous
marshland, a strip of ever watery, impenetrable, and
indeterminable country.   It is just by the comparison with the realm of darkness on the edge of
the world of knowledge that the bright, accessible
region of that world rises in value.—We must once
more become good friends of the "everyday matters,"
and not, as hitherto, despise them and look beyond
them at clouds and monsters of the night.   In forests
and caverns, in marshy tracts and under dull skies,
on the lowest rungs of the ladder of culture, man
has lived for æons, and lived in poverty.   There
he has learnt to despise the present, his neighbours,

his life, and himself, and we, the inhabitants of the brighter fields of Nature and mind, still inherit in our blood some taint of this contempt for everyday matters.

17.

PROFOUND INTERPRETATIONS.—He who has interpreted a passage in an author " more profoundly " than was intended, has not interpreted the author but has obscured him.   Our metaphysicians are in the same relation, or even in a worse relation, to the text of Nature.   For, to apply their profound interpretations, they often alter the text to suit their purpose—or, in other words, corrupt the text.   A curious example of the corruption and obscuration of an author's text is furnished by the ideas of Schopenhauer on the pregnancy of women.   " The sign of a continuous will to life in time," he says, " is copulation ; the sign of the light of knowledge which is associated anew with this will and holds the possibility of a deliverance, and that too in the highest degree of clearness, is the renewed incarnation of the will to life.   This incarnation is betokened by pregnancy, which is therefore frank and open, and even proud, whereas copulation hides itself like a criminal."   He declares that every woman, if surprised in the sexual act, would be likely to die of shame, but " displays her pregnancy without a trace of shame, nay even with a sort of pride."   Now, firstly, this condition cannot easily be displayed more aggressively than it displays itself, and when

Schopenhauer gives prominence only to the intentional character of the display, he is fashioning his text to suit the interpretation. Moreover, his statement of the universality of the phenomenon is not true. He speaks of "every woman." Many women, especially the younger, often appear painfully ashamed of their condition, even in the presence of their nearest kinsfolk. And when women of riper years, especially in the humbler classes, do actually appear proud of their condition, it is because they would give us to understand that they are still desirable to their husbands. That a neighbour on seeing them or a passing stranger should say or think " Can it be possible ? "—that is an alms always acceptable to the vanity of women of low mental capacity. In the reverse instance, to conclude from Schopenhauer's proposition, the cleverest and most intelligent women would tend more than any to exult openly in their condition. For they have the best prospect of giving birth to an intellectual prodigy, in whom "the will" can once more "negative" itself for the universal good. Stupid women, on the other hand, would have every reason to hide their pregnancy more modestly than anything they hide.—It cannot be said that this view corresponds to reality. Granted, however, that Schopenhauer was right on the general principle that women show more self-satisfaction when pregnant than at any other time, a better explanation than this lies to hand. One might imagine the clucking of a hen even before she lays an egg, saying, " Look ! look ! I shall lay an egg ! I shall lay an egg ! "

18.

THE MODERN DIOGENES.—Before we look for man, we must have found the lantern.—Will it have to be the Cynic's lantern?

19.

IMMORALISTS.—Moralists must now put up with being rated as immoralists, because they dissect morals. He, however, who would dissect must kill, but only in order that we may know more, judge better, live better, not in order that all the world may dissect. Unfortunately, men still think that every moralist in his every action must be a pattern for others to imitate. They confound him with the preacher of morality. The older moralists did not dissect enough and preached too often, whence that confusion and the unpleasant consequences for our latter-day moralists are derived.

20.

A CAUTION AGAINST CONFUSION.—There are moralists who treat the strong, noble, self-denying attitude of such beings as the heroes of Plutarch, or the pure, enlightened, warmth-giving state of soul peculiar to truly good men and women, as difficult scientific problems. They investigate the origin of such phenomena, indicating the complex element in the apparent simplicity, and directing their gaze to the tangled skein of motives, the delicate web of conceptual illusions, and the sentiments of individuals or of groups, that are a legacy of ancient days gradually increased. Such moralists are very different from those with whom they are most commonly confounded, from those petty minds that do not believe at all in these modes of thought and states of soul, and imagine their own poverty to be hidden somewhere behind the glamour of greatness and purity. The moralists say, "Here are problems," and these pitiable creatures say, "Here are impostors and deceptions." Thus the latter deny the existence of the very things which the former are at pains to explain.

21.

MAN AS THE MEASURER.—Perhaps all human morality had its origin in the tremendous excitement that seized primitive man when he discovered measure and measuring, scales and weighing (for the word *Mensch* [man] means " the measurer "—he wished to *name* himself after his greatest discovery!). With these ideas they mounted into regions that are quite beyond all measuring and weighing, but did not appear to be so in the beginning.

22.

THE PRINCIPLE OF EQUILIBRIUM.—The robber and the man of power who promises to protect a community from robbers are perhaps at bottom beings of the same mould, save that the latter attains his ends by other means than the former— that is to say, through regular imposts paid to him by the community, and no longer through forced contributions. (The same relation exists between

merchant and pirate, who for a long period are one
and the same person: where the one function appears to them inadvisable, they exercise the other.
Even to-day mercantile morality is really nothing
but a refinement on piratical morality—buying in
the cheapest market, at prime cost if possible, and
selling in the dearest.) The essential point is that
the man of power promises to maintain the equilibrium against the robber, and herein the weak find
a possibility of living. For either they must group
themselves into an equivalent power, or they must
subject themselves to some one of equivalent power
(*i.e.* render service in return for his efforts). The
latter course is generally preferred, because it really
keeps two dangerous beings in check—the robber
through the man of power, and the man of power
through the standpoint of advantage ; for the latter
profits by treating his subjects with graciousness
and tolerance, in order that they may support not
only themselves but their ruler. As a matter of
fact, conditions may still be hard and cruel enough,
yet in comparison with the complete annihilation
that was formerly always a possibility, men breathe
freely.—The community is at first the organisation of the weak to counterbalance menacing forces.
An organisation to outweigh those forces would be
more advisable, if its members grew strong enough
to destroy the adverse power: and when it is a
question of one mighty oppressor, the *attempt will*
certainly be made. But if the one man is the head
of a clan, or if he has a large following, a rapid and
decisive annihilation is improbable, and a long or
permanent feud is only to be expected. This feud,

however, involves the least desirable condition for
the community, for it thereby loses the time to provide for its means of subsistence with the necessary
regularity, and sees the product of all work hourly
threatened.   Hence the community prefers to raise
its power of attack and defence to the exact plane
on which the power of its dangerous neighbour
stands, and to give him to understand that an equal
weight now lies in its own side of the scales—so
why not be good friends?—Thus equilibrium is a
most important conception for the understanding
of the ancient doctrines of law and morals.   Equilibrium is, in fact, the basis of justice.   When justice
in ruder ages says, " An eye for an eye, a tooth
for a tooth," it presupposes the attainment of this
equilibrium and tries to maintain it by means of
this compensation ; so that, when crime is committed, the injured party will not take the revenge
of blind anger.   By means of the *jus talionis* the
equilibrium of the disturbed relations of power is
restored, for in such primitive times an eye or an
arm more means a bit more power, more weight.
—In a community where all consider themselves
equal, disgrace and punishment await crime—that
is, violations of the principle of equilibrium.   Disgrace is thrown into the scale as a counter-weight
against the encroaching individual, who has gained
profit by his encroachment, and now suffers losses
(through disgrace) which annul and outweigh the
previous profits.   Punishment, in the same way,
sets up a far greater counter-weight against the preponderance which every criminal hopes to obtain—
imprisonment as against a deed of violence, restitu-

tion and fines as against theft.   Thus the sinner is
reminded that his action has excluded him from the
community and from its moral advantages, since
the community treats him as an inferior, a weaker
brother, an outsider.   For this reason punishment
is not merely retaliation, but has something more,
something of the cruelty of the state of nature, and
of this it would serve as a reminder.

23.

WHETHER THE ADHERENTS OF THE DOCTRINE
OF FREE WILL HAVE A RIGHT TO PUNISH?—Men
whose vocation it is to judge and punish try to
establish in every case whether an evil-doer is really
responsible for his act, whether he was able to apply
his reasoning powers, whether he acted with motives
and not unconsciously or under constraint.   If he is
punished, it is because he preferred the worse to the
better motives, which he must consequently have
known.   Where this knowledge is wanting, man is,
according to the prevailing view, not responsible—
unless his ignorance, *e.g.* his *ignorantia legis*, be the
consequence of an intentional neglect to learn what
he ought: in that case he already preferred the
worse to the better motives at the time when he
refused to learn, and must now pay the penalty of
his unwise choice.   If, on the other hand, perhaps
through stupidity or shortsightedness, he has never
seen the better motives, he is generally not punished, for people say that he made a wrong choice,
he acted like a brute beast.   The intentional rejection of the better reason is now needed before we

treat the offender as fit to be punished. But how can
any one be intentionally more unreasonable than he
ought to be?   Whence comes the decision, if the
scales are loaded with good and bad motives?   So
the origin is not error or blindness, not an internal
or external constraint?   (It should furthermore be
remembered that every so-called "external constraint" is nothing more than the internal constraint
of fear and pain.) Whence? is the repeated question.
So reason is not to be the cause of action, because
reason cannot decide against the better motives?
Thus we call "free will" to our aid.   Absolute
discretion is to decide, and a moment is to intervene
when no motive exercises an influence, when the
deed is done as a miracle, resulting from nothing.
This assumed discretion is punished in a case
where no discretion should rule.   Reason, which
knows law, prohibition, and command, should have
left no choice, they say, and should have acted
as a constraint and a higher power.   Hence the
offender is punished because he makes use of "free
will"—in other words, has acted without motive
where he should have been guided by motives.
But why did he do it?   This question must not even
be asked; the deed was done without a "Why?"
without motive, without origin, being a thing pur-
poseless, unreasoned.—However, according to the
above-named preliminary condition of punishability,
such a deed should not be punished at all!   Moreover, even this reason for punishing should not
hold good, that in this case something had *not* been
done, had been omitted, that reason had not been
used at all: for at any rate the omission was unin-

tentional, and only intentional omission is considered punishable. The offender has indeed preferred the worse to the better motives, but without motive and purpose: he has indeed failed to apply his reason, but not exactly with the object of not applying it. The very assumption made in the case of punishable crime, that the criminal intentionally renounced his reason, is removed by the hypothesis of " free will." According to your own principles, you must not punish, you adherents of the doctrine of free will!—These principles are, however, nothing but a very marvellous conceptual mythology, and the hen that hatched them has brooded on her eggs far away from all reality.

24.

JUDGING THE CRIMINAL AND HIS JUDGE.—The criminal, who knows the whole concatenation of circumstances, does not consider his act so far beyond the bounds of order and comprehension as does his judge. His punishment, however, is measured by the degree of astonishment that seizes the judge when he finds the crime incomprehensible. —If the defending counsel's knowledge of the case and its previous history extends far enough, the so-called extenuating circumstances which he duly pleads must end by absolving his client from all guilt. Or, to put it more plainly, the advocate will, step by step, tone down and finally remove the astonishment of the judge, by forcing every honest listener to the tacit avowal, " He was bound to act as he did, and if we punished, we should be punishing eternal Necessity."—Measuring the punishment by the degree of knowledge we possess or can obtain of the previous history of the crime— is that not in conflict with all equity?

25.

EXCHANGE AND EQUITY.—In an exchange, the only just and honest course would be for either party to demand only so much as he considers his commodity to be worth, allowance being made for trouble in acquisition, scarcity, time spent and so forth, besides the subjective value. As soon as you make your price bear a relation to the other's need, you become a refined sort of robber and ex-tortioner.—If money is the sole medium of ex-change, we must remember that a shilling is by no means the same thing in the hands of a rich heir, a farm labourer, a merchant, and a university student. It would be equitable for every one to receive much or little for his money, according as he has done much or little to earn it. In practice, as we all know, the reverse is the case. In the world of high finance the shilling of the idle rich man can buy more than that of the poor, industrious man.

26.

LEGAL CONDITIONS AS MEANS.—Law, where it rests upon contracts between equals, holds good so long as the power of the parties to the contract remains equal or similar. Wisdom created law to end all feuds and useless expenditure among men on an equal footing. Quite as definite an end is put to this waste, however, when one party has

become decidedly weaker than the other.   Subjec-
tion enters and law ceases, but the result is the
same as that attained by law.   For now it is the
wisdom of the superior which advises to spare the
inferior and not uselessly to squander his strength.
Thus the position of the inferior is often more favourable than that of the equal.—Hence legal conditions are temporary *means* counselled by wisdom,
and not ends.

27.

EXPLANATION OF MALICIOUS JOY.—Malicious
joy arises when a man consciously finds himself
in evil plight and feels anxiety or remorse or pain.
The misfortune that overtakes B. makes him equal
to A., and A. is reconciled and no longer envious.
—If A. is prosperous, he still hoards up in his
memory B.'s misfortune as a capital, so as to throw
it in the scale as a counter-weight when he himself suffers adversity.   In this case too he feels
" malicious joy " (*Schadenfreude*).   The sentiment
of equality thus applies its standard to the domain
of luck and chance.   Malicious joy is the commonest
expression of victory and restoration of equality,
even in a higher state of civilisation.   This emotion
has only been in existence since the time when
man learnt to look upon another as his equal—in
other words, since the foundation of society.

28.

THE ARBITRARY ELEMENT IN THE AWARD OF
PUNISHMENT. — To   most   criminals   punishment

comes just as illegitimate children come to women.
They have done the same thing a hundred times
without any bad consequences. Suddenly comes
discovery, and with discovery punishment. Yet
habit should make the deed for which the
criminal is punished appear more excusable, for he
has developed a propensity that is hard to resist.
Instead of this, the criminal is punished more
severely if the suspicion of habitual crime rests on
him, and habit is made a valid reason against all
extenuation.   On the other hand, a model life,
wherein crime shows up in more terrible contrast,
should make the guilt appear more heavy! But
here the custom is to soften the punishment.
Everything is measured not from the standpoint
of the criminal but from that of society and its
losses and dangers.   The previous utility of an
individual is weighed against his one nefarious
action, his previous criminality is added to that
recently discovered, and punishment is thus meted
out as highly as possible.   But if we thus punish or
reward a man's past (for in the former case the
diminution of punishment is a reward) we ought
to go farther back and punish and reward the
cause of his past—I mean parents, teachers, society.
In many instances we shall then find the *judges*
somehow or other sharing in the guilt.   It is arbitrary to stop at the criminal himself when we
punish his past : if we will not grant the absolute
excusability of every crime, we should stop at each
individual case and probe no farther into the past
—in other words, isolate guilt and not connect it
with previous actions.   Otherwise we sin against

logic. The teachers of free will should draw the inevitable conclusion from their doctrine of " free will " and boldly decree : " No action has a past."

29.

ENVY AND HER NOBLER SISTER. — Where equality is really recognised and permanently established, we see the rise of that propensity that is generally considered immoral, and would scarcely be conceivable in a state of nature—envy. The envious man is susceptible to every sign of individual superiority to the common herd, and wishes to depress every one once more to the level —or raise himself to the superior plane. Hence arise two different modes of action, which Hesiod designated good and bad Eris. In the same way, in a condition of equality there arises indignation if A. is prosperous above and B. unfortunate beneath their deserts and equality. These latter, however, are emotions of nobler natures. They feel the want of justice and equity in things that are independent of the arbitrary choice of men—or, in other words, they desire the equality recognised by man to be recognised as well by Nature and chance. They are angry that men of equal merits should not have equal fortune.

30.

THE ENVY OF THE GODS.—" The envy of the Gods " arises when a despised person sets himself on an equality with his superior (like Ajax), or is made equal with him by the favour of fortune (like Niobe, the too favoured mother). In the social class system this envy demands that no one shall have merits above his station, that his prosperity shall be on a level with his position, and especially that his self-consciousness shall not outgrow the limits of his rank. Often the victorious general, or the pupil who achieves a masterpiece, has experienced "the envy of the gods."

31.

VANITY AS AN ANTI-SOCIAL AFTERGROWTH.— As men, for the sake of security, have made themselves equal in order to found communities, but as also this conception is imposed by a sort of constraint and is entirely opposed to the instincts of the individual, so, the more universal security is guaranteed, the more do new offshoots of the old instinct for predominance appear. Such offshoots appear in the setting-up of class distinctions, in the demand for professional dignities and privileges, and, generally speaking, in vanity (manners, dress, speech, and so forth). So soon as danger to the community is apparent, the majority, who were unable to assert their preponderance in a time of universal peace, once more bring about the condition of equality, and for the time being the absurd privileges and vanities disappear. If the community, however, collapses utterly and anarchy reigns supreme, there arises the state of nature: an absolutely ruthless inequality as recounted by Thucydides in the case of Corcyra. Neither a natural justice nor a natural injustice exists.

32.

EQUITY.—Equity is a development of justice, and arises among such as do not come into conflict with the communal equality. This more subtle recognition of the principle of equilibrium is applied to cases where nothing is prescribed by law. Equity looks forwards and backwards, its maxim being, "Do unto others as you would that they should do unto you." *Aequum* means: "This principle is conformable to our equality; it tones down even our small differences to an appearance of equality, and expects us to be indulgent in cases where we are not compelled to pardon."

33.

ELEMENTS OF REVENGE.—The word "revenge" is spoken so quickly that it almost seems as if it could not contain more than one conceptual and emotional root. Hence we are still at pains to find this root. Our economists, in the same way, have never wearied of scenting a similar unity in the word "value," and of hunting after the primitive root idea of value. As if all words were not pockets, into which this or that or several things have been stuffed at once! So "revenge" is now one thing, now another, and sometimes more composite. Let us first distinguish that defensive counter-blow, which we strike, almost unconsciously, even at inanimate objects (such as machinery in motion) that have hurt us. The notion is to set a check to the object that has hurt us, by bringing the machine to a stop.   Sometimes the force of this counter-blow, in order to attain its object, will have to be strong enough to shatter the machine.   If the machine be too strong to be disorganised by one man, the latter will all the same strike the most violent blow he can —as a sort of last attempt.   We behave similarly towards persons who hurt us, at the immediate sensation of the hurt.   If we like to call this an act of revenge, well and good : but we must remember that here self-preservation alone has set its cog-wheels of reason in motion, and that after all we do not think of the doer of the injury but only of ourselves. We act without any idea of doing injury in return, only with a view to getting away safe and sound. —It needs time to pass in thought from oneself to one's adversary and ask oneself at what point he is most vulnerable.   This is done in the second variety of revenge, the preliminary idea of which is to consider the vulnerability and susceptibility of the other. The intention then is to give pain.   On the other hand, the idea of securing himself against further injury is in this case so entirely outside the avenger's horizon, that he almost regularly brings about his own further injury and often foresees it in cold blood.   If in the first sort of revenge it was the fear of a second blow that made the counter-blow as strong as possible, in this case there is an almost complete indifference to what one's adversary will do : the strength of the counter-blow is only determined by what he has *already* done to us.   Then what has he done ?   What profit is it to us if he is now suffering, after we have suffered through him ?   This is a case of readjustment, whereas the first act of revenge only serves the purpose of self-preservation. It may be that through our adversary we have lost property, rank, friends, children —these losses are not recovered by revenge, the readjustment only concerns a subsidiary loss which is added to all the other losses. The revenge of readjustment does not preserve one from further injury, it does not make good the injury already suffered—except in one case. If our honour has suffered through our adversary, revenge can restore it. But in any case honour *has* suffered an injury if intentional harm has been done us, because our adversary proved thereby that he was not afraid of us. By revenge we prove that we are not afraid of him either, and herein lies the settlement, the readjustment. (The intention of showing their complete lack of fear goes so far in some people that the dangers of revenge—loss of health or life or other losses—are in their eyes an indispensable condition of every vengeful act. Hence they practise the duel, although the law also offers them aid in obtaining satisfaction for what they have suffered. They are not satisfied with a safe means of recovering their honour, because this would not prove their fearlessness.)—In the first-named variety of revenge it is just fear that strikes the counter-blow; in the second case it is the absence of fear, which, as has been said, wishes to manifest itself in the counter-blow.—Thus nothing appears more different than the motives of the two courses of action which are designated by the one word "revenge." Yet it often happens that the avenger is not precisely certain as to what really prompted his deed : perhaps he struck the counter-blow from fear and the instinct of self-preservation, but in the background, when he has time to reflect upon the standpoint of wounded honour, he imagines that he has avenged himself for the sake of his honour—this motive is in any case more *reputable* than the other.   An essential point is whether he sees his honour injured in the eyes of others (the world) or only in the eyes of his offenders: in the latter case he will prefer secret, in the former open revenge.   Accordingly, as he enters strongly or feebly into the soul of the doer and the spectator, his revenge will be more bitter or more tame.   If he is entirely lacking in this sort of imagination, he will not think at all of revenge, as the feeling of " honour " is not present in him, and accordingly cannot be wounded.   In the same way, he will not think of revenge if he despises the offender and the spectator ; because as objects of his contempt they cannot give him honour, and accordingly cannot rob him of honour.   Finally, he will forego revenge in the not uncommon case of his loving the offender. It is true that he then suffers loss of honour in the other's eyes, and will perhaps become less worthy of having his love returned.   But even to renounce all requital of love is a sacrifice that love is ready to make when its only object is to avoid hurting the beloved object: this would mean hurting oneself more than one is hurt by the sacrifice.—Accordingly, every one will avenge himself, unless he be bereft of honour or inspired by contempt or by love for the offender.   Even if he turns to the law-courts, he desires revenge as a private individual ; but also, as a thoughtful, prudent man of society, he desires the revenge of society upon one who does not respect it.   Thus by legal punishment private honour as well as that of society is restored—that is to say, punishment is revenge.   Punishment undoubtedly contains the first-mentioned element of revenge, in as far as by its means society helps to preserve itself, and strikes a counter-blow in self-defence. Punishment desires to prevent further injury, to scare other offenders.   In this way the two elements of revenge, different as they are, are united in punishment, and this may perhaps tend most of all to maintain the above-mentioned confusion of ideas, thanks to which the individual avenger generally does not know what he really wants.

34.

THE VIRTUES THAT DAMAGE US.—As members of communities we think we have no right to exercise certain virtues which afford us great honour and some pleasure as private individuals (for example, indulgence and favour towards miscreants of all kinds)— in short, every mode of action whereby the advantage of society would suffer through our virtue.   No bench of judges, face to face with its conscience, may permit itself to be gracious.   This privilege is reserved for the king as an individual, and we are glad when he makes use of it, proving that we should like to be gracious individually, but not collectively.   Society recognises only the virtues profitable to her, or at least not injurious to her—virtues like justice, which are exercised without loss, or, in fact, at compound interest.   The virtues that damage us cannot have

originated in society, because even now opposition
to them arises in every small society that is in the
making.   Such virtues are therefore those of men
of unequal standing, invented by the superior individuals; they are the virtues of rulers, and the idea
underlying them is: " I am mighty enough to put
up with an obvious loss ; that is a proof of my power."
Thus they are virtues closely akin to pride.

35.

THE CASUISTRY OF ADVANTAGE.—There would
be no moral casuistry if there were no casuistry of
advantage.   The most free and refined intelligence
is often incapable of choosing between two alterna-
tives in such a way that his choice necessarily involves the greater advantage.   In such cases we
choose because we must, and afterwards often feel
a kind of emotional sea-sickness.

36.

TURNING HYPOCRITE. — Every beggar turns
hypocrite, like every one who makes his living out
of indigence, be it personal or public.—The beggar
does not feel want nearly so keenly as he must make
others feel it, if he wishes to make a living by mendi-
cancy.

37.

A SORT OF CULT OF THE PASSIONS.—You
hypochondriacs, you philosophic blind-worms talk
of the formidable nature of human passions, in
order to inveigh against the dreadsomeness of the

whole world-structure. As if the passions were always and everywhere formidable! As if this sort of terror must always exist in the world!—Through a carelessness in small matters, through a deficiency in observation of self and of the rising generation, you have yourselves allowed your passions to develop into such unruly monsters that you are frightened now at the mere mention of the word "passion"! It rests with you and it rests with us to divest the passions of their formidable features and so to dam them that they do not become devastating floods.—We must not exalt our errors into eternal fatalities. Rather shall we honestly endeavour to convert all the passions of humanity into sources of joy.*

38.

THE STING OF CONSCIENCE.—The sting of conscience, like the gnawing of a dog at a stone, is mere foolishness.

39.

ORIGIN OF RIGHTS.—Rights may be traced to traditions, traditions to momentary agreements. At some time or other men were mutually content with the consequences of making an agreement, and, again, too indolent formally to renew it. Thus they went on living as if it had constantly been renewed, and gradually, when oblivion cast its

---

* The play on *Freudenschaften* (*i.e.* pleasure-giving passions) and *Leidenschaften* (*i.e.* pain-giving passions) is often used by Nietzsche, and is untranslateable.—TR.

veil over the origin, they thought they possessed
a sacred, unalterable foundation on which every
generation would be compelled to build. Tradi-
tion was now a constraint, even if it no more involved the profit originally derived from making the
agreement.—Here the weak have always found their
strong fortress. They are inclined to immortalise
the momentary agreement, the single act of favour
shown towards them.

40.

THE SIGNIFICANCE OF OBLIVION IN MORAL
SENTIMENT.—The same actions that in primitive
society first aimed at the common advantage were
later on performed from other motives : from fear
or reverence of those who demanded and recommended them ; or from habit, because men had seen
them done about them from childhood upwards ;
or from kindness, because the practising of them
caused delight and approving looks on all sides ;
or from vanity, because they were praised. Such
actions, in which the fundamental motive, that of
utility, has been *forgotten*, are then called moral ;
not, indeed, because they are done from those other
motives, but because they are not done with a conscious purpose of utility.—Whence the hatred of
utility that suddenly manifests itself here, and
by which all praiseworthy actions formally ex-
clude all actions for the sake of utility?—Clearly
society, the rallying-point of all morality and of
all maxims in praise of moral action, has had to
battle too long and too fiercely with the selfishness
and obstinacy of the individual not to rate every

motive morally higher than utility. Hence it looks as if morals had not sprung from utility, whereas in fact morals are originally the public utility, which had great difficulty in prevailing over the interests of the unit and securing a loftier reputation.

41.

THE HEIRS TO THE WEALTH OF MORALITY.—Even in the domain of morals there is an inherited wealth, which is owned by the gentle, the good-tempered, the compassionate, the indulgent. They have inherited from their forefathers their gentle mode of action, but not common sense (the source of that mode of action). The pleasant thing about this wealth is that one must always bestow and communicate a portion of it, if its presence is to be felt at all. Thus this wealth unconsciously aims at bridging the gulf between the morally rich and the morally poor, and, what is its best and most remarkable feature, not for the sake of a future mean between rich and poor, but for the sake of a universal prosperity and superfluity.—Such may be the prevailing view of inherited moral wealth, but it seems to me that this view is maintained more *in majorem gloriam* of morality than in honour of truth. Experience at least establishes a maxim which must serve, if not as a refutation, at any rate as an important check upon that generalisation. Without the most exquisite intelligence, says experience, without the most refined capacity for choice and a strong propensity to observe the mean, the morally rich will become spendthrifts of morality.

For by abandoning themselves without restraint to their compassionate, gentle, conciliatory, harmonising instincts, they make all about them more careless, more covetous, and more sentimental. The children of these highly moral spendthrifts easily and (sad to relate) at best become pleasant but futile wasters.

42.

THE JUDGE AND EXTENUATING CIRCUMSTANCES.—"One should behave as a man of honour even towards the devil and pay his debts," said an old soldier, when the story of Faust had been related to him in rather fuller detail. "Hell is the right place for Faust!" "You are terrible, you men!" cried his wife; "how can that be? After all, his only fault was having no ink in his ink-stand! It is indeed a sin to write with blood, but surely for that such a handsome man ought not to burn in Hell-fire?"

43.

PROBLEM OF THE DUTY OF TRUTH.—Duty is an imperious sentiment that forces us to action. We call it good, and consider it outside the pale of discussion. The origin, limits, and justification of duty we will not debate or allow to be debated. But the thinker considers everything an evolution and every evolution a subject for discussion, and is accordingly without duty so long as he is merely a thinker. As such, he would not recognise the duty of seeing and speaking the truth; he would not *feel* the sentiment at all. He asks, whence comes it and whither will it go? But even this questioning appears to him questionable. Surely, however, the consequence would be that the thinker's machinery would no longer work properly if he could really feel himself unencumbered by duty in the search for knowledge? It would appear, then, that for fuel the same element is necessary as must be investigated by means of the machine.— Perhaps the formula will be: granted there were a duty of recognising truth, what is then the truth in regard to every other kind of duty?—But is not a hypothetical sense of duty a contradiction in terms?

44.

GRADES OF MORALS. — Morality is primarily a means of preserving the community and saving it from destruction. Next it is a means of maintaining the community on a certain plane and in a certain degree of benevolence. Its motives are fear and hope, and these in a more coarse, rough, and powerful form, the more the propensity towards the perverse, one-sided, and personal still persists. The most terrible means of intimidation must be brought into play so long as milder forms have no effect and that twofold species of preservation cannot be attained. (The strongest intimidation, by the way, is the invention of a hereafter with a hell everlasting.) For this purpose we must have racks and torturers of the soul. Further grades of morality, and accordingly means to the end referred to, are the commandments of a God (as in the Mosaic law). Still further and higher are the commandments of an absolute sense of duty with

a " Thou shalt "—all rather roughly hewn yet *broad*
steps, because on the finer, narrower steps men
cannot yet set their feet. Then comes a morality
of inclination, of taste, finally of insight—which is
beyond all the illusory motives of morality, but
has convinced itself that humanity for long periods
could be allowed no other.

45.

THE MORALITY OF PITY IN THE MOUTHS OF THE
INTEMPERATE.—All those who are not sufficiently
masters of themselves and do not know morality
as a self-control and self-conquest continuously
exercised in things great and small, unconsciously
come to glorify the good, compassionate, benevolent
impulses of that instinctive morality which has no
head, but seems merely to consist of a heart and
helpful hands. It is to their interest even to cast
suspicion upon a morality of reason and to set up
the other as the sole morality.

46.

SEWERS OF THE SOUL.—Even the soul must
have its definite sewers, through which it can allow
its filth to flow off: for this purpose it may use
persons, relations, social classes, its native country,
or the world, or finally—for the wholly arrogant (I
mean our modern " pessimists ")—*le bon Dieu.*

47.

A KIND OF REST AND CONTEMPLATION.—Be-
ware lest your rest and contemplation resemble that

of a dog before a butcher's stall, prevented by fear from advancing and by greed from retiring, and opening its eyes wide as though they were mouths.

48.

PROHIBITIONS WITHOUT REASONS.—A prohibition, the reason of which we do not understand or admit, is almost a command, not only for the stiff-necked but for the thirster after knowledge. We at once make an experiment in order to learn *why* the prohibition was made. Moral prohibitions, like those of the Decalogue, are only suited to ages when reason lies vanquished. Nowadays a prohibition like "Thou shalt not kill," "Thou shalt not commit adultery," laid down without reasons, would have an injurious rather than a beneficial effect.

49.

CHARACTER PORTRAIT.—What sort of a man is it that can say of himself : " I despise very easily, but never hate. I at once find out in every man something which can be honoured and for which I honour him : the so-called amiable qualities attract me but little "?

50.

PITY AND CONTEMPT.—The expression of pity is regarded as a sign of contempt, because one has clearly ceased to be an object of *fear* as soon as one becomes an object of pity. One has sunk below the level of the equilibrium. For this equilibrium does not satisfy human vanity, which is only satisfied by the feeling that one is imposing respect and awe. Hence it is difficult to explain why pity is so highly prized, just as we need to explain why the unselfish man, who is originally despised or feared as being artful, is praised.

51.

THE CAPACITY OF BEING SMALL.—We must be as near to flowers, grasses, and butterflies as a child, that is, not much bigger than they. We adults have grown up beyond them and have to stoop to them. I think the grasses hate us when we confess our love for them.—He who would have a share in all good things must understand at times how to be small.

52.

THE SUM-TOTAL OF CONSCIENCE.—The sum-total of our conscience is all that has regularly been demanded of us, without reason, in the days of our childhood, by people whom we respected or feared. From conscience comes that feeling of obligation ("This I must do, this omit") which does not ask, Why must I?—In all cases where a thing is done with "because" and "why," man acts without conscience, but not necessarily on that account *against* conscience.—The belief in authority is the source of conscience; which is therefore not the voice of God in the heart of man, but the voice of some men in man.

53.

CONQUEST OF THE PASSIONS.—The man who has overcome his passions has entered into possession of the most fruitful soil, like the colonist who has become lord over bogs and forests. To sow the seed of spiritual good works on the soil of the vanquished passions is the next and most urgent task. The conquest itself is a means, not an end: if it be not so regarded, all kind of weeds and devil's crop quickly spring up upon the fertile soil that has been cleared, and soon the growth is all wilder and more luxuriant than before.

54.

SKILL IN SERVICE.—All so-called practical men have skill in service, whether it be serving others or themselves; this is what makes them practical. Robinson owned a servant even better than Friday —his name was Crusoe.

55.

DANGER IN SPEECH TO INTELLECTUAL FREE- DOM.—Every word is a preconceived judgment.

56.

INTELLECT AND BOREDOM.—The proverb, " The Hungarian is far too lazy to feel bored," gives food for thought. Only the highest and most active animals are capable of being bored.—The boredom of God on the seventh day of Creation would be a subject for a great poet.

57.

INTERCOURSE WITH ANIMALS.—The origin of our morality may still be observed in our relations with animals. Where advantage or the reverse do not come into play, we have a feeling of complete irresponsibility. For example, we kill or wound insects or let them live, and as a rule think no more about it. We are so clumsy that even our gracious acts towards flowers and small animals are almost always murderous: this does not in the least detract from our pleasure in them.—To-day is the festival of the small animals, the most sultry day of the year. There is a swarming and crawling around us, and we, without intention, but also without reflection, crush here and there a little fly or winged beetle.—If animals do us harm, we strive to *annihilate* them in every possible way. The means are often cruel enough, even without our really intending them to be so—it is the cruelty of thoughtlessness. If they are useful, we turn them to advantage, until a more refined wisdom teaches us that certain animals amply reward a different mode of treatment, that of tending and breeding. Here responsibility first arises. Torturing is avoided in the case of the domestic animal. One man is indignant if another is cruel to his cow, quite in accordance with the primitive communal morality, which sees the commonwealth in danger whenever an individual does wrong. He who perceives any transgression in the community fears indirect harm to himself. Thus we fear in this case for the quality of meat, agriculture, and means of communication if we see the domestic animals ill-treated. Moreover, he who is harsh to animals awakens a suspicion that he is also harsh to men who are weak, inferior, and incapable of revenge. He is held to be ignoble and deficient in the finer form of pride. Thus arises a foundation of moral judgments and sentiments, but the greatest contribution is made by superstition. Many animals incite men by glances, tones, and gestures to transfer themselves into them in imagination, and some religions teach us, under certain circumstances, to see in animals the dwelling-place of human and divine souls : whence they recommend a nobler caution or even a reverential awe in intercourse with animals. Even after the disappearance of this superstition the sentiments awakened by it continue to exercise their influence, to ripen and to blossom.—Christianity, as is well known, has shown itself in this respect a poor and retrograde religion.

58.

NEW ACTORS.—Among human beings there is no greater banality than death. Second in order, because it is possible to die without being born, comes birth, and next comes marriage. But these hackneyed little tragi-comedies are always presented, at each of their unnumbered and innumerable performances, by new actors, and accordingly do not cease to find interested spectators : whereas we might well believe that the whole audience of the world-theatre had long since hanged themselves to every tree from sheer boredom at these performances. So much depends on new actors, so little on the piece.

59.

WHAT IS " BEING OBSTINATE " ?—The shortest way is not the straightest possible, but that wherein

favourable winds swell our sails.   So says the wisdom of seamen.   Not to follow his course is obstinate, firmness of character being then adulterated
by stupidity.

60.

THE WORD "VANITY."—It is annoying that
certain words, with which we moralists positively
cannot dispense, involve in themselves a kind of
censorship of morals, dating from the times when
the most ordinary and natural impulses were de-
nounced.   Thus that fundamental conviction that
on the waves of society we either find navigable
waters or suffer shipwreck far more through what
we appear than through what we are (a conviction
that must act as guiding principle of all action in
relation to society) is branded with the general word
" vanity."   In other words, one of the most weighty
and significant of qualities is branded with an expression which denotes it as essentially empty and
negative : a great thing is designated by a diminutive, ay, even slandered by the strokes of caricature.
There is no help for it ; we must use such words, but
then we must shut our ears to the insinuations of
ancient habits.

61.

THE FATALISM OF THE TURK.—The fatalism of
the Turk has this fundamental defect, that it contrasts man and fate as two distinct things.   Man,
says this doctrine, may struggle against fate and
try to baffle it, but in the end fate will always gain
the victory.   Hence the most rational course is to

resign oneself or to live as one pleases. As a matter of fact, every man is himself a piece of fate. When he thinks that he is struggling against fate in this way, fate is accomplishing its ends even in that struggle. The combat is a fantasy, but so is the resignation in fate—all these fantasies are included in fate.—The fear felt by most people of the doctrine that denies the freedom of the will is a fear of the fatalism of the Turk. They imagine that man will become weakly resigned and will stand before the future with folded hands, because he cannot alter anything of the future. Or that he will give a free rein to his caprices, because the predestined cannot be made worse by that course. The follies of men are as much a piece of fate as are his wise actions, and even that fear of belief in fate is a fatality. You yourself, you poor timid creature, are that indomitable *Moira*, which rules even the Gods; whatever may happen, you are a curse or a blessing, and in any case the fetters wherein the strongest lies bound : in you the whole future of the human world is predestined, and it is no use for you to be frightened of yourself.

62.

THE ADVOCATE OF THE DEVIL.—" Only by our own suffering do we become wise, only by others' suffering do we become good "—so runs that strange philosophy which derives all morality from pity and all intellectuality from the isolation of the individual. Herein this philosophy is the unconscious pleader for all human deterioration. For pity needs suffering, and isolation contempt of others.

63.

THE MORAL CHARACTER-MASKS. — In ages when the character-masks of different classes are definitely fixed, like the classes themselves, moralists will be seduced into holding the moral character-masks, too, as absolute, and in delineating them accordingly. Thus Molière is intelligible as the contemporary of the society of Louis XIV.: in our society of transitions and intermediate stages he would seem an inspired pedant.

64.

THE MOST NOBLE VIRTUE.—In the first era of the higher humanity courage is accounted the most noble virtue, in the next justice, in the third temperance, in the fourth wisdom. In which era do *we* live? In which do *you* live?

65.

A NECESSARY PRELIMINARY.—A man who will not become master of his irritability, his venomous and vengeful feelings, and his lust, and attempts to become master in anything else, is as stupid as the farmer who lays out his field beside a torrent without guarding against that torrent.

66.

WHAT IS TRUTH?—*Schwarzert* (Melanchthon): We often preach our faith when we have lost it, and leave not a stone unturned to find it—and then we often do not preach worst!

Luther: Brother, you are really speaking like an angel to-day.

Schwarzert: But that is the idea of your enemies, and they apply it to you.

Luther: Then it would be a lie from the devil's hind-quarters.

67.

THE HABIT OF CONTRASTS.—Superficial, in-exact observation sees contrasts everywhere in nature (for instance, "hot and cold"), where there are no contrasts, only differences of degree. This bad habit has induced us to try to understand and interpret even the inner nature, the intellectual and moral world, in accordance with such contrasts. An infinite amount of cruelty, arrogance, harshness, estrangement, and coldness has entered into human emotion, because men imagined they saw contrasts where there were only transitions.

68.

CAN WE FORGIVE?—How can we forgive them at all, if they know not what they do? We have nothing to forgive. But does a man ever fully know what he is doing? And if this point at least remains always debatable, men never have anything to forgive each other, and indulgence is for the reasonable man an impossible thing. Finally, if the evil-doers had really known what they did, we should still only have a right to forgive if we had a right to accuse and to punish. But we have not that right.

69.

HABITUAL SHAME.—Why do we feel shame when some virtue or merit is attributed to us which, as the saying goes, "we have not deserved"? Because we appear to have intruded upon a territory to which we do not belong, from which we should be excluded, as from a holy place or holy of holies, which ought not to be trodden by our foot. Through the errors of others we have, nevertheless, penetrated to it, and we are now swayed partly by fear, partly by reverence, partly by surprise ; we do not know whether we ought to fly or to enjoy the blissful moment with all its gracious advantages. In all shame there is a mystery, which seems desecrated or in danger of desecration through us. All *favour* begets shame.—But if it be remembered that we have never really "deserved" anything, this feeling of shame, provided that we surrender ourselves to this point of view in a spirit of Christian contemplation, becomes habitual, because upon such a one God seems continually to be conferring his blessing and his favours. Apart from this Christian interpretation, the state of habitual shame will be possible even to the entirely godless sage, who clings firmly to the basic non-responsibility and non-meritoriousness of all action and being. If he be treated as if he had deserved this or that, he will seem to have won his way into a higher order of beings, who do actually deserve something, who are free and can really bear the burden of responsibility for their own volition and capacity. Whoever says to him, "You have deserved it," appears to cry out to him, "You are not a human being, but a God."

70.

THE MOST UNSKILFUL TEACHER.—In one man all his real virtues are implanted on the soil of his spirit of contradiction, in another on his incapacity to say "no"—in other words, on his spirit of acquiescence. A third has made all his morality grow out of his pride as a solitary, a fourth from his strong social instinct. Now, supposing that the seeds of the virtues in these four cases, owing to mischance or unskilful teachers, were not sown on the soil of their nature, which provides them with the richest and most abundant mould, they would become weak, unsatisfactory men (devoid of morality). And who would have been the most unskilful of teachers, the evil genius of these men? The moral fanatic, who thinks that the good can only grow out of the good and on the soil of the good.

71.

THE CAUTIOUS STYLE.—*A.* But if this were known to *all*, it would be injurious to the *majority*. You yourself call your opinions dangerous to those in danger, and yet you make them public?

B. I write so that neither the mob, nor the *populi*, nor the parties of all kinds can read me. So my opinions will never be "public opinions."

A. How do you write, then?

B. Neither usefully nor pleasantly—for the three classes I have mentioned.

72.

DIVINE MISSIONARIES. — Even Socrates feels himself to be a divine missionary, but I am not sure whether we should not here detect a tincture of that Attic irony and fondness for jesting whereby this odious, arrogant conception would be toned down. He talks of the fact without unction—his images of the gadfly and the horse are simple and not sacerdotal. The real religious task which he has set himself—to *test* God in a hundred ways and see whether he spoke the truth—betrays a bold and free attitude, in which the missionary walked by the side of his God. This testing of God is one of the most subtle compromises between piety and free-thinking that has ever been devised.—Nowadays we do not even need this compromise any longer.

73.

HONESTY IN PAINTING.—Raphael, who cared a great deal for the Church (so far as she could pay him), but, like the best men of his time, cared little for the objects of the Church's belief, did not advance one step to meet the exacting, ecstatic piety of many of his patrons. He remained honest even in that exceptional picture which was originally intended for a banner in a procession—the Sistine Madonna. Here for once he wished to paint a vision, but such a vision as even noble youths without "faith" may and will have—the vision of the future wife, a wise, high-souled, silent, and very beautiful woman, carrying her first-born in her arms. Let men of an older generation, accustomed to prayer and devotion, find here, like the worthy elder on the left, something superhuman to revere.   We younger men (so Raphael seems to call to us) are occupied with the beautiful maiden on the right, who says to the spectator of the picture, with her challenging and by no means devout look, "The mother and her child—is not that a pleasant, inviting sight?"   The face and the look are reflected in the joy in the faces of the beholders.   The artist who devised all this enjoys himself in this way, and adds his own delight to the delight of the art-lover.   As regards the " messianic " expression in the face of the child, Raphael, honest man, who would not paint any state of soul in which he did not believe, has amiably cheated his religious admirers.   He painted that freak of nature which is very often found, the man's eye in the child's face, and that, too, the eye of a brave, helpful man who sees distress.   This eye should be accompanied by a beard.   The fact that a beard is wanting, and that two different ages are seen in one countenance, is the pleasing paradox which believers have interpreted in accordance with their faith in miracles.   The artist could only expect as much from their art of exposition and interpretation.

74.

PRAYER.—On two hypotheses alone is there any sense in prayer, that not quite extinct custom of olden times.   It would have to be possible either to fix or alter the will of the godhead, and the devotee would have to know best himself what he needs and should really desire.   Both hypotheses, axiomatic and traditional in all other religions, are denied by Christianity. If Christianity neverthe-less maintained prayer side by side with its belief in the all-wise and all-provident divine reason (a belief that makes prayer really senseless and even blasphemous), it showed here once more its admir-able "wisdom of the serpent." For an outspoken command, "Thou shalt not pray," would have led Christians by way of boredom to the denial of Christianity. In the Christian *ora et labora ora* plays the rôle of pleasure. Without *ora* what could those unlucky saints who renounced *labora* have done? But to have a chat with God, to ask him for all kinds of pleasant things, to feel a slight amusement at one's own folly in still having any wishes at all, in spite of so excellent a father—all that was an admirable invention for saints.

75.

A HOLY LIE.—The lie that was on Arria's lips when she died (*Paete, non dolet* *) obscures all the truths that have ever been uttered by the dying. It is the only holy *lie* that has become famous, whereas elsewhere the odour of sanctity has clung only to *errors*.

76.

THE MOST NECESSARY APOSTLE. — Among twelve apostles one must always be hard as stone, in order that upon him the new church may be built.

---

* The wife of the Stoic Thrasea Paetus, when their com-plicity in the great conspiracy of 65 A.D. against Nero was discovered, is reported to have said as she committed suicide, " It doesn't hurt, Paetus."—TR.

77.

WHICH IS MORE TRANSITORY, THE BODY OR THE SPIRIT ?—In legal, moral, and religious institutions the external and concrete elements—in other words, rites, gestures, and ceremonies—are the most permanent. They are the body to which a new spirit is constantly being superadded. The cult, like an unchangeable text, is ever interpreted anew. Concepts and emotions are fluid, customs are solid.

78.

THE BELIEF IN DISEASE *QUA* DISEASE.— Christianity first painted the devil on the wall of the world. Christianity first brought the idea of sin into the world. The belief in the remedies, which is offered as an antidote, has gradually been shaken to its very foundations. But the belief in the disease, which Christianity has taught and propagated, still exists.

79.

SPEECH AND WRITINGS OF RELIGIOUS MEN.— If the priest's style and general expression, both in speaking and writing, do not clearly betray the religious man, we need no longer take his views upon religion and his pleading for religion seriously. These opinions have become powerless for him if, judging by his style, he has at command irony, arrogance, malice, hatred, and all the changing eddies of mood, just like the most irreligious of men—how far more powerless will they be for his hearers and readers! In short, he will serve to make the latter still more irreligious.

80.

THE DANGER IN PERSONALITY. — The more God has been regarded as a personality in himself, the less loyal have we been to him. Men are far more attached to their thought-images than to their best beloved. That is why they sacrifice themselves for State, Church, and even for God—so far as he remains *their* creation, their thought, and is not too much looked upon as a personality. In the latter case they almost always quarrel with him. After all, it was the most pious of men who let slip that bitter cry: " My God, why hast thou forsaken me? "

81.

WORLDLY JUSTICE.—It is possible to unhinge worldly justice with the doctrine [of the complete non-responsibility and innocence of every man. An attempt has been made in the same direction on the basis of the opposite doctrine of the full responsibility and guilt of every man. It was the founder of Christianity who wished to abolish worldly justice and banish judgment and punishment from the world. For he understood all guilt as " sin "—that is, an outrage against God and not against the world. On the other hand, he considered every man in a broad sense, and almost in every sense, a sinner. The guilty, however, are not to be the judges of their peers—so his rules of equity decided. Thus all dispensers of worldly justice were in his eyes as culpable as those they condemned, and their air of guiltlessness appeared to him hypocritical and pharisaical. Moreover, he looked to the motives and not to the results of actions, and thought that only one was keen-sighted enough to give a verdict on motives—himself or, as he expressed it, God.

82.

AN AFFECTATION IN PARTING.—He who wishes to sever his connection with a party or a creed thinks it necessary for him to refute it. This is a most arrogant notion. The only thing necessary is that he should clearly see what tentacles hitherto held him to this party or creed and no longer hold him, what views impelled him to it and now impel him in some other directions. We have not joined the party or creed on strict grounds of knowledge. We should not affect this attitude on parting from it either.

83.

SAVIOUR AND PHYSICIAN.—In his knowledge of the human soul the founder of Christianity was, as is natural, not without many great deficiencies and prejudices, and, as physician of the soul, was addicted to that disreputable, laical belief in a universal medicine. In his methods he sometimes resembles that dentist who wishes to heal all pain by extracting the tooth. Thus, for example, he assails sensuality with the advice: "If thine eye offend thee, pluck it out."—Yet there still remains the distinction

that the dentist at least attains his object—painlessness for the patient—although in so clumsy a fashion
that he becomes ridiculous; whereas the Christian
who follows that advice and thinks he has killed
his sensuality, is wrong, for his sensuality still lives
in an uncanny, vampire form, and torments him in
hideous disguises.

84.

PRISONERS.—One morning the prisoners entered
the yard for work, but the warder was not there.
Some, as their manner was, set to work at once;
others stood idle and gazed defiantly around.
Then one of them strode forward and cried, "Work
as much as you will or do nothing, it all comes to
the same.   Your secret machinations have come to
light; the warder has been keeping his eye on you
of late, and will cause a terrible judgment to be
passed upon you in a few days' time.   You know
him—he is of a cruel and resentful disposition.
But now, listen: you have mistaken me hitherto.
I am not what I seem, but far more—I am the son
of the warder, and can get anything I like out of
him.   I can save you—nay, I will save you.   But
remember this: I will only save those of you who
believe that I am the son of the prison warder.
The rest may reap the fruits of their unbelief."
"Well," said an old prisoner after an interval of
silence, "what can it matter to you whether we
believe you or not?   If you are really the son, and
can do what you say, then put in a good word for
us all.   That would be a real kindness on your
part.   But have done with all talk of belief and

unbelief!" "What is more," cried a younger man, "I don't believe him: he has only got a bee in his bonnet. I'll wager that in a week's time we shall find ourselves in the same place as we are to-day, and the warder will know nothing." "And if the warder ever knew anything, he knows it no longer," said the last of the prisoners, coming down into the yard at that moment, "for he has just died suddenly." "Ah ha!" cried several in confusion, "ah ha! Sir Son, Sir Son, how stands it now with your title? Are we by any chance *your* prisoners now?" "I told you," answered the man gently, " I will set free all who believe in me, as surely as my father still lives."—The prisoners did not laugh, but shrugged their shoulders and left him to himself.

85.

THE PERSECUTORS OF GOD.—Paul conceived and Calvin followed up the idea that countless creatures have been predestined to damnation from time immemorial, and that this fair world was made in order that the glory of God might be manifested therein. So heaven and hell and mankind merely exist to satisfy the vanity of God! What a cruel, insatiable vanity must have smouldered in the soul of the first or second thinker of such a thought!—Paul, then, after all, remained Saul—the persecutor of God.

86.

SOCRATES.—If all goes well, the time will come when, in order to advance themselves on the path

of moral reason, men will rather take up the
Memorabilia of Socrates than the Bible, and when
Montaigne and Horace will be used as pioneers and
guides for the understanding of Socrates, the simplest
and most enduring of interpretative sages.   In him
converge the roads of the most different philosophic modes of life, which are in truth the modes of
the different temperaments, crystallised by reason
and habit and all ultimately directed towards the
delight in life and in self.   The apparent conclusion is that the most peculiar thing about Socrates
was his share in all the temperaments.   Socrates
excels the founder of Christianity by virtue of his
merry style of seriousness and by that wisdom of
sheer roguish pranks which constitutes the best state
of soul in a man.   Moreover, he had a superior intelligence.

87.

LEARNING TO WRITE WELL.—The age of good
speaking is over, because the age of city-state culture
is over.   The limit allowed by Aristotle to the
great city—in which the town-crier must be able
to make himself heard by the whole assembled
community—troubles us as little as do any city-
communities, us who even wish to be understood
beyond the boundaries of nations.   Therefore
every one who is of a good European turn of mind
must learn to *write* well, and to write better and
better.   He cannot help himself, he must learn
that: even if he was born in Germany, where bad
writing is looked upon as a national privilege.
Better writing means better thinking; always to

discover matter more worthy of communication; to be able to communicate it properly; to be translate-able into the tongues of neighbouring nations; to make oneself comprehensible to foreigners who learn our language; to work with the view of making all that is good common property, and of giving free access everywhere to the free; finally, to pave the way for that still remote state of things, when the great task shall come for good Europeans—guidance and guardianship of the universal world-culture.—Whoever preaches the opposite doctrine of not troubling about good writing and good reading (both virtues grow together and decline together) is really showing the peoples a way of becoming more and more *national*.   He is intensi-fying the malady of this century, and is a foe to good Europeans, a foe to free spirits.

88.

THE THEORY OF THE BEST STYLE.—The theory of the best style may at one time be the theory of finding the expression by which we transfer every mood of ours to the reader and the listener.   At another, it may be the theory of finding expressions for the more desirable human moods, the communi-cation and transference of which one desires most —for the mood of a man moved from the depth of his heart, intellectually cheerful, bright, and sincere, who has conquered his passions.   This will be the theory of the best style, a theory that corresponds to the good man.

89.

PAYING ATTENTION TO MOVEMENT. — The movement of the sentences shows whether the author be tired. Individual expressions may nevertheless be still strong and good, because they were invented earlier and for their own sake, when the thought first flashed across the author's mind. This is frequently the case with Goethe, who too often dictated when he was tired.

90.

"ALREADY" AND "STILL."—*A*. German prose is still very young. Goethe declares that Wieland is its father.

B. So young and already so ugly!

C. But, so far as I am aware, Bishop Ulfilas already wrote German prose, which must therefore be fifteen hundred years old.

B. So old and still so ugly!

91.

ORIGINAL GERMAN.—German prose, which is really not fashioned on any pattern and must be considered an original creation of German taste, should give the eager advocate of a future original German culture an indication of how real German dress, German society, German furniture, German meals would look without the imitation of models. —Some one who had long reflected on these vistas finally cried in great horror, "But, Heaven help us, perhaps we already have that original culture— only we don't like to talk about it!"

92.

FORBIDDEN BOOKS.—One should never read anything written by those arrogant wiseacres and puzzle-brains who have the detestable vice of logical paradox. They apply *logical* formulæ just where everything is really improvised at random and built in the air. ("Therefore" with them means, "You idiot of a reader, this 'therefore' does not exist for you, but only for me." The answer to this is: "You idiot of a writer, then why do you write?")

93.

DISPLAYING ONE'S WIT.—Every one who wishes to display his wit thereby proclaims that he has also a plentiful lack of wit. That vice which clever Frenchmen have of adding a touch of *dédain* to their best ideas arises from a desire to be considered richer than they really are. They wish to be carelessly generous, as if weary of continual spending from overfull treasuries.

94.

FRENCH AND GERMAN LITERATURE.—The misfortune of the French and German literature of the last hundred years is that the Germans ran away too early from the French school, and the French, later on, went too early to the German school.

95.

OUR PROSE.—None of the present-day cultured nations has so bad a prose as the German. When

clever, *blasé* Frenchmen say, " There is no German
prose," we ought really not to be angry, for this
criticism is more polite than we deserve.   If we look
for reasons, we come at last to the strange phenomenon that the German knows only improvised
prose and has no conception of any other.   He
simply cannot understand the Italian, who says that
prose is as much harder than poetry as the repre-
sentation of naked beauty is harder to the sculptor
than that of draped beauty.   Verse, images, rhythm,
and rhyme need honest effort—that even the German
realises, and he is not inclined to set a very high
value on extempore poetry.   But the notion of working at a page of prose as at a statue sounds to him
like a tale from fairyland.

96.

THE GRAND STYLE.—The grand style comes into
being when the beautiful wins a victory over the
monstrous.

97.

DODGING.—We do not realise, in the case of distinguished minds, wherein lies the excellence of their
expression, their turn of phrase, until we can say
what word every mediocre writer would inevitably
have hit upon in expressing the same idea.   All great
artists, in steering their car, show themselves prone
to dodge and leave the track, but never to fall over.

98.

SOMETHING LIKE BREAD.—Bread neutralises
and takes out the taste of other food, and is there-

fore necessary to every long meal.   In all works of art there must be something like bread, in order that they may produce divers effects.   If these effects followed one another without occasional pauses and intervals, they would soon make us weary and provoke disgust—in fact, a long meal of art would then be impossible.

99.

JEAN PAUL.—Jean Paul knew a great deal, but had no science; understood all manner of tricks of art, but had no art; found almost everything enjoyable, but had no taste; possessed feeling and seriousness, but in dispensing them poured over them a nauseous sauce of tears; had even wit, but, unfortunately for his ardent desire for it, far too little— whence he drives the reader to despair by his very lack of wit.   In short, he was the bright, rank-smelling weed that shot up overnight in the fair pleasaunces of Schiller and Goethe.   He was a good, comfortable man, and yet a destiny, a destiny in a dressing-gown.*

100.

PALATE FOR OPPOSITES.—In order to enjoy a work of the past as its contemporaries enjoyed it, one must have a palate for the prevailing taste of the age which it attacked.

---

* It is interesting to compare this judgment with Carlyle's praise of Jean Paul.   The dressing-gown is an allusion to Jean Paul's favourite costume.—TR.

101.

SPIRITS-OF-WINE AUTHORS.—Many writers are neither spirit nor wine, but spirits of wine. They can flare up, and then they give warmth.

102.

THE INTERPRETATIVE SENSE.—The sense of taste, as the true interpretative sense, often talks the other senses over to its point of view and imposes upon them its laws and customs. At table one can receive disclosures about the most subtle secrets of the arts ; it suffices to observe what tastes good and when and after what and how long it tastes good.

103.

LESSING.—Lessing had a genuine French talent, and, as writer, went most assiduously to the French school. He knows well how to arrange and display his wares in his shop-window. Without this true art his thoughts, like the objects of them, would have remained rather in the dark, nor would the general loss be great. His art, however, has taught many (especially the last generation of German scholars) and has given enjoyment to a countless number. It is true his disciples had no need to learn from him, as they often did, his unpleasant tone with its mingling of petulance and candour.—Opinion is now unanimous on Lessing as " lyric poet," and will some day be unanimous on Lessing as " dramatic poet."

104.

UNDESIRABLE READERS.—How an author is vexed by those stolid, awkward readers who always fall at every place where they stumble, and always hurt themselves when they fall!

105.

POETS' THOUGHTS.—Real thoughts of real poets always go about with a veil on, like Egyptian women; only the deep *eye* of thought looks out freely through the veil.—Poets' thoughts are as a rule not of such value as is supposed. We have to pay for the veil and for our own curiosity into the bargain.

106.

WRITE SIMPLY AND USEFULLY.—Transitions, details, colour in depicting the passions—we make a present of all these to the author because we bring them with us and set them down to the credit of his book, provided he makes us some compensation.

107.

WIELAND.—Wieland wrote German better than any one else, and had the genuine adequacies and inadequacies of the master. His translations of the letters of Cicero and Lucian are the best in the language. His ideas, however, add nothing to our store of thought. We can endure his cheerful moralities as little as his cheerful immoralities, for both are very closely connected. The men who enjoyed them were at bottom better men than we are, but also a good deal heavier. They *needed* an author of this sort. The Germans did not need Goethe, and therefore cannot make proper use of him. We have only to consider the best of our statesmen and artists in this light. None of them had or *could* have had Goethe as their teacher.

108.

RARE FESTIVALS.—Pithy conciseness, repose, and maturity—where you find these qualities in an author, cry halt and celebrate a great festival in the desert. It will be long before you have such a treat again.

109.

THE TREASURE OF GERMAN PROSE.—Apart from Goethe's writings and especially Goethe's conversations with Eckermann (the best German book in existence), what German prose literature remains that is worth reading over and over again? Lichtenberg's *Aphorisms*, the first book of Jung-Stilling's *Story of My Life*, Adalbert Stifter's *St. Martin's Summer* and Gottfried Keller's *People of Seldwyla* —and there, for the time being, it comes to an end.

110.

LITERARY AND COLLOQUIAL STYLE.—The art of writing demands, first and foremost, substitutions for the means of expression which speech alone possesses—in other words, for gestures, accent, intonation, and look. Hence literary style is quite different from colloquial style, and far more difficult, because it has to make itself as intelligible as the latter with fewer accessaries. Demosthenes delivered his speeches differently from what we read; he worked them up for reading purposes.—Cicero's speeches ought to be "demosthenised" with the same object, for at present they contain more of the Roman Forum than we can endure.

III.

CAUTION IN QUOTATION.—Young authors do not know that a good expression or idea only looks well among its peers; that an excellent quotation may spoil whole pages, nay the whole book; for it seems to cry warningly to the reader, "Mark you, I am the precious stone, and round about me is lead —pale, worthless lead!" Every word, every idea only desires to live in its own company—that is the moral of a choice style.

112.

HOW SHOULD ERRORS BE ENUNCIATED?—We may dispute whether it be more injurious for errors to be enunciated badly or as well as the best truths. It is certain that in the former case they are doubly harmful to the brain and are less easily removed from it. But, on the other hand, they are not so certain of effect as in the latter case. They are, in fact, less contagious.

113.

LIMITING AND WIDENING.—Homer limited and diminished the horizon of his subject, but allowed individual scenes to expand and blossom out. Later, the tragedians are constantly renewing this process. Each takes his material in ever smaller and smaller fragments than his predecessor did, but

each attains a greater wealth of blooms within the
narrow hedges of these sequestered garden en-
closures.

114.

LITERATURE AND MORALITY MUTUALLY EX-
PLANATORY.—We can show from Greek literature
by what forces the Greek spirit developed, how it
entered upon different channels, and where it became enfeebled. All this also depicts to us how
Greek morality proceeded, and how all morality will
proceed : how it was at first a constraint and displayed cruelty, then became gradually milder ; how
a pleasure in certain actions, in certain forms and
conventions arose, and from this again a propensity
for solitary exercise, for solitary possession ; how the
track becomes crowded and overcrowded with competitors; how satiety enters in, new objects of struggle
and ambition are sought, and forgotten aims are
awakened to life; how the drama is repeated, and the
spectators become altogether weary of looking on,
because the whole gamut seems to have been run
through—and then comes a stoppage, an expira-
tion, and the rivulets are lost in the sand.   The end,
or at any rate *an* end, has come.

115.

WHAT LANDSCAPES GIVE PERMANENT DE-
LIGHT.—Such and such a landscape has features
eminently suited for painting, but I cannot find the
formula for it; it remains beyond my grasp as a
whole.   I notice that all landscapes which please
me permanently have a simple geometrical scheme

of lines underneath all their complexity.   Without such a mathematical substratum no scenery becomes artistically pleasing.   Perhaps this rule may be applied symbolically to human beings.

116.

READING ALOUD. — The ability to read aloud involves of necessity the ability to declaim.   Everywhere we must apply pale tints, but we must determine the degree of pallor in close relation to the richly and deeply coloured background, that always hovers before our eyes and acts as our guide—in other words, in accordance with the way in which we should *declaim* the same passages.   That is why we must be able to declaim.

117.

THE DRAMATIC SENSE.—He who has not the four subtler senses of art tries to understand everything with the fifth sense, which is the coarsest of all —the dramatic sense.

118.

HERDER.—Herder fails to be all that he made people think he was and himself wished to think he was.   He was no great thinker or discoverer, no newly fertile soil with the unexhausted strength of a virgin forest.   But he possessed in the highest degree the power of scenting the future, he saw and picked the first-fruits of the seasons earlier than all others, and they then believed that he had made them grow.   Between darkness and light, youth and age,

his mind was like a hunter on the watch, looking
everywhere for transitions, depressions, convulsions,
the outward and visible signs of internal growth.
The unrest of spring drove him to and fro, but he
was himself not the spring.—At times, indeed, he
had some inkling of this, and yet would fain not
have believed it — he, the ambitious priest, who
would have so gladly been the intellectual pope of
his epoch ! This is his despair. He seems to have
lived long as a pretender to several kingdoms or
even to a universal monarchy. He had his following which believed in him, among others the young
Goethe. But whenever crowns were really distri-
buted, he was passed over. Kant, Goethe, and then
the first true German historians and scholars robbed
him of what he thought he had reserved for himself
(although in silence and secret he often thought the
reverse). Just when he doubted in himself, he
gladly clothed himself in dignity and enthusiasm :
these were often in him mere garments, which had
to hide a great deal and also to deceive and comfort
him. He really had fire and enthusiasm, but his
ambition was far greater ! It blew impatiently at
the fire, which flickered, crackled, and smoked—his
style flickers, crackles, and smokes—but he yearned
for the great flame which never broke out. He did
not sit at the table of the genuine creators, and his
ambition did not admit of his sitting modestly
among those who simply enjoy. Thus he was a
restless spirit, the taster of all intellectual dishes,
which were collected by the Germans from every
quarter and every age in the course of half a century.
Never really happy and satisfied, Herder was also

too often ill, and then at times envy sat by his bed, and hypocrisy paid her visit as well.   He always had an air of being scarred and crippled, and he lacked simple, stalwart manliness more completely than any of the so-called "classical writers."

119.

SCENT OF WORDS.—Every word has its scent; there is a harmony and discord of scents, and so too of words.

120.

THE FAR-FETCHED STYLE.—The natural style is an offence to the lover of the far-fetched style.

121.

A VOW.—I will never again read an author of whom one can suspect that he *wanted* to make a book, but only those writers whose thoughts unexpectedly became a book.

122.

THE ARTISTIC CONVENTION.—Three-fourths of Homer is convention, and the same is the case with all the Greek artists, who had no reason for falling into the modern craze for originality.   They had no fear of convention, for after all convention was a link between them and their public.   Conventions are the artistic means *acquired* for the understanding of the hearer; the common speech, learnt with much toil, whereby the artist can really communicate his ideas.   All the more when he wishes, like

the Greek poets and musicians, to conquer at once
with each of his works (since he is accustomed to
compete publicly with one or two rivals), the first
condition is that he must be understood at once,
and this is only possible by means of convention.
What the artist devises beyond convention he offers
of his own free will and takes a risk, his success at
best resulting in the setting-up of a new convention.   As a rule originality is marvelled at, sometimes even worshipped, but seldom understood.   A
stubborn avoidance of convention means a desire
not to be understood.   What, then, is the object of
the modern craze for originality?

123.

ARTISTS' AFFECTATION OF SCIENTIFIC ME-
THOD.—Schiller, like other German artists, fancied
that if a man had intellect he was entitled to impro-
vise even with the pen on all difficult subjects.   So
there we see his prose essays—in every way a model
of how *not* to attack scientific questions of æsthetics
and ethics, and a danger for young readers who, in
their admiration for Schiller the poet, have not the
courage to think meanly of Schiller the thinker and
author.—The temptation to traverse for once the
forbidden paths, and to have his say in science as
well, is easy and pardonable in the artist.   For
even the ablest artist from time to time finds his
handicraft and his workshop unendurable.   This
temptation is so strong that it makes the artist show
all the world what no one wishes to see, that his little
chamber of thought is cramped and untidy.   Why

not, indeed ?   He does not live there.   He proceeds
to show that the storeroom of his knowledge is
partly empty, partly filled with lumber.   Why not,
indeed ?   This condition does not really become
the artist-child badly.   In particular, the artist
shows that for the very easiest exercises of scientific
method, which are accessible even to beginners, his
joints are too stiff and untrained.   Even of that he
need not really be ashamed !   On the other hand,
he often develops no mean art in imitating all the
mistakes, vices, and base pedantries that are practised in the scientific community, in the belief that
these belong to the appearance of the thing, if not to
the thing itself.   This is the very point that is so
amusing in artists' writing, that the artist involuntarily acts as his vocation demands : he parodies
the scientific and inartistic natures.   Towards science
he should show no attitude but that of parody, in
so far as he is an artist and only an artist.

124.

THE FAUST-IDEA. — A little sempstress is seduced and plunged into despair : a great scholar of
all the four Faculties is the evil-doer.   That cannot
have happened in the ordinary course, surely ?   No,
certainly not !   Without the aid of the devil incar-
nate, the great scholar would never have achieved
the deed.—Is this really destined to be the greatest
German " tragic idea," as one hears it said among
Germans ?—But for Goethe even this idea was too
terrible.   His kind heart could not avoid placing
the little sempstress, " the good soul that forgot

itself but once," near to the saints, after her involuntary death. Even the great scholar, "the good
man" with "the dark impulse," is brought into
heaven in the nick of time, by a trick which is
played upon the devil at the decisive moment. In
heaven the lovers find themselves again. Goethe
once said that his nature was too conciliatory for
really tragic subjects.

125.

ARE THERE "GERMAN CLASSICS"?—Sainte-
Beuve observes somewhere that the word "classic"
does not suit the genius of certain literatures. For
instance, nobody could talk seriously of "German
classics."—What do our German publishers, who
are about to add fifty more to the fifty German
classics we are told to accept, say to that? Does
it not almost seem as if one need only have been
dead for the last thirty years, and lie a lawful prey
to the public,* in order to hear suddenly and unexpectedly the trumpet of resurrection as a "Classic"?
And this in an age and a nation where at least five
out of the six great fathers of its literature are undoubtedly antiquated or becoming antiquated—without there being any need for the age or the nation to
be ashamed of this. For those writers have given
way before the strength of our time—let that be considered in all fairness!—Goethe, as I have indicated,
I do not include. He belongs to a higher species
than "national literatures": hence life, revival,

* The German copyright expires thirty years after publication.—TR.

and decay do not enter into the reckoning in his
relations with his countrymen.   He lived and now
lives but for the few ; for the majority he is nothing
but a flourish of vanity which is trumpeted from
time to time across the border into foreign ears.
Goethe, not merely a great and good man, but a
culture, is in German history an interlude without a
sequel.   Who, for instance, would be able to point
to any trace of Goethe's influence in German politics
of the last seventy years (whereas the influence,
certainly of Schiller, and perhaps of Lessing, can be
traced in the political world)?   But what of those
five others?   Klopstock, in a most honourable way,
became out of date even in his own lifetime, and so
completely that the meditative book of his later
years, *The Republic of Learning*, has never been
taken seriously from that day to this.   Herder's
misfortune was that his writings were always either
new or antiquated.   Thus for stronger and more
subtle minds (like Lichtenberg) even Herder's
masterpiece, his *Ideas for the History of Mankind*,
was in a way antiquated at the very moment of its
appearance.   Wieland, who lived to the full and
made others live likewise, was clever enough to
anticipate by death the waning of his influence.
Lessing, perhaps, still lives to-day—but among a
young and ever younger band of scholars.   Schiller
has fallen from the hands of young men into those
of boys, of all German boys.   It is a well-known
sign of obsolescence when a book descends to
people of less and less mature age.—Well, what is
it that has thrust these five into the background,
so that well-educated men of affairs no longer read

them ?   A better taste, a riper knowledge, a higher
reverence for the real and the true : in other words,
the very virtues which these five (and ten or twenty
others of lesser repute) first re-planted in Germany,
and which now, like a mighty forest, cast over their
graves not only the shadow of awe, but something
of the shadow of oblivion.—But classical writers
are not planters of intellectual and literary virtues.
They bring those virtues to perfection and are their
highest luminous peaks, and being brighter, freer,
and purer than all that surrounds them, they remain
shining above the nations when the nations themselves perish.   There may come an elevated stage
of humanity, in which the Europe of the peoples
is a dark, forgotten thing, but Europe lives on in
thirty books, very old but never antiquated—in the
classics.

126.

INTERESTING, BUT NOT BEAUTIFUL. — This
countryside conceals its meaning, but it has one
that we should like to guess.   Everywhere that I
look, I read words and hints of words, but I do not
know where begins the sentence that solves the
riddle of all these hints.   So I get a stiff neck in
trying to discover whether I should start reading
from this or that point.

127.

AGAINST INNOVATORS IN LANGUAGE.—The use
of neologisms or archaisms, the preference for the
rare and the bizarre, the attempt to enrich rather
than to limit the vocabulary, are always signs either

of an immature or of a corrupted taste. A noble poverty but a masterly freedom within the limits of that modest wealth distinguishes the Greek artists in oratory. They wish to have less than the people has—for the people is richest in old and new—but they wish to have that little *better*. The reckoning up of their archaic and exotic forms is soon done, but we never cease marvelling if we have an eye for their light and delicate manner in handling the commonplace and apparently long outworn elements in word and phrase.

128.

GLOOMY AND SERIOUS AUTHORS. — He who commits his sufferings to paper becomes a gloomy author, but he becomes a serious one if he tells us what he *has* suffered and why he is now enjoying a pleasurable repose.

129.

HEALTHINESS OF TASTE.—How is it that health is less contagious than disease—generally, and particularly in matters of taste? Or are there epidemics of health?

130.

A RESOLUTION.—Never again to read a book that is born and christened (with ink) at the same moment.

131.

IMPROVING OUR IDEAS.—Improving our style means improving our ideas, and nothing else. He who does not at once concede this can never be convinced of the point.

132.

CLASSICAL BOOKS.—The weakest point in every classical book is that it is written too much in the mother tongue of its author.

133.

BAD BOOKS.—The book should demand pen, ink, and desk, but usually it is pen, ink, and desk that demand the book.   That is why books are of so little account at present.

134.

PRESENCE OF SENSE.—When the public reflects on paintings, it becomes a poet ; when on poems, an investigator.   At the moment when the artist summons it it is always lacking in the right sense, and accordingly in presence of sense, not in presence of mind.

135.

CHOICE IDEAS.—The choice style of a momentous period does not only select its words but its ideas— and both from the customary and prevailing usage. Venturesome ideas, that smell too fresh, are to the maturer taste no less repugnant than new and reckless images and phrases.   Later on both choice ideas and choice words soon smack of mediocrity, because the scent of the choice vanishes quickly, and then nothing but the customary and commonplace element is tasted.

136.

MAIN REASON FOR CORRUPTION OF STYLE.—
The desire to display more sentiment than one
really feels for a thing corrupts style, in language
and in all art. All great art shows rather the
opposite tendency. Like every man of moral
significance, it loves to check emotion on its way
and not let it run its course to the very end. This
modesty of letting emotion but half appear is most
clearly to be observed, for example, in Sophocles.
The features of sentiment seem to become beautified
when sentiment feigns to be more shy than it
really is.

137.

AN EXCUSE FOR THE HEAVY STYLE. — The
lightly uttered phrase seldom falls on the ear with
the full weight of the subject. This is, however, due
to the bad training of the ear, which by education
must pass from what has hitherto been called music
to the school of the higher harmony—in other words,
to conversation.

138.

BIRD'S-EYE VIEWS. — Here torrents rush from
every side into a ravine: their movement is so swift
and stormy, and carries the eye along so quickly,
that the bare or wooded mountain slopes around
seem not to sink down but to fly down. We are in
an agonised tension at the sight, as if behind all
this were hidden some hostile element, before which
all must fly, and against which the abyss alone gave
protection. This landscape cannot be painted, un-

less we hover above it like a bird in the open air. Here for once the so-called bird's-eye view is not an artistic caprice, but the sole possibility.

139.

RASH COMPARISONS.—If rash comparisons are not proofs of the wantonness of the writer, they are proofs of the exhaustion of his imagination. In any case they bear witness to his bad taste.

140.

DANCING IN CHAINS. — In the case of every Greek artist, poet, or writer we must ask : What is the new constraint which he imposes upon himself and makes attractive to his contemporaries, so as to find imitators? For the thing called "invention" (in metre, for example) is always a self-imposed fetter of this kind. " Dancing in chains "—to make that hard for themselves and then to spread a false notion that it is easy—that is the trick that they wish to show us. Even in Homer we may perceive a wealth of inherited formulæ and laws of epic narration, within the circle of which he had to dance, and he himself created new conventions for them that came after. This was the discipline of the Greek poets: first to impose upon themselves a manifold constraint by means of the earlier poets ; then to invent in addition a new constraint, to impose it upon themselves and cheerfully to overcome it, so that constraint and victory are perceived and admired.

141.

AUTHORS' COPIOUSNESS.—The last quality that a good author acquires is copiousness: whoever has it to begin with will never become a good author. The noblest racehorses are lean until they are permitted to rest from their victories.

142.

WHEEZING HEROES.—Poets and artists who suffer from a narrow chest of the emotions generally make their heroes wheeze. They do not know what easy breathing means.

143.

THE SHORT-SIGHTED.*—The short-sighted are the deadly foes of all authors who let themselves go. These authors should know the wrath with which these people shut the book in which they observe that its creator needs fifty pages to express five ideas. And the cause of their wrath is that they have endangered what remains of their vision almost without compensation. A short-sighted person said, "All authors let themselves go." "Even the Holy Ghost?" "Even the Holy Ghost." But he had a right to, for he wrote for those who had lost their sight altogether.

144.

THE STYLE OF IMMORTALITY.—Thucydides and Tacitus both imagined immortal life for their works when they executed them. That might be guessed

* Nietzsche himself was extremely short-sighted—TR.

(if not known otherwise) from their style. The one thought to give permanence to his ideas by salting them, the other by boiling them down; and neither, it seems, made a miscalculation.

145.

AGAINST IMAGES AND SIMILES.—By images and similes we convince, but we do not prove. That is why science has such a horror of images and similes. Science does not want to convince or make plausible, and rather seeks to provoke cold distrust by its mode of expression, by the bareness of its walls. For distrust is the touchstone for the gold of certainty.

146.

CAUTION.—In Germany, he who lacks thorough knowledge should beware of writing. The good German does not say in that case " he is ignorant," but " he is of doubtful character."—This hasty conclusion, by the way, does great credit to the Germans.

147.

PAINTED SKELETONS. — Painted skeletons are those authors who try to make up for their want of flesh by artistic colourings.

148.

THE GRAND STYLE AND SOMETHING BETTER. —It is easier to learn how to write the grand style than how to write easily and simply. The reasons for this are inextricably bound up with morality.

149.

SEBASTIAN BACH.—In so far as we do not hear
Bach's music as perfect and experienced connoisseurs of counterpoint and all the varieties of the fugal
style (and accordingly must dispense with real artistic
enjoyment), we shall feel in listening to his music
—in Goethe's magnificent phrase—as if "we were
present at God's creation of the world." In other
words, we feel here that something great is in the
making but not yet made—our mighty modern music,
which by conquering nationalities, the Church, and
counterpoint has conquered the world. In Bach
there is still too much crude Christianity, crude
Germanism, crude scholasticism. He stands on
the threshold of modern European music, but turns
from thence to look at the Middle Ages.

150.

HÄNDEL.—Händel, who in the invention of his
music was bold, original, truthful, powerful, inclined
to and akin to all the heroism of which a *nation* is
capable, often proved stiff, cold, nay even weary of
himself in composition. He applied a few well-tried
methods of execution, wrote copiously and quickly,
and was glad when he had finished—but that joy
was not the joy of God and other creators in the
eventide of their working day.

151.

HAYDN.—So far as genius can exist in a man
who is merely *good*, Haydn had genius. He went

just as far as the limit which morality sets to intellect, and only wrote music that has "no past."

152.

BEETHOVEN AND MOZART.—Beethoven's music
often appears like a deeply emotional meditation
on unexpectedly hearing once more a piece long
thought to be forgotten, "Tonal Innocence": it is
music about music. In the song of the beggar and
child in the street, in the monotonous airs of vagrant
Italians, in the dance of the village inn or in carnival
nights he discovers his melodies. He stores them
together like a bee, snatching here and there some
notes or a short phrase. To him these are hallowed
memories of "the better world," like the ideas of
Plato.—Mozart stands in quite a different relation
to his melodies. He finds his inspiration not in
hearing music but in gazing at life, at the most
stirring life of southern lands. He was always
dreaming of Italy, when he was not there.

153.

RECITATIVE.—Formerly recitative was dry, but
now we live in the age of moist recitative. It has
fallen into the water, and the waves carry it whither-
soever they list.

154.

"CHEERFUL" MUSIC.—If for a long time we
have heard no music, it then goes like a heavy
southern wine all too quickly into the blood and
leaves behind it a soul dazed with narcotics, half-

awake, longing for sleep. This is particularly the
case with cheerful music, which inspires in us bitterness and pain, satiety and home-sickness together, and forces us to sip again and again as at
a sweetened draught of poison. The hall of gay,
noisy merriment then seems to grow narrow, the
light to lose its brightness and become browner.
At last we feel as if this music were penetrating
to a prison where a poor wretch cannot sleep for
home-sickness.

155.

FRANZ SCHUBERT.—Franz Schubert, inferior as
an artist to the other great musicians, had nevertheless the largest share of inherited musical wealth.
He spent it with a free hand and a kind heart, so
that for a few centuries musicians will continue to
nibble at his ideas and inspirations. In his works
we find a store of *unused* inventions ; the greatness
of others will lie in making use of those inventions.
If Beethoven may be called the ideal listener for
a troubadour, Schubert has a right to be called the
ideal troubadour.

156.

MODERN MUSICAL EXECUTION.—Great tragic
or dramatic execution of music acquires its character
by imitating the gesture of the great sinner, such
as Christianity conceives and desires him : the slow-
stepping, passionately brooding man, distracted by
the agonies of conscience, now flying in terror,
now clutching with delight, now standing still in
despair—and all the other marks of great sinful-

ness. Only on the Christian assumption that all men are great sinners and do nothing but sin could we justify the application of this style of execution to *all* music. So far, music would be the reflection of all the actions and impulses of man, and would continually have to express by gestures the language of the great sinner. At such a performance, a listener who was not enough of a Christian to understand this logic might indeed cry out in horror, " For the love of Heaven, how did sin find its way into music ? "

157.

FELIX MENDELSSOHN. — Felix Mendelssohn's music is the music of the good taste that enjoys all the good things that have ever existed. It always points behind. How could it have much " in front," much of a future ?—But did he want it to have a future ? He possessed a virtue rare among artists, that of gratitude without *arrière-pensée*. This virtue, too, always points behind.

158.

A MOTHER OF ARTS.—In our sceptical age, real devotion requires almost a brutal heroism of ambition. Fanatical shutting of the eyes and bending of the knee no longer suffice. Would it not be possible for ambition—in its eagerness to be the last devotee of all the ages—to become the begetter of a final church music, as it has been the begetter of the final church architecture ? (They call it the Jesuit style.)

159.

FREEDOM IN FETTERS—A PRINCELY FREEDOM.
—Chopin, the last of the modern musicians, who
gazed at and worshipped beauty, like Leopardi;
Chopin, the Pole, the inimitable (none that came
before or after him has a right to this name)—
Chopin had the same princely punctilio in convention that Raphael shows in the use of the simplest
traditional colours. The only difference is that
Chopin applies them not to colour but to melodic
and rhythmic traditions. He admitted the validity
of these traditions because he was born under the
sway of etiquette. But in these fetters he plays and
dances as the freest and daintiest of spirits, and, be
it observed, he does not spurn the chain.

160.

CHOPIN'S BARCAROLLE.—Almost all states and
modes of life have a moment of rapture, and good
artists know how to discover that moment. Such
a moment there is even in life by the seashore—that
dreary, sordid, unhealthy existence, dragged out in
the neighbourhood of a noisy and covetous rabble.
This moment of rapture Chopin in his Barcarolle
expressed in sound so supremely that Gods themselves, when they heard it, might yearn to lie long
summer evenings in a boat.

161.

ROBERT SCHUMANN.—"The Stripling," as the
romantic songsters of Germany and France of the

first three decades of this century imagined him—this stripling was completely translated into song and melody by Robert Schumann, the eternal youth, so long as he felt himself in full possession of his powers. There are indeed moments when his music reminds one of the eternal " old maid."

162.

DRAMATIC SINGERS.—"Why does this beggar sing?" "Probably he does not know how to wail." "Then he does right." But our dramatic singers, who wail because they do not know how to sing —are they also in the right?

163.

DRAMATIC MUSIC.—For him who does not see what is happening on the stage, dramatic music is a monstrosity, just as the running commentary to a lost text is a monstrosity. Such music requires us to have ears where our eyes are. This, however, is doing violence to Euterpe, who, poor Muse, wants to have her eyes and ears where the other Muses have theirs.

164.

VICTORY AND REASONABLENESS. — Unfortunately in the æsthetic wars, which artists provoke by their works and apologias for their works, just as is the case in real war, it is might and not reason that decides. All the world now assumes as a historical fact that, in his dispute with Piccini, Gluck was in the right. At any rate, he was victorious, and had might on his side.

165.

OF THE PRINCIPLE OF MUSICAL EXECUTION.—
Do the modern musical performers really believe
that the supreme law of their art is to give every
piece as much high-relief as is possible, and to make
it speak at all costs a dramatic language?   Is not
this principle, when applied for example to Mozart,
a veritable sin against the spirit—the gay, sunny,
airy, delicate spirit—of Mozart, whose seriousness
was of a kindly and not awe-inspiring order, whose
pictures do not try to leap from the wall and drive
away the beholder in panic?   Or do you think that
all Mozart's music is identical with the statue-music
in *Don Juan*?   And not only Mozart's, but all
music?—You reply that the advantage of your
principle lies in its greater *effect*.   You would be
right if there did not remain the counter-question,
" *On whom* has the effect operated, and *on whom*
should an artist of the first rank desire to produce
his effect?"   Never on the populace!   Never on
the immature!   Never on the morbidly sensitive!
Never on the diseased!   And above all—never on
the *blasé*!

166.

THE MUSIC OF TO-DAY.— This ultra-modern
music, with its strong lungs and weak nerves, is
frightened above all things of itself.

167.

WHERE MUSIC IS AT HOME.—Music reaches its
high-water mark only among men who have not the

ability or the right to argue.   Accordingly, its chief
promoters are princes, whose aim is that there should
be not much criticism nor even much thought in
their neighbourhood.   Next come societies which,
under some pressure or other (political or religious),
are forced to become habituated to silence, and
so feel all the greater need of spells to charm away
emotional ennui—these spells being generally eternal
love-making and eternal music.   Thirdly, we must
reckon whole nations in which there is no " society,"
but all the greater number of individuals with a
bent towards solitude, mystical thinking, and a reverence for all that is inexpressible ; these are the
genuine " musical souls."   The Greeks, as a nation
delighting in talking and argument, accordingly put
up with music only as an *hors d'œuvre* to those arts
which really admit of discussion and dispute.   About
music one can hardly even *think* clearly.   The Py-
thagoreans, who in so many respects were exceptional
Greeks, are said to have been great musicians.   This
was the school that invented a five-years' silence,*
but did not invent a dialectic.

168.

SENTIMENTALITY IN MUSIC.—We may be ever
so much in sympathy with serious and profound
music, yet nevertheless, or perhaps all the more for
that reason, we shall at occasional moments be over-
powered, entranced, and almost melted away by its

---

* In the sixth century B.C. Pythagoras founded at Croton a
" school " somewhat resembling a monastic order.   Among the
ordeals for novitiates was enforced silence for five years.—TR.

opposite—I mean, by those simple Italian operatic airs which, in spite of all their monotony of rhythm and childishness of harmony, seem at times to sing to us like the very soul of music. Admit this or not as you please, you Pharisees of good taste, it is so, and it is my present task to propound the riddle that it is so, and to nibble a little myself at the solution.—In childhood's days we tasted the honey of many things for the first time. Never was honey so good as then ; it seduced us to life, into abundant life, in the guise of the first spring, the first flower, the first butterfly, the first friendship. Then—perhaps in our ninth year or so—we heard our first music, and this was the first that we understood ; thus the simplest and most childish tunes, that were not much more than a sequel to the nurse's lullaby and the strolling fiddler's tune, were our first experience. (For even the most trifling "revelations" of art need preparation and study; there is no "immediate" effect of art, whatever charming fables the philosophers may tell.) Our sensation on hearing these Italian airs is associated with those first musical raptures, the strongest of our lives. The bliss of childhood and its flight, the feeling that our most precious possession can never be brought back, all this moves the chords of the soul more strongly than the most serious and profound music can move them.—This mingling of æsthetic pleasure with moral pain, which nowadays it is customary to call (rather too haughtily, I think) "sentimentality"—it is the mood of Faust at the end of the first scene—this "sentimentality" of the listener is all to the advantage of Italian music. It is a feeling which the ex-

perienced connoisseurs in art, the pure "æsthetes," like
to ignore.—Moreover, almost all music has a magical
effect only when we hear it speak the language of
our own *past*. Accordingly, it seems to the layman
that all the old music is continually growing better,
and that all the latest is of little value. For the latter
arouses no "sentimentality," that most essential
element of happiness, as aforesaid, for every man
who cannot approach this art with pure æsthetic
enjoyment.

169.

AS FRIENDS OF MUSIC.—Ultimately we are and
remain good friends with music, as we are with the
light of the moon. Neither, after all, tries to sup-
plant the sun : they only want to illumine our nights
to the best of their powers. Yet we may jest and
laugh at them, may we not? Just a little, at least,
and from time to time? At the man in the moon,
at the woman in the music?

170.

ART IN AN AGE OF WORK.—We have the conscience of an industrious epoch. This debars us
from devoting our best hours and the best part
of our days to art, even though that art be the
greatest and worthiest. Art is for us a matter of
leisure, of recreation, and we consecrate to it the
residue of our time and strength. This is the cardinal fact that has altered the relation of art to life.
When art makes its great demands of time and
strength upon its recipients, it has to battle against
the conscience of the industrious and efficient, it is

relegated to the idle and conscienceless, who, by
their very nature, are not exactly suited to great
art, and consider its claims arrogant. It might,
therefore, be all over with art, since it lacks air and
the power to breathe. But perhaps the great art
attempts, by a sort of coarsening and disguising, to
make itself at home in that other atmosphere, or at
least to put up with it—an atmosphere which is really
a natural element only for petty art, the art of recreation, of pleasant distraction. This happens nowadays almost everywhere. Even the exponents of
great art promise recreation and distraction; even
they address themselves to the exhausted; even they
demand from him the evening hours of his working-
day—just like the artists of the entertaining school,
who are content to smooth the furrowed brow and
brighten the lack-lustre eye. What, then, are the
devices of their mightier brethren? These have in
their medicine-chests the most powerful excitants,
which might give a shock even to a man half-dead:
they can deafen you, intoxicate you, make you
shudder, or bring tears to your eyes. By this
means they overpower the exhausted man and
stimulate him for one night to an over-lively condition, to an ecstasy of terror and delight. This
great art, as it now lives in opera, tragedy, and music
—have we a right to be angry with it, because of
its perilous fascination, as we should be angry with
a cunning courtesan? Certainly not. It would far
rather live in the pure element of morning calm, and
would far rather make its appeal to the fresh, ex-
pectant, vigorous morning-soul of the beholder or
listener. Let us be thankful that it prefers living

thus to vanishing altogether. But let us also confess that an era that once more introduces free and
complete high-days and holidays into life will have
no use for *our* great art.

171.

THE EMPLOYEES OF SCIENCE AND THE OTHERS.
—Really efficient and successful men of science might
be collectively called " The Employees." If in youth
their acumen is sufficiently practised, their memory is
full, and hand and eye have acquired sureness, they
are appointed by an older fellow-craftsman to a
scientific position where their qualities may prove
useful. Later on, when they have themselves gained
an eye for the gaps and defects in their science, they
place themselves in whatever position they are needed.
These persons all exist for the sake of science. But
there are rarer spirits, spirits that seldom succeed
or fully mature—" for whose sake science exists "
—at least, in their view. They are often unpleasant,
conceited, or cross-grained men, but almost always
prodigies to a certain extent. They are neither
employees nor employers; they make use of what
those others have worked out and established,
with a certain princely carelessness and with little
and rare praise—just as if the others belonged
to a lower order of beings. Yet they possess
the same qualities as their fellow-workers, and
that sometimes in a less developed form. Moreover, they have a peculiar limitation, from which
the others are free; this makes it impossible to
put them into a place and to see in them useful
tools. They can only live in their own air and on

their own soil. This limitation suggests to them what elements of a science " are theirs "—in other words, what they can carry home into their house and atmosphere : they think that they are always collecting their scattered " property." If they are prevented from building at their own nest, they perish like shelterless birds. The loss of freedom causes them to wilt away. If they show, like their colleagues, a fondness for certain regions of science, it is always only regions where the fruits and seeds necessary to them can thrive. What do they care whether science, taken as a whole, has untilled or badly tilled regions? They lack all impersonal interest in a scientific problem. As they are themselves personal through and through, all their knowledge and ideas are remoulded into a person, into a living complexity, with its parts interdependent, overlapping, jointly nurtured, and with a peculiar atmosphere and scent as a whole.—Such natures, with their system of personal knowledge, produce the illusion that a science (or even the whole of philosophy) is finished and has reached its goal. The life in their system works this magic, which at times has been fatal to science and deceptive to the really efficient workers above described, and at other times, when drought and exhaustion prevailed, has acted as a kind of restorative, as if it were the air of a cool, refreshing resting-place.—These men are usually called *philosophers*.

172.

RECOGNITION OF TALENT.—As I went through the village of S., a boy began to crack his whip with all his might—he had made great progress in this art, and he knew it. I threw him a look of recognition —in reality it hurt me cruelly. We do the same in our recognition of many of the talents. We do good to them when they hurt us.

173.

LAUGHING AND SMILING.—The more joyful and assured the mind becomes, the more man loses the habit of loud laughter. In compensation, there is an intellectual smile continually bubbling up in him, a sign of his astonishment at the innumerable concealed delights of a good existence.

174.

THE TALK OF INVALIDS.—Just as in spiritual grief we tear our hair, strike our foreheads, lacerate our cheeks or even (like Œdipus) gouge our eyes out, so against violent physical pain we call to our aid a bitter, violent emotion, through the recollection of slanderous and malignant people, through the denigration of our future, through the sword-pricks and acts of malice which we mentally direct against the absent. And at times it is true that one devil drives out another—but then we have the other.—Hence a different sort of talk, tending to alleviate pain, should be recommended invalids : reflections upon the kindnesses and courtesies that can be performed towards friend and foe.

175.

MEDIOCRITY AS A MASK.—Mediocrity is the happiest mask which the superior mind can wear, because it does not lead the great majority—that is, the mediocre—to think that there is any disguise. Yet the superior mind assumes the mask just for their sake—so as not to irritate them, nay, often from a feeling of pity and kindness.

176.

THE PATIENT.—The pine tree seems to listen, the fir tree to wait, and both without impatience. They do not give a thought to the petty human being below who is consumed by his impatience and his curiosity.

177.

THE BEST JOKER.—My favourite joke is the one that takes the place of a heavy and rather hesitating idea, and that at once beckons with its finger and winks its eye.

178.

THE ACCESSARIES OF ALL REVERENCE.—Wherever the past is revered, the over-cleanly and over-tidy people should not be admitted. Piety does not feel content without a little dust, dirt, and dross.

179.

THE GREAT DANGER OF SAVANTS.—It is just the most thorough and profound savants who are in peril of seeing their life's goal set ever lower and lower, and, with a feeling of this in their minds, to become ever more discouraged and more unendurable in the latter half of their lives. At first they plunge into their science with spacious hopes and set themselves daring tasks, the ends of which are

already anticipated by their imaginations. Then
there are moments as in the lives of the great
maritime discoverers—knowledge, presentiment, and
power raise each other higher and higher, until a new
shore first dawns upon the eye in the far distance.
But now the stern man recognises more and more
how important it is that the individual task of the
inquirer should be limited as far as possible, so
that it may be entirely accomplished and the intolerable waste of force from which earlier periods
of science suffered may be avoided. In those days
everything was done ten times over, and then the
eleventh always had the last and best word. Yet
the more the savant learns and practises this art of
solving riddles in their entirety, the more pleasure
he finds in so doing. But at the same time his demands upon what is here called "entirety" grow
more exacting. He sets aside everything that must
remain in this sense incomplete, he acquires a disgust and an acute scent for the half-soluble—for
all that can only give a kind of certainty in a
general and indefinite form. His youthful plans
crumble away before his eyes. There remains
scarcely anything but a few little knots, in untying which the master now takes his pleasure and
shows his strength. Then, in the midst of all this
useful, restless activity, he, now grown old, is suddenly then often overcome by a deep misgiving, a
sort of torment of conscience. He looks upon
himself as one changed, as if he were diminished,
humbled, transformed into a dexterous *dwarf*; he
grows anxious as to whether mastery in small
matters be not a convenience, an escape from the

summons to greatness in life and form.   But he cannot pass *beyond* any longer—the time for that has
gone by.

180.

TEACHERS IN THE AGE OF BOOKS.—Now that
self-education and mutual education are becoming
more widespread, the teacher in his usual form must
become almost unnecessary.   Friends eager to learn,
who wish to master some branch of knowledge together, find in our age of books a shorter and more
natural way than " school " and " teachers."

181.

VANITY AS THE GREATEST UTILITY.—Originally the strong individual uses not only Nature but
even societies and weaker individuals as objects of
rapine.   He exploits them, so far as he can, and
then passes on.   As he lives from hand to mouth,
alternating between hunger and superfluity, he kills
more animals than he can eat, and robs and maltreats men more than is necessary.   His manifestation of power is at the same time one of revenge
against his cramped and worried existence.   Furthermore, he wishes to be held more powerful than he
is, and thus misuses opportunities; the accretion of
fear that he begets being an accretion of power.   He
soon observes that he stands or falls not by what
he *is* but by what he is *thought* to be.   Herein lies
the origin of vanity.   The man of power seeks by
every means to increase others' faith in his power.—
The thralls who tremble before him and serve him
know, for their part, that they are worth just so

much as they appear to him to be worth, and so they work with an eye to this valuation rather than to their own self-satisfaction. We know vanity only in its most weakened forms, in its idealisations and its small doses, because we live in a late and very emasculated state of society. Originally vanity is the great utility, the strongest means of preservation. And indeed vanity will be greater, the cleverer the individual, because an increase in the belief in power is easier than an increase in the power itself, but only for him who has intellect or (as must be the case under primitive conditions) who is cunning and crafty.

182.

WEATHER-SIGNS OF CULTURE.—There are so few decisive weather-signs of culture that we must be glad to have at least one unfailing sign at hand for use in house and garden. To test whether a man belongs to us (I mean to the free spirits) or not, we must test his sentiments regarding Christianity. If he looks upon Christianity with other than a critical eye, we turn our backs to him, for he brings us impure air and bad weather.—It is no longer our task to teach such men what a sirocco wind is. They have Moses and the prophets of weather and of enlightenment.* If they will not listen to these, then——

183.

THERE IS A PROPER TIME FOR WRATH AND PUNISHMENT.—Wrath and punishment are our in-

* In the German *Aufklärung* there is a play on the sense "clearing up" (of weather) and "enlightenment."—TR.

heritance from the animals. Man does not become of age until he has restored to the animals this gift of the cradle.—Herein lies buried one of the mightiest ideas that men can have, the idea of a progress of all progresses.—Let us go forward together a few millenniums, my friends! There is still reserved for mankind a great deal of joy, the very scent of which has not yet been wafted to the men of our day! Indeed, we may promise ourselves this joy, nay summon and conjure it up as a necessary thing, so long as the development of human reason does not stand still. Some day we shall no longer be reconciled to the logical sin that lurks in all wrath and punishment, whether exercised by the individual or by society—some day, when head and heart have learnt to live as near together as they now are far apart. That they no longer stand so far apart as they did originally is fairly palpable from a glance at the whole course of humanity. The individual who can review a life of introspective work will become conscious of the *rapprochement* arrived at, with a proud delight at the distance he has bridged, in order that he may thereupon venture upon more ample hopes.

184.

ORIGIN OF PESSIMISTS.—A snack of good food often decides whether we are to look to the future with hollow eye or in hopeful mood. The same influence extends to the very highest and most intellectual states. Discontent and reviling of the world are for the present generation an inheritance from starveling ancestors. Even in our artists and

poets we often notice that, however exuberant their
life, they are not of good birth, and have often, from
oppressed and ill-nourished ancestors, inherited in
their blood and brain much that comes out as the
subject and even the conscious colouring of their
work.   The culture of the Greeks is a culture of men
of wealth, in fact, inherited wealth.   For a few centuries
they lived better than we do (better in every sense,
in particular far more simply in food and drink).
Then the brain finally became so well-stored and
subtle, and the blood flowed so quickly, like a joyous,
clear wine, that the best in them came to light no
longer as gloomy, distorted, and violent, but full of
beauty and sunshine.

185.

OF REASONABLE DEATH.—Which is more reasonable, to stop the machine when the works have done
the task demanded of them, or to let it run on until
it stands still of its own accord—in other words, is
destroyed ?   Is not the latter a waste of the cost of
upkeep, a misuse of the strength and care of those
who serve?   Are men not here throwing away that
which would be sorely needed elsewhere ?   Is not a
kind of contempt of the machines propagated, in that
many of them are so uselessly tended and kept up?—
I am speaking of involuntary (natural) and voluntary
(reasonable) death.   Natural death is independent
of all reason and is really an irrational death, in
which the pitiable substance of the shell determines
how long the kernel is to exist or not ; in which,
accordingly, the stunted, diseased and dull-witted

jailer is lord, and indicates the moment at which his distinguished prisoner shall die. Natural death is the suicide of nature—in other words, the annihilation of the most rational being through the most irrational element that is attached thereto. Only through religious illumination can the reverse appear; for then, as is equitable, the higher reason (God) issues its orders, which the lower reason has to obey. Outside religious thought natural death is not worth glorifying. The wise dispensation and disposal of death belongs to that now quite incomprehensible and immoral-sounding morality of the future, the dawn of which it will be an ineffable delight to behold.

186.

RETROGRADE INFLUENCES.—All criminals force society back to earlier stages of culture than that in which they are placed for the time being. Their influence is retrograde. Let us consider the tools that society must forge and maintain for its defence: the cunning detectives, the jailers, the hangmen. Nor should we forget the public counsel for prosecution and defence. Finally we may ask ourselves whether the judge himself and punishment and the whole legal procedure are not oppressive rather than elevating in their reaction upon all who are not law-breakers. For we shall never succeed in arraying self-defence and revenge in the garb of innocence, and so long as men are used and sacrificed as a means to the end of society, all loftier humanity will deplore this necessity.

187.

WAR AS A REMEDY.—For nations that are growing weak and contemptible war may be prescribed
as a remedy, if indeed they really want to go on
living.   National consumption as well as individual
admits of a brutal cure.   The eternal will to live
and inability to die is, however, in itself already a
sign of senility of emotion.   The more fully and
thoroughly we live, the more ready we are to sacrifice life for a single pleasurable emotion.   A people
that lives and feels in this wise has no need of war.

188.

INTELLECTUAL AND PHYSICAL TRANSPLANTA-
TION AS REMEDIES.—The different cultures are so
many intellectual climates, every one of which is
peculiarly harmful or beneficial to this or that
organism.   History as a whole, as the knowledge
of different cultures, is the science of remedies, but
not the science of the healing art itself.   We still
need a physician who can make use of these
remedies, in order to send every one—temporarily
or permanently—to the climate that just suits
him.   To live in the present, within the limits of a
single culture, is insufficient as a universal remedy :
too many highly useful kinds of men, who cannot
breathe freely in this atmosphere, would perish.
With the aid of history we must give them air and
try to preserve them : even men of lower cultures
have their value.—Add to this cure of intellects that
humanity, on considerations of bodily health, must
strive to discover by means of a medical geography

what kinds of degeneration and disease are caused by each region of the earth, and conversely, what ingredients of health the earth affords : and then, gradually, nations, families, and individuals must be transplanted long and permanently enough for them to become masters of their inherited physical infirmities. The whole world will finally be a series of sanatoria.

189.

REASON AND THE TREE OF MANKIND.—What you all fear in your senile short-sightedness, regarding the over-population of the world, gives the more hopeful a mighty task. Man is some day to become a tree overshadowing the whole earth, with millions upon millions of buds that shall all grow to fruits side by side, and the earth itself shall be prepared for the nourishment of this tree. That the shoot, tiny as yet, may increase in sap and strength ; that the sap may flow in countless channels for the nutrition of the whole and the parts—from these and similar tasks we must derive our standard for measuring whether a man of to-day is useful or worthless. The task is unspeakably great and adventurous : let us all contribute our share to prevent the tree from rotting before its time ! The historically trained mind will no doubt succeed in calling up the human activities of all the ages before its eyes, as the community of ants with its cunningly wrought mounds stands before our eyes. Superficially judged, mankind as a whole, like ant-kind, might admit of our speaking of "instinct." On a closer examination we observe how whole nations, nay whole centuries, take pains to discover and test new means of benefiting the great mass of humanity, and thus finally the great common fruit-tree of the world. Whatever injury the individual nations or periods may suffer in this testing process, they have each become wise through this injury, and from them the tide of wisdom slowly pours over the principles of whole races and whole epochs. Ants too go astray and make blunders. Through the folly of its remedies, mankind may well go to rack and ruin before the proper time. There is no sure guiding instinct for the former or the latter. Rather must we boldly face the great task of preparing the earth for a plant of the most ample and joyous fruitfulness—a task set by reason to reason !

190.

THE PRAISE OF DISINTERESTEDNESS AND ITS ORIGIN. — Between two neighbouring chieftains there was a long-standing quarrel : they laid waste each other's territories, stole cattle, and burnt down houses, with an indecisive result on the whole, because their power was fairly equal. A third, who from the distant situation of his property was able to keep aloof from these feuds, yet had reason to dread the day when one of the two neighbours should gain a decisive preponderance, at last intervened between the combatants with ceremonial goodwill. Secretly he lent a heavy weight to his peace proposal by giving either to understand that he would henceforth join forces with the other against the one who strove to break the peace.

They met in his presence, they hesitatingly placed into his hand the hands that had hitherto been the tools and only too often the causes of hatred—and then they really and seriously tried to keep the peace. Either saw with astonishment how suddenly his prosperity and his comfort increased; how he now had as neighbour a dealer ready to buy and sell instead of a treacherous or openly scornful evil-doer; how even, in unforeseen troubles, they could reciprocally save each other from distress, instead of, as before, making capital out of this distress of his neighbour and enhancing it to the highest degree. It even seemed as if the human type had improved in both countries, for the eyes had become brighter, the forehead had lost its wrinkles; all now felt confidence in the future—and nothing is more advantageous for the souls and bodies of men than this confidence. They saw each other every year on the anniversary of the alliance, the chieftains as well as their retinue, and indeed before the eyes of the mediator, whose mode of action they admired and revered more and more, the greater the profit that they owed to him became. Then his mode of action was called *disinterested.* They had looked far too fixedly at the profit they had reaped themselves hitherto to see anything more of their neighbour's method of dealing than that his condition in consequence of this had not altered so much as their own; he had rather remained the same: and thus it appeared that the former had not had his profit in view. For the first time people said to themselves that disinterestedness was a virtue. It is true that in minor private matters similar circumstances

had arisen, but men only had eyes for this virtue
when it was depicted on the walls in a large script
that was legible to the whole community.   Moral
qualities are not recognised as virtues, endowed
with names, held in esteem, and recommended as
worthy of acquisition until the moment when they
have *visibly* decided the happiness and destiny of
whole societies.   For then the loftiness of sentiment and the excitation of the inner creative forces
is in many so great, that offerings are brought to
this quality, offerings from the best of what each
possesses.   At its feet the serious man lays his
seriousness, the dignified man his dignity, women
their gentleness, the young all the wealth of hope
and futurity that in them lies; the poet lends it
words and names, sets it marching in the procession
of similar beings, gives it a pedigree, and finally, as
is the way of artists, adores the picture of his fancy
as a new godhead—he even teaches others to adore.
Thus in the end, with the co-operation of universal
love and gratitude, a virtue becomes, like a statue,
a repository of all that is good and honourable, a
sort of temple and divine personage combined.   It
appears thenceforward as an individual virtue, as
an absolute entity, which it was not before, and
exercises the power and privileges of a sanctified
super-humanity.—In the later days of Greece the
cities were full of such deified human abstractions
(if one may so call them).   The nation, in its own
fashion, had set up a Platonic " Heaven of Ideas "
on earth, and I do not think that its inhabitants
were felt to be less alive than any of the old
Homeric divinities.

191.

DAYS OF DARKNESS.—" Days of Darkness " is the name given in Norway to the period when the sun remains below the horizon the whole day long. The temperature then falls slowly but continually.— A fine simile for all thinkers for whom the sun of the human future is temporarily eclipsed.

192.

THE PHILOSOPHY OF LUXURY.—A garden, figs, a little cheese, and three or four good friends—that was the luxury of Epicurus.

193.

THE EPOCHS OF LIFE.—The real epochs of life are those brief periods of cessation midway between the rise and decline of a dominating idea or emotion. Here once again there is satisfaction : all the rest is hunger and thirst—or satiety.

194.

DREAMS.—Our dreams, if for once in a way they succeed and are complete—generally a dream is a bungled piece of work—are symbolic concatenations of scenes and images in place of a narrative poetical language. They paraphrase our experiences or expectations or relations with poetic boldness and definiteness, so that in the morning we are always astonished at ourselves when we remember the nature of our dream. In dreams we use up too much artistry—and hence are often too poor in artistry in the daytime.

195.

NATURE AND SCIENCE. — As in nature, so in
science the worse and less fertile soils are first
cultivated—because the means that science in its
early stages has at command are fairly sufficient for
this purpose.   The working of the most fertile soils
requires an enormous, carefully developed, perse-
vering method, tangible individual results, and an
organised body of well-trained workers.   All these
are found together only at a late stage.—Impatience and ambition often grasp too early at these
most fertile soils, but the results are then from the
first null and void.   In nature such losses would
usually be avenged by the starvation of the settlers.

196.

THE SIMPLE LIFE.—A simple mode of life is
nowadays difficult, requiring as it does far more reflection and gift for invention than even very clever
people possess.   The most honourable will perhaps
still say, " I have not the time for such lengthy
reflection.   The simple life is for me too lofty a goal :
I will wait till those wiser than I have discovered
it."

197.

PEAKS AND NEEDLE-POINTS.—The poor fertility,
the frequent celibacy, and in general the sexual
coldness of the highest and most cultivated spirits,
as that of the classes to which they belong, is
essential in human economy.   Intelligence recognises and makes use of the fact that at an acme of

intellectual development the danger of a neurotic offspring is very great.   Such men are the peaks of mankind — they ought no longer to run out into needle-points.

198.

NATURA NON FACIT SALTUM.—However strongly man may develop upwards and seem to leap from one contradiction to another, a close observation will reveal the dovetails where the new building grows out of the old.   This is the biographer's task : he must reflect upon his subject on the principle that nature takes no jumps.

199.

CLEAN, BUT——   He who clothes himself with rags washed clean dresses cleanly, to be sure, but is still ragged.

200.

THE SOLITARY SPEAKS.—In compensation for much disgust, disheartenment, boredom—such as a lonely life without friends, books, duties, and passions must involve—we enjoy those short spans of deep communion with ourselves and with Nature. He who fortifies himself completely against boredom fortifies himself against himself too.   He will never drink the most powerful elixir from his own innermost spring.

201.

FALSE RENOWN.—I hate those so-called natural beauties which really have significance only through science, especially geographical science, but are in-

significant in an æsthetic sense : for example, the
view of Mont Blanc from Geneva. This is an insignificant thing without the auxiliary mental joy of
science : the nearer mountains are all more beautiful
and fuller of expression, but " not nearly so high,"
adds that absurd depreciatory science. The eye
here contradicts science : how can it truly rejoice in
the contradiction ?

202.

THOSE THAT TRAVEL FOR PLEASURE. — Like
animals, stupid and perspiring, they climb mountains : people forgot to tell them that there were
fine views on the way.

203.

TOO MUCH AND TOO LITTLE.—Men nowadays
live too much and think too little. They have
hunger and dyspepsia together, and become thinner
and thinner, however much they eat. He who now
says " Nothing has happened to me " is a blockhead.

204.

END AND GOAL.—Not every end is the goal.
The end of a melody is not its goal, and yet if
a melody has not reached its end, it has also not
reached its goal. A parable.

205.

NEUTRALITY OF NATURE ON A GRAND SCALE.
—The neutrality of Nature on a grand scale (in

mountain, sea, forest, and desert) is pleasing, but
only for a brief space.   Afterwards we become impatient.   "Have they all nothing to say to *us*?
Do *we* not exist so far as they are concerned?"
There arises a feeling that a *lèse-majesté* is committed against humanity.

206.

FORGETTING OUR PURPOSE.—In a journey we
commonly forget its goal.   Almost every vocation
is chosen and entered upon as means to an end, but
is continued as the ultimate end.   Forgetting our
purpose is the most frequent form of folly.

207.

SOLAR ORBIT OF AN IDEA.—When an idea is
just rising on the horizon, the soul's temperature is
usually very low.   Gradually the idea develops in
warmth, and is hottest (that is to say, exerts its
greatest influence) when belief in the idea is already
on the wane.

208.

HOW TO HAVE EVERY MAN AGAINST YOU.—
If some one now dared to say, "He that is not
for me is against me," he would at once have all
against him.—This sentiment does credit to our era.

209.

BEING ASHAMED OF WEALTH.—Our age endures
only a single species of rich men—those who are

ashamed of their wealth. If we hear it said of
any one that he is very rich, we at once feel a similar
sentiment to that experienced at the sight of a re-
pulsively swollen invalid, one suffering from diabetes
or dropsy. We must with an effort remember our
humanity, in order to go about with this rich man
in such a way that he does not notice our feeling of
disgust. But as soon as he prides himself at all on
his wealth, our feelings are mingled with an almost
compassionate surprise at such a high degree of
human unreason. We would fain raise our hands
to heaven and cry, "Poor deformed and over-
burdened creature, fettered a hundredfold, to whom
every hour brings or may bring something unpleasant, in whose frame twitches every event that
occurs in scores of countries, how can you make us
believe that you feel at ease in your position? If
you appear anywhere in public, we know that it
is a sort of running the gauntlet amid countless
glances that have for you only cold hate or im-
portunity or silent scorn. You may earn more
easily than others, but it is only a superfluous
earning, which brings little joy, and the guarding
of what you have earned is now, at any rate, a more
troublesome business than any toilsome process of
earning. You are continually suffering, because you
are continually losing. What avails it you that they
are always injecting you with fresh artificial blood?
That does not relieve the pain of those cupping-
glasses that are fixed, for ever fixed, on your neck!—
But, to be quite fair to you, it is difficult or perhaps
impossible for you *not* to be rich. You *must* guard,
you *must* earn more; the inherited bent of your

character is the yoke fastened upon you.   But do not on that account deceive us—be honestly and visibly ashamed of the yoke you wear, as in your soul you are weary and unwilling to wear it.   This shame is no disgrace."

210.

EXTRAVAGANT PRESUMPTIONS.—There are men so presumptuous that they can only praise a greatness which they publicly admire by representing it as steps and bridges that lead to themselves.

211.

ON THE SOIL OF INSULT.—He who wishes to deprive men of a conception is generally not satisfied with refuting it and drawing out of it the illogical worm that resides within.   Rather, when the worm has been killed, does he throw the whole fruit as well into the mire, in order to make it ignoble in men's sight and to inspire disgust.   Thus he thinks that he has found a means of making the usual "third-day resurrection" of conceptions an impossibility.—He is wrong, for on the very soil of insult, in the midst of the filth, the kernel of the conception soon produces new seeds.—The right thing then, is not to scorn and bespatter what one wishes finally to remove, but to lay it tenderly on ice again and again, having regard to the fact that conceptions are very tenacious of life.   Here we must act according to the maxim : " One refutation is no refutation."

212.

THE LOT OF MORALITY.—Since spiritual bondage is being relaxed, morality (the inherited, traditional, instinctive mode of action in accordance
with moral sentiments) is surely also on the decline.
This, however, is not the case with the individual
virtues, moderation, justice, repose; for the greatest
freedom of the conscious intellect leads at some
time, even unconsciously, back to these virtues, and
then enjoins their practice as expedient.

213.

THE FANATIC OF DISTRUST AND HIS SURETY.
—*The Elder*: You wish to make the tremendous
venture and instruct mankind in the great things?
What is your surety?

Pyrrho: It is this: I intend to warn men
against myself; I intend to confess all the defects of
my character quite openly, and reveal to the world
my hasty conclusions, my contradictions, and my
foolish blunders. "Do not listen to me," I will say
to them, "until I have become equal to the meanest
among you, nay am even less than he. Struggle
against truth as long as you can, from your disgust
with her advocate. I shall be your seducer and
betrayer if you find in me the slightest glimmering
of respectability and dignity."

The Elder: You promise too much; you cannot
bear this burden.

Pyrrho: Then I will tell men even that, and say
that I am too weak, and cannot keep my promise.
The greater my unworthiness, the more will they

mistrust the truth, when it passes through my lips.

The Elder: You propose to teach distrust of truth?

Pyrrho: Yes; distrust as it never was yet on earth, distrust of anything and everything. This is the only road to truth. The right eye must not trust the left eye, and for some time light must be called darkness: this is the path that you must tread. Do not imagine that it will lead you to fruit trees and fair pastures. You will find on this road little hard grains — these are truths. For years and years you will have to swallow handfuls of lies, so as not to die of hunger, although you know that they are lies. But those grains will be sown and planted, and perhaps, perhaps some day will come the harvest. No one may *promise* that day, unless he be a fanatic.

The Elder: Friend, friend! Your words too are those of a fanatic!

Pyrrho: You are right! I will be distrustful of all words.

The Elder: Then you will have to be silent.

Pyrrho: I shall tell men that I have to be silent, and that they are to mistrust my silence.

The Elder: So you draw back from your undertaking?

Pyrrho: On the contrary—you have shown me the door through which I must pass.

The Elder: I don't know whether we yet completely understand each other?

Pyrrho: Probably not.

The Elder: If only you understand yourself!

(Pyrrho turns round and laughs.)

The Elder : Ah, friend !   Silence and laughter—
is that now your whole philosophy ?

Pyrrho : There might be a worse.

214.

EUROPEAN BOOKS.—In reading Montaigne, La
Rochefoucauld, La Bruyère, Fontenelle (especially
the *Dialogues des Morts*), Vauvenargues, and Cham-
fort we are nearer to antiquity than in any group
of six authors of other nations.   Through these
six the spirit of the last centuries before Christ
has once more come into being, and they collectively form an important link in the great and
still continuous chain of the Renaissance.   Their
books are raised above all changes of national
taste and philosophical nuances from which as a
rule every book takes and must take its hue in
order to become famous.   They contain more real
ideas than all the books of German philosophers
put together : ideas of the sort that breed ideas——
I am at a loss how to define to the end : enough to
say that they appear to me writers who wrote
neither for children nor for visionaries, neither for
virgins nor for Christians, neither for Germans nor
for——   I am again at a loss how to finish my list.
To praise them in plain terms, I may say that
had they been written in Greek, they would have
been understood by Greeks.   How much, on the
other hand, would even a Plato have understood
of the writings of our best German thinkers—Goethe
and Schopenhauer, for instance—to say nothing
of the repugnance that he would have felt to

their style, particularly to its obscure, exaggerated, and occasionally dry-as-dust elements?   And these are defects from which these two among German thinkers suffer least and yet far too much (Goethe as thinker was fonder than he should have been of embracing the cloud, and Schopenhauer almost constantly wanders, not with impunity, among symbols of objects rather than among the objects themselves). — On the other hand, what clearness and graceful precision there is in these Frenchmen ! The Greeks, whose ears were most refined, could not but have approved of this art, and one quality they would even have admired and reverenced— the French verbal wit: they were extremely fond of this quality, without being particularly strong in it themselves.

215.

FASHION AND MODERNITY. — Wherever ignorance, uncleanness, and superstition are still rife, where communication is backward, agriculture poor, and the priesthood powerful, national costumes are still worn.   Fashion, on the other hand, rules where the opposite conditions prevail.   Fashion is accordingly to be found next to the virtues in modern Europe.   Are we to call it their seamy side?— Masculine dress that is fashionable and no longer national proclaims of its wearer: firstly, that he does not wish to appear as an individual or as member of a class or race; that he has made an intentional suppression of these kinds of vanity a law unto himself: secondly, that he is a worker, and has little time for dressing and self-adornment,

and moreover regards anything expensive or lux-
urious in material and cut as out of harmony with
his work: lastly, that by his clothes he indicates the more learned and intellectual callings as
those to which he stands or would like to stand
nearest as a European — whereas such national
costumes as still exist would exhibit the occupations of brigand, shepherd, and soldier as the most
desirable and distinguished. Within this general
character of masculine fashion exist the slight
fluctuations demanded by the vanity of young
men, the dandies and dawdlers of our great
cities — in other words, Europeans who have
not yet reached maturity.—European women are
as yet far less mature, and for this reason the
fluctuations with them are much greater. They
also will not have the national costume, and hate
to be recognised by their dress as German, French,
or Russian. They are, however, very desirous of
creating an impression as individuals. Then, too,
their dress must leave no one in doubt that they
belong to one of the more reputable classes of
society (to "good" or "high" or "great" society),
and on this score their pretensions are all the
greater if they belong scarcely or not at all to that
class. Above all, the young woman does not want
to wear what an older woman wears, because she
thinks she loses her market value if she is suspected
of being somewhat advanced in years. The older
woman, on the other hand, would like to deceive
the world as long as possible by a youthful garb.
From this competition must continually arise
temporary fashions, in which the youthful element

is unmistakably and inimitably apparent. But after the inventive genius of the young female artists has run riot for some time in such indiscreet revelations of youth (or rather, after the inventive genius of older, courtly civilisations and of still existing peoples—in fact, of the whole world of dress—has been pressed into the service, and, say, the Spaniards, Turks, and ancient Greeks have been yoked together for the glorification of fair flesh), then they at last discover, time and again, that they have not been good judges of their own interest ; that if they wish to have power over men, the game of hide-and-seek with the beautiful body is more likely to win than naked or half-naked honesty.   And then the wheel of taste and vanity turns once more in an opposite direction.   The rather older young women find that their kingdom has come, and the competition of the dear, absurd creatures rages again from the beginning.—But the more women advance mentally, and no longer among themselves concede the pre-eminence to an unripe age, the smaller their fluctuations of costume grow and the less elaborate their adornment.   A just verdict in this respect must not be based on ancient models—in other words, not on the standard of the dress of women who dwell on the shores of the Mediterranean—but must have an eye to the climatic conditions of the central and northern regions, where the intellectual and creative spirit of Europe now finds its most natural home.— Generally speaking, therefore, it is not change that will be the characteristic mark of fashion and modernity, for change is retrograde, and betokens

the still unripened men and women of Europe; but
rather the repudiation of national, social, and individual vanity.   Accordingly, it is commendable,
because involving a saving of time and strength,
if certain cities and districts of Europe think and
invent for all the rest in the matter of dress, in
view of the fact that a sense of form does not
seem to have been bestowed upon all.   Nor is
it really an excessive ambition, so long as these
fluctuations still exist, for Paris, for example, to
claim to be the sole inventor and innovator in this
sphere.   If a German, from hatred of these claims
on the part of a French city, wishes to dress differently,—as, for example, in the Dürer style,—let
him reflect that he then has a costume which
the Germans of olden times wore, but which the
Germans have not in the slightest degree invented.
For there has never been a style of dress that
characterised the German as a German.   Moreover,
let him observe how he looks in his costume, and
whether his altogether modern face, with all its hues
and wrinkles, does not raise a protest against a
Dürer fashion of dress.—Here, where the concepts
" modern" and " European " are almost identical, we
understand by " Europe " a far wider region than
is embraced by the Europe of geography, the little
peninsula of Asia.   In particular, we must include
America, in so far as America is the daughter of
our civilisation.   On the other hand, not all Europe
falls under the heading of cultured " Europe," but
only those nations and divisions of nations which
have their common past in Greece, Rome, Judaism,
and Christianity.

216.

"GERMAN VIRTUE."—There is no denying that from the end of the eighteenth century a current of moral awakening flowed through Europe. Then only Virtue found again the power of speech. She learnt to discover the unrestrained gestures of exaltation and emotion, she was no longer ashamed of herself, and she created philosophies and poems for her own glorification. If we look for the sources of this current, we come upon Rousseau, but the mythical Rousseau, the phantom formed from the impression left by his writings (one might almost say again, his mythically interpreted writings) and by the indications that he provided himself. He and his public constantly worked at the fashioning of this ideal figure. The other origin lies in the resurrection of the Stoical side of Rome's greatness, whereby the French so nobly carried on the task of the Renaissance. With striking success they proceeded from the reproduction of antique forms to the reproduction of antique characters. Thus they may always claim a title to the highest honours, as the nation which has hitherto given the modern world its best books and its best men. How this twofold archetype, the mythical Rousseau and the resurrected spirit of Rome, affected France's weaker neighbours, is particularly noticeable in Germany, which, in consequence of her novel and quite unwonted impulse to seriousness and loftiness in will and self-control, finally came to feel astonishment at her own new-found virtue, and launched into the world the concept "German virtue," as if this were the most

original and hereditary of her possessions. The first
great men who transfused into their own blood that
French impulse towards greatness and consciousness
of the moral will were more honest, and more grateful. Whence comes the moralism of Kant? He is
continually reminding us: from Rousseau and the
revival of Stoic Rome. The moralism of Schiller
has the same source and the same glorification of
the source. The moralism of Beethoven in notes is
a continual song in praise of Rousseau, the antique
French, and Schiller. " Young Germany " was the
first to forget its gratitude, because in the meantime
people had listened to the preachers of hatred of
the French. The "young German " came to the fore
with more consciousness than is generally allowed
to youths. When he investigated his paternity,
he might well think of the proximity of Schiller,
Schleiermacher, and Fichte. But he should have
looked for his grandfathers in Paris and Geneva,
and it was very short-sighted of him to believe what
he believed: that virtue was not more than thirty
years old. People became used to demanding that
the word "German " should connote " virtue," and
this process has not been wholly forgotten to
this day.—Be it observed further that this moral
awakening, as may almost be guessed, has resulted
only in drawbacks and obstacles to the *recognition*
of moral phenomena. What is the entire German
philosophy, starting from Kant, with all its French,
English, and Italian offshoots and by-products? A
semi-theological attack upon Helvetius, a rejection
of the slowly and laboriously acquired views and
signposts of the right road, which in the end he

collected and expressed so well.   To this day Helvetius is the best-abused of all good moralists and good men in Germany.

217.

CLASSIC AND ROMANTIC.—Both classically and romantically minded spirits—two species that always exist—cherish a vision of the future; but the former derive their vision from the strength of their time, the latter from its weakness.

218.

THE MACHINE AS TEACHER.—Machinery teaches in itself the dovetailed working of masses of men, in activities where each has but one thing to do.   It is the model of party organisations and of warfare. On the other hand, it does not teach individual self-glorification, for it makes of the many a machine, and of each individual a tool for one purpose.   Its most general effect is to teach the advantage of centralisation.

219.

UNABLE TO SETTLE. — One likes to live in a small town.   But from time to time just this small town drives us out into bare and lonely Nature, especially when we think we know it too well.   Finally, in order to refresh ourselves from Nature, we go to the big town.   A few draughts from this cup and we see its dregs, and the circle begins afresh, with the small town as starting-point.—So the moderns live ;

they are in all things rather too thorough to be able
to settle like the men of other days.

220.

REACTION AGAINST THE CIVILISATION OF
MACHINERY.—The machine, itself a product of the
highest mental powers, sets in motion hardly any
but the lower, unthinking forces of the men who
serve it. True, it unfetters a vast quantity of force
which would otherwise lie dormant. But it does not
communicate the impulse to climb higher, to improve, to become artistic. It creates activity and
monotony, but this in the long-run produces a
counter-effect, a despairing ennui of the soul, which
through machinery has learnt to hanker after the
variety of leisure.

221.

THE DANGER OF ENLIGHTENMENT.—All the
half-insane, theatrical, bestially cruel, licentious, and
especially sentimental and self-intoxicating elements which go to form the true revolutionary substance, and became flesh and spirit, before the
revolution, in Rousseau—all this composite being,
with factitious enthusiasm, finally set even "enlightenment" upon its fanatical head, which thereby began
itself to shine as in an illuminating halo. Yet, enlightenment is essentially foreign to that phenomenon, and, if left to itself, would have pierced silently
through the clouds like a shaft of light, long content
to transfigure individuals alone, and thus only slowly
transfiguring national customs and institutions as
well. But now, bound hand and foot to a violent and

abrupt monster, enlightenment itself became violent and abrupt. Its danger has therefore become almost greater than its useful quality of liberation and illumination, which it introduced into the great revolutionary movement. Whoever grasps this will also know from what confusion it has to be extricated, from what impurities to be cleansed, in order that it may then by itself continue the work of enlightenment and also nip the revolution in the bud and nullify its effects.

222.

PASSION IN THE MIDDLE AGES.—The Middle Ages are the period of great passions. Neither antiquity nor our period possesses this widening of the soul. Never was the capacity of the soul greater or measured by larger standards. The physical, primeval sensuality of the barbarian races and the over-soulful, over-vigilant, over-brilliant eyes of Christian mystics, the most childish and youthful and the most over-ripe and world-weary, the savageness of the beast of prey and the effeminacy and excessive refinement of the late antique spirit—all these elements were then not seldom united in one and the same person. Thus, if a man was seized by a passion, the rapidity of the torrent must have been greater, the whirl more confused, the fall deeper than ever before.—We modern men may be content to feel that we have suffered a loss here.

223.

ROBBING AND SAVING.—All intellectual movements whereby the great may hope to rob and the small to save are sure to prosper. That is why, for instance, the German Reformation made progress.

224.

GLADSOME SOULS.—When even a remote hint of drink, drunkenness, and an evil-smelling kind of jocularity was given, the souls of the old Germans waxed gladsome. Otherwise they were depressed, but here they found something they really understood.

225.

DEBAUCHERY AT ATHENS.—Even when the fish-market of Athens acquired its thinkers and poets, Greek debauchery had a more idyllic and refined appearance than Roman or German debauchery ever had. The voice of Juvenal would have sounded there like a hollow trumpet, and would have been answered by a good-natured and almost childish outburst of laughter.

226.

CLEVERNESS OF THE GREEK.—As the desire for victory and pre-eminence is an ineradicable trait of human nature, older and more primitive than any respect of or joy in equality, the Greek State sanctioned gymnastic and artistic competitions among equals. In other words, it marked out an arena where this impulse to conquer would find a vent without jeopardising the political order. With the final decline of gymnastic and artistic contests the Greek State fell into a condition of profound unrest and dissolution.

227.

THE "ETERNAL EPICURUS." — Epicurus has lived in all periods, and lives yet, unbeknown to those who called and still call themselves Epicureans, and without repute among philosophers. He has himself even forgotten his own name—that was the heaviest luggage that he ever cast off.

228.

THE STYLE OF SUPERIORITY. — "University slang," the speech of the German students, has its origin among the students who do not study. The latter know how to acquire a preponderance over their more serious fellows by exposing all the farcical elements of culture, respectability, erudition, order, and moderation, and by having words taken from these realms always on their lips, like the better and more learned students, but with malice in their glance and an accompanying grimace. This language of superiority—the only one that is original in Germany—is nowadays unconsciously used by statesmen and newspaper critics as well. It is a continual process of ironical quotation, a restless, cantankerous squinting of the eye right and left, a language of inverted commas and grimaces.

229.

THE RECLUSE.—We retire into seclusion, but not from personal misgivings, as if the political and social conditions of the day did not satisfy us; rather because by our retirement we try to save and

collect forces which will some day be urgently
needed by culture, the more this present is *this
present*, and, as such, fulfils its task.   We form a
capital and try to make it secure, but, as in times
of real danger, our method is to bury our hoard.

230.

TYRANTS OF THE INTELLECT.—In our times,
any one who expressed a single moral trait so
thoroughly as the characters of Theophrastus and
Molière do, would be considered ill, and be spoken
of as possessing "a fixed idea."   The Athens of the
third century, if we could visit it, would appear
to us populated by fools.   Nowadays the democracy of ideas rules in every brain—there the multitude collectively is lord.   A single idea that tried
to be lord is now called, as above stated, "a fixed
idea."   This is our method of murdering tyrants—
we hint at the madhouse.

231.

A MOST DANGEROUS EMIGRATION.—In Russia
there is an emigration of the intelligence.   People
cross the frontier in order to read and write good
books.   Thus, however, they are working towards
turning their country, abandoned by the intellect,
into a gaping Asiatic maw, which would fain
swallow our little Europe.

232.

POLITICAL FOOLS.—The almost religious love of
the king was transferred by the Greeks, when the

monarchy was abolished, to the *polis*.   An idea can be loved more than a person, and does not thwart the lover so often as a beloved human being (for the more men know themselves to be loved, the less considerate they usually become, until they are no longer worthy of love, and a rift really arises). Hence the reverence for State and *polis* was greater than the reverence for princes had ever been.   The Greeks are the political fools of ancient history—to-day other nations boast that distinction.

233.

AGAINST NEGLECT OF THE EYES.—Might one not find among the cultured classes of England, who read the *Times*, a decline in their powers of sight every ten years?

234.

GREAT WORKS AND GREAT FAITH.—One man had great works, but his comrade had great faith in these works.   They were inseparable, but obviously the former was entirely dependent upon the latter.

235.

THE SOCIABLE MAN.—" I don't get on well with myself," said some one in explanation of his fondness for society.   " Society has a stronger digestion than I have, and can put up with me."

236.

SHUTTING THE MIND'S EYES.—If we are practised and accustomed to reflect upon our actions, we must nevertheless close the inner eye while performing an action (be this even only writing letters or eating or drinking). Even in conversation with average people we must know how to obscure our own mental vision in order to attain and grasp average thinking. This shutting of the eyes is a conscious act and can be achieved by the will.

237.

THE MOST TERRIBLE REVENGE.—If we wish to take a thorough revenge upon an opponent, we must wait until we have our hand quite full of truths and equities, and can calmly use the whole lot against him. Hence the exercise of revenge may be identified with the exercise of equity. It is the most terrible kind of revenge, for there is no higher court to which an appeal can be made. Thus did Voltaire revenge himself on Piron, with five lines that sum up Piron's whole life, work, and character: every word is a truth. So too he revenged himself upon Frederick the Great in a letter to him from Ferney.

238.

TAXES OF LUXURY.—In shops we buy the most necessary and urgent things, and have to pay very dear, because we pay as well for what is also to be had there cheap, but seldom finds a customer—articles of luxury that minister to pleasure. Thus luxury lays a constant tax upon the man of simple life who does without luxuries.

239.

WHY BEGGARS STILL LIVE.—If all alms were given only out of compassion, the whole tribe of beggars would long since have died of starvation.

240.

WHY BEGGARS STILL LIVE.—The greatest of almsgivers is cowardice.

241.

HOW THE THINKER MAKES USE OF A CONVERSATION.—Without being eavesdroppers, we can hear a good deal if we are able to see well, and at the same time to let ourselves occasionally get out of our own sight. But people do not know how to make use of a conversation. They pay far too much attention to what *they* want to say and reply, whereas the true listener is often contented to make a provisional answer and to say something merely as a payment on account of politeness, but on the other hand, with his memory lurking in ambush, carries away with him all that the other said, together with his tones and gestures in speaking.—In ordinary conversation every one thinks *he* is the leader, just as if two ships, sailing side by side and giving each other a slight push here and there, were each firmly convinced that the other ship was following or even being towed.

242.

THE ART OF EXCUSING ONESELF.—If some one excuses himself to us, he has to make out a very

good case, otherwise we readily come to feel ourselves the culprits, and experience an unpleasant
emotion.

243.

IMPOSSIBLE INTERCOURSE.—The ship of your
thoughts goes too deep for you to be able to travel
with it in the waters of these friendly, decorous,
obliging people. There are too many shallows and
sandbanks: you would have to tack and turn, and
would find yourself continually at your wits' end,
and they would soon also be in perplexity as to
your perplexity, the reason for which they cannot
divine.

244.

THE FOX OF FOXES.—A true fox not only calls
sour the grapes he cannot reach, but also those he
has reached and snatched from the grasp of others.

245.

IN INTIMATE INTERCOURSE.—However closely
men are connected, there are still all the four
quarters of the heavens in their common horizon,
and at times they become aware of this fact.

246.

THE SILENCE OF DISGUST.—Behold! some one
undergoes a thorough and painful transformation
as thinker and human being, and makes a public
avowal of the change. And those who hear him
see nothing, and still believe he is the same as
before! This common experience has already dis-

gusted many writers. They had rated the intellectuality of mankind too highly, and made a vow
to be silent as soon as they became aware of their
mistake.

247.

BUSINESS SERIOUSNESS.—The business of many
rich and eminent men is their form of recreation
from too long periods of habitual leisure. They then
become as serious and impassioned as other people
do in their rare moments of leisure and amusement.

248.

THE EYE'S DOUBLE SENSE.—Just as a sudden
scaly ripple runs over the waters at your feet, so
there are similar sudden uncertainties and ambigu-
ities in the human eye.   They lead to the question :
is it a shudder, or a smile, or both?

249.

POSITIVE AND NEGATIVE.—This thinker needs
no one to refute him—he is quite capable of doing
that himself.

250.

THE REVENGE OF THE EMPTY NETS.—Above
all we should beware of those who have the bitter
feeling of the fisherman who after a hard day's work
comes home in the evening with nets empty.

251.

NON-ASSERTION OF OUR RIGHTS.—The exertion
of power is laborious and demands courage.   That

is why so many do not assert their most valid rights, because their rights are a kind of power, and they are too lazy or too cowardly to exercise them. *Indulgence* and *patience* are the names given to the virtues that cloak these faults.

252.

BEARERS OF LIGHT.—In Society there would be no sunshine if the born flatterers (I mean the so-called amiable people) did not bring some in with them.

253.

WHEN MOST BENEVOLENT.—When a man has been highly honoured and has eaten a little, he is most benevolent.

254.

TO THE LIGHT.—Men press forward to the light not in order to see better but to shine better.—The person before whom we shine we gladly allow to be called a light.

255.

THE HYPOCHONDRIAC.—The hypochondriac is a man who has just enough intellect and pleasure in the intellect to take his sorrows, his losses, and his mistakes seriously.   But the field on which he grazes is too small : he crops it so close that in the end he has to look for single stalks.   Thus he finally becomes envious and avaricious—and only then is he unbearable.

256.

GIVING IN RETURN.—Hesiod advises us to give the neighbour who has helped us good measure and, if possible, fuller measure in return, as soon as we have the power. For this is where the neighbour's pleasure comes in, since his former benevolence brings him interest. Moreover, he who gives in return also has his pleasure, inasmuch as, by giving a little more than he got, he redeems the slight humiliation of being compelled to seek aid.

257.

MORE SUBTLE THAN IS NECESSARY.—Our sense of observation for how far others perceive our weaknesses is far more subtle than our sense of observation for the weaknesses of others. It follows that the first-named sense is more subtle than is necessary.

258.

A KIND OF BRIGHT SHADOWS.—Close to the nocturnal type of man we almost regularly find, as if bound up with him, a bright soul. This is, as it were, the negative shadow cast by the former.

259.

NOT TO TAKE REVENGE.—There are so many subtle sorts of revenge that one who has occasion to take revenge can really do or omit to do what he likes. In any case, the whole world will agree, after a time, that he *has* avenged himself. Hence the avoidance of revenge is hardly within man's power. He must not even so much as say that he does not *want* to do so, since the contempt for revenge is interpreted and felt as a sublime and exquisite form of revenge.—It follows that we must do nothing superfluous.

260.

THE MISTAKE OF THOSE WHO PAY HOMAGE.—
Every one thinks he is paying a most agreeable com-
pliment to a thinker when he says that he himself
hit upon exactly the same idea and even upon the
same expression.   The thinker, however, is seldom
delighted at hearing such news, nay, rather, he often
becomes distrustful of his own thoughts and expressions.   He silently resolves to revise both some
day.   If we wish to pay homage to any one, we
must beware of expressing our agreement, for this
puts us on the same level.—Often it is a matter of
social tact to listen to an opinion as if it were not
ours or even travelled beyond the limits of our own
horizon—as, for example, when an old man once in
a while opens the storehouse of his acquired knowledge.

261.

LETTERS.—A letter is an unannounced visit, and
the postman is the intermediary of impolite surprises.
Every week we ought to have one hour for receiving
letters, and then go and take a bath.

262.

PREJUDICED.—Some one said: I have been prejudiced against myself from childhood upwards, and
hence I find some truth in every censure and some
absurdity in every eulogy.   Praise I generally value
too low and blame too high.

263.

THE PATH TO EQUALITY. — A few hours of mountain-climbing make a blackguard and a saint two rather similar creatures. Weariness is the shortest path to equality and fraternity—and finally liberty is bestowed by sleep.

264.

CALUMNY.—If we begin to trace to its source a real scandalous misrepresentation, we shall rarely look for its origin in our honourable and straight-forward enemies; for if they invented anything of the sort about us, they, as being our enemies, would gain no credence. Those, however, to whom for a time we have been most useful, but who, from some reason or other, may be secretly sure that they will obtain no more from us—such persons are in a position to start the ball of slander rolling. They gain credence, firstly, because it is assumed that they would invent nothing likely to do them damage; secondly, because they have learnt to know us intimately.—As a consolation, the much-slandered man may say to himself: Calumnies are diseases of others that break out in your body. They prove that Society is a (moral) organism, so that you can prescribe to *yourself* the cure that will in the end be useful to others.

265.

THE CHILD'S KINGDOM OF HEAVEN. — The happiness of a child is as much of a myth as the happiness of the Hyperboreans of whom the Greeks fabled.   The Greeks supposed that, if indeed happiness dwells anywhere on our earth, it must certainly dwell as far as possible from us, perhaps over yonder at the edge of the world.   Old people have the same thought—if man is at all capable of being happy, he must be happy as far as possible from our age, at the frontiers and beginnings of life.   For many a man the sight of children, through the veil of this myth, is the greatest happiness that he can feel.   He enters himself into the forecourt of heaven when he says, "Suffer the little children to come unto me, for of them is the kingdom of heaven."   The myth of the child's kingdom of heaven holds good, in some way or other, wherever ·in the modern world some sentimentality exists.

266.

THE IMPATIENT.—It is just the growing man who does not want things in the growing stage. He is too impatient for that.   The youth will not wait until, after long study, suffering, and privation, his picture of men and things is complete.   Accordingly, he confidently accepts another picture that lies ready to his hand and is recommended to him, and pins his faith to that, as if it must give him at once the lines and colours of his own painting.   He presses a philosopher or a poet to his bosom, and must from that time forth perform long stretches of forced labour and renounce his own self.   He learns much in the process, but he often forgets what is most worth learning and knowing—his self.   He remains all his life a partisan.

Ah, a vast amount of tedious work has to be done before you find your own colours, your own brush, your own canvas!—Even then you are very far from being a master in the art of life, but at least you are the boss in your own workshop.

267.

THERE ARE NO TEACHERS.—As thinkers we ought only to speak of self-teaching.   The instruction of the young by others is either an experiment performed upon something as yet unknown and unknowable, or else a thorough levelling process, in order to make the new member of society conform to the customs and manners that prevail for the time being.   In both cases the result is accordingly unworthy of a thinker—the handiwork of parents and teachers, whom some valiantly honest person * has called "*nos ennemis naturels.*"   One day, when, as the world thinks, we have long since finished our education, we *discover ourselves.*   Then begins the task of the thinker, and then is the time to summon him to our aid—not as a teacher, but as a self-taught man who has experience.

268.

SYMPATHY WITH YOUTH.—We are sorry when we hear that some one who is still young is losing his teeth or growing blind.   If we knew all the irrevocable and hopeless feelings hidden in his whole being, how great our sorrow would be!   Why do

---

* Stendhal.—TR.

we really suffer on this account? Because youth
has to continue the work we have undertaken, and
every flaw and failing in its strength is likely to
injure *our* work, that will fall into its hands. It is
the sorrow at the imperfect guarantee of our immortality : or, if we only feel ourselves as executors
of the human mission, it is the sorrow that this
mission must pass to weaker hands than ours.

269.

THE AGES OF LIFE.—The comparison of the
four ages of life with the four seasons of the year
is a venerable piece of folly. Neither the first
twenty nor the last twenty years of a life correspond
to a season of the year, assuming that we are not
satisfied with drawing a parallel between white hair
and snow and similar colour-analogies. The first
twenty years are a preparation for life in general,
for the whole year of life, a sort of long New Year's
Day. The last twenty review, assimilate, bring into
union and harmony all that has been experienced
till then : as, in a small degree, we do on every
New Year's Eve with the whole past year. But in
between there really lies an interval which suggests
a comparison with the seasons—the time from the
twentieth to the fiftieth year (to speak here of decades in the lump, while it is an understood thing
that every one must refine for himself these rough
outlines). Those three decades correspond to three
seasons—summer, spring, and autumn. Winter
human life has none, unless we like to call the (unfortunately) often intervening hard, cold, lonely,

hopeless, unfruitful periods of disease the winters of man.   The twenties, hot, oppressive, stormy, impetuous, exhausting years, when we praise the day in the evening, when it is over, as we wipe the sweat from our foreheads—years in which work seems to us cruel but necessary—these twenties are the summer of life.   The thirties, on the other hand, are its spring-time, with the air now too warm, now too cold, ever restless and stimulating, bubbling sap, bloom of leaves, fragrance of buds everywhere, many delightful mornings and evenings, work to which the song of birds awakens us, a true work of the heart, a kind of joy in our own robustness, strengthened by the savour of hopeful anticipation.   Lastly the forties, mysterious like all that is stationary, like a high, broad plateau, traversed by a fresh breeze, with a clear, cloudless sky above it, which always has the same gentle look all day and half the night—the time of harvest and cordial gaiety—that is the autumn of life.

270.

WOMEN'S INTELLECT IN MODERN SOCIETY.— What women nowadays think of men's intellect may be divined from the fact that in their art of adornment they think of anything but of emphasising the intellectual side of their faces or their single intellectual features.   On the contrary, they conceal such traits, and understand, for example by an arrangement of their hair over their forehead, how to give themselves an appearance of vivid, eager sensuality and materialism, just when they but slightly possess those qualities.   Their conviction that intellect in women frightens men goes so far that they even gladly deny the keenness of the most intellectual sense and purposely invite the reputation of short-sightedness. They think they will thereby make men more confiding. It is as if a soft, attractive twilight were spreading itself around them.

271.

GREAT AND TRANSITORY.—What moves the observer to tears is the rapturous look of happiness with which a fair young bride gazes upon her husband. We feel all the melancholy of autumn in thinking of the greatness and of the transitoriness of human happiness.

272.

SENSE AND SACRIFICE.—Many a woman has the *intelletto del sacrifizio*,* and no longer enjoys life when her husband refuses to sacrifice her. With all her wit, she then no longer knows—whither? and without perceiving it, is changed from sacrificial victim to sacrificial priest.

273.

THE UNFEMININE.—"Stupid as a man," say the women; "Cowardly as a woman," say the men. Stupidity in a woman is unfeminine.

274.

MASCULINE AND FEMININE TEMPERAMENT AND MORTALITY. — That the male sex has a worse

---

* A transposition of *sacrifizio dell' intelletto*, the Jesuit maxim.—TR.

temperament than the female follows from the fact that male children have a greater mortality than female, clearly because they "leap out of their skins" more easily.   Their wildness and unbearableness soon make all the bad stuff in them deadly.

275.

THE AGE OF CYCLOPEAN BUILDING.—The democratisation of Europe is a resistless force.   Even he who would stem the tide uses those very means that democratic thought first put into men's hands, and he makes these means more handy and workable.   The most inveterate enemies of democracy (I mean the spirits of upheaval) seem only to exist in order, by the fear that they inspire, to drive forward the different parties faster and faster on the democratic course.   Now we may well feel sorry for those who are working consciously and honourably for this future.   There is something dreary and monotonous in their faces, and the grey dust seems to have been wafted into their very brains.   Nevertheless, posterity may possibly some day laugh at our anxiety, and see in the democratic work of several generations what we see in the building of stone dams and walls—an activity that necessarily covers clothes and face with a great deal of dust, and perhaps unavoidably makes the workmen, too, a little dull-witted; but who would on that account desire such work undone?   It seems that the democratisation of Europe is a link in the chain of those mighty prophylactic principles which are the thought of the modern era, and whereby we rise up in revolt against the Middle Ages. Now, and now only, is the age of Cyclopean building! A final security in the foundations, that the future may build on them without danger! Henceforth, an impossibility of the orchards of culture being once more destroyed overnight by wild, senseless mountain torrents! Dams and walls against barbarians, against plagues, against physical and spiritual serfdom! And all this understood at first roughly and literally, but gradually in an ever higher and more spiritual sense, so that all the principles here indicated may appear as the intellectual preparation of the highest artist in horticulture, who can only apply himself to his own task when the other is fully accomplished!—True, if we consider the long intervals of time that here lie between means and end, the great, supreme labour, straining the powers and brains of centuries, that is necessary in order to create or to provide each individual means, we must not bear too hardly upon the workers of the present when they loudly proclaim that the wall and the fence are already the end and the final goal. After all, no one yet sees the gardener and the fruit, for whose sake the fence exists.

276.

THE RIGHT OF UNIVERSAL SUFFRAGE.—The people has not granted itself universal suffrage but, wherever this is now in force, it has received and accepted it as a temporary measure. But in any case the people has the right to restore the gift, if it does not satisfy its anticipations. This dissatisfaction seems universal nowadays, for when, at any occasion where the vote is exercised, scarce two-thirds, nay perhaps not even the majority of all voters, go to the polls, that very fact is a vote against the whole suffrage system.—On this point, in fact, we must pronounce a much sterner verdict. A law that enacts that the majority shall decide as to the welfare of all cannot be built up on the foundation that it alone has provided, for it is bound to require a far broader foundation, namely the unanimity of all. Universal suffrage must not only be the expression of the will of a majority, but of the whole country. Thus the dissent of a very small minority is already enough to set aside the system as impracticable; and the abstention from voting is in fact a dissent of this kind, which ruins the whole institution. The "absolute veto" of the individual, or—not to be too minute—the veto of a few thousands, hangs over the system as the consequence of justice. On every occasion when it is employed, the system must, according to the variety of the division, first prove that it has still a right to exist.

277.

FALSE CONCLUSIONS.—What false conclusions are drawn in spheres where we are not at home, even by those of us who are accustomed as men of science to draw right conclusions! It is humiliating! Now it is clear that in the great turmoil of worldly doings, in political affairs, in all sudden and urgent matters such as almost every day brings up, these false conclusions must decide. For no one

feels at home with novelties that have sprung up in
the night. All political work, even with great statesmen, is an improvisation that trusts to luck.

278.

PREMISSES OF THE AGE OF MACHINERY.—The
press, the machine, the railway, the telegraph are
premisses of which no one has yet dared to draw
the conclusions that will follow in a thousand years.

279.

A DRAG UPON CULTURE.—When we are told that
here men have no time for productive occupations,
because military manœuvres and processions take
up their days, and the rest of the population must
feed and clothe them, their dress, however, being
striking, often gay and full of absurdities; that there
only a few distinguished qualities are recognised,
individuals resemble each other more than elsewhere,
or at any rate are treated as equals, yet obedience
is exacted and yielded without reasoning, for men
command and make no attempt to convince; that
here punishments are few, but these few cruel and
likely to become the final and most terrible; that
there treason ranks as the capital offence, and even
the criticism of evils is only ventured on by the most
audacious; that there, again, human life is cheap,
and ambition often takes the form of setting life in
danger—when we hear all this, we at once say, "This
is a picture of a barbarous society that rests on a
hazardous footing." One man perhaps will add, " It
is a portrait of Sparta." But another will become

meditative and declare that this is a description of
our modern military system, as it exists in the midst
of our altogether different culture and society, a
living anachronism, the picture, as above said, of a
community resting on a hazardous footing ; a posthumous work of the past, which can only act as a
drag upon the wheels of the present.—Yet at times
even a drag upon culture is vitally necessary—that
is to say, when culture is advancing too rapidly
downhill or (as perhaps in this case) *uphill*.

280.

MORE REVERENCE FOR THEM THAT KNOW.—
In the competition of production and sale the public
is made judge of the product.   But the public has
no special knowledge, and judges by the appearance
of the wares.   In consequence, the art of appearance
(and perhaps the taste for it) must increase under the
dominance of competition, while on the other hand
the quality of every product must deteriorate.   The
result will be—so far as reason does not fall in value
—that one day an end will be put to that competition, and a new principle will win the day.   Only
the master of the craft should pronounce a verdict
on the work, and the public should be dependent on
the belief in the personality of the judge and his
honesty.   Accordingly, no anonymous work !   At
least an expert should be there as guarantor and
pledge his name if the name of the creator is lacking or is unknown.   The cheapness of an article
is for the layman another kind of illusion and de-
ceit, since only durability can decide that a thing

is cheap and to what an extent.   But it is difficult,
and for a layman impossible, to judge of its durability.—Hence that which produces an effect on the
eye and costs little at present gains the advantage
—this being naturally machine-made work.   Again,
machinery—that is to say, the cause of the greatest
rapidity and facility in production—favours the most
saleable kind of article.   Otherwise it involves no
tangible profit; it would be too little used and
too often stand idle.   But as to what is most saleable, the public, as above said, decides: it must be
the most exchangeable—in other words, the thing
that appears good and also appears cheap.   Thus
in the domain of labour our motto must also hold
good: " More respect for them that know ! "

281.

THE DANGER OF KINGS.—Democracy has it in
its power, without any violent means, and only by
a lawful pressure steadily exerted, to make kingship
and emperorship hollow, until only a zero remains,
perhaps with the significance of every zero in that,
while nothing in itself, it multiplies a number ten-
fold if placed on the right side.   Kingship and emperorship would remain a gorgeous ornament upon
the simple and appropriate dress of democracy, a
beautiful superfluity that democracy allows itself,
a relic of all the historically venerable, primitive ornaments, nay the symbol of history itself, and in
this unique position a highly effective thing if, as
above said, it does not stand alone, but is put on the
right side.—In order to avoid the danger of this

nullification, kings hold by their teeth to their dignity as war-lords.   To this end they need wars, or
in other words exceptional circumstances, in which
that slow, lawful pressure of the democratic forces
is relaxed.

282.

THE TEACHER A NECESSARY EVIL. — Let us
have as few people as possible between the productive minds and the hungry and recipient minds !
The middlemen almost unconsciously adulterate the
food which they supply.   For their work as middlemen they want too high a fee for themselves, and
this is drawn from the original, productive spirits
—namely, interest, admiration, leisure, money, and
other advantages.—Accordingly, we should always
look upon the teacher as a necessary evil, just like
the merchant ; as an evil that we should make as
small as possible.—Perhaps the prevailing distress
in Germany has its main cause in the fact that too
many wish to live and live well by trade (in other
words, desiring as far as possible to diminish prices
for the producer and raise prices for the consumer,
and thus to profit by the greatest possible loss to
both).   In the same way, we may certainly trace a
main cause of the prevailing intellectual poverty in
the superabundance of teachers.   It is because of
teachers that so little is learnt, and that so badly.

283.

THE TAX OF HOMAGE.—Him whom we know
and honour,—be he physician, artist, or artisan,—
who does and produces something for us, we gladly

pay as highly as we can, often a fee beyond our
means.   On the other hand, we pay the unknown
as low a price as possible ; here is a contest in which
every one struggles and makes others struggle for a
foot's breadth of land.   In the work of the known
there is something that cannot be bought, the sentiment and ingenuity put into his work for our own
sake.   We think we cannot better express our sense
of obligation than by a sort of sacrifice on our part.
—The heaviest tax is the tax of homage.   The more
competition prevails, the more we buy for the unknown and work for the unknown, the lower does this
tax become, whereas it is really the standard for the
loftiness of man's spiritual intercourse.

284.

THE MEANS TOWARDS GENUINE PEACE.—No
government will nowadays admit that it maintains
an army in order to satisfy occasionally its passion
for conquest.   The army is said to serve only
defensive purposes.   This morality, which justifies
self-defence, is called in as the government's advocate.   This means, however, reserving morality for
ourselves and immorality for our neighbour, because
he must be thought eager for attack and conquest
if our state is forced to consider means of self-
defence.—At the same time, by our explanation of
our need of an army (because he denies the lust of
attack just as our state does, and ostensibly also
maintains his army for defensive reasons), we proclaim him a hypocrite and cunning criminal, who
would fain seize by surprise, without any fighting,

a harmless and unwary victim. In this attitude all states face each other to-day. They presuppose evil intentions on their neighbour's part and good intentions on their own. This hypothesis, however, is an *inhuman* notion, as bad as and worse than war. Nay, at bottom it is a challenge and motive to war, foisting as it does upon the neighbouring state the charge of immorality, and thus provoking hostile intentions and acts. The doctrine of the army as a means of self-defence must be abjured as completely as the lust of conquest. Perhaps a memorable day will come when a nation renowned in wars and victories, distinguished by the highest development of military order and intelligence, and accustomed to make the heaviest sacrifice to these objects, will voluntarily exclaim, "We will break our swords," and will destroy its whole military system, lock, stock, and barrel. Making ourselves defenceless (after having been the most strongly defended) from a loftiness of sentiment—that is the means towards genuine peace, which must always rest upon a pacific disposition. The so-called armed peace that prevails at present in all countries is a sign of a bellicose disposition, of a disposition that trusts neither itself nor its neighbour, and, partly from hate, partly from fear, refuses to lay down its weapons. Better to perish than to hate and fear, and twice as far better to perish than to make one-self hated and feared—this must some day become the supreme maxim of every political community !— Our liberal representatives of the people, as is well known, have not the time for reflection on the nature of humanity, or else they would know that they are working in vain when they work for "a gradual diminution of the military burdens." On the contrary, when the distress of these burdens is greatest, the sort of God who alone can help here will be nearest. The tree of military glory can only be destroyed at one swoop, with one stroke of lightning. But, as you know, lightning comes from the cloud and from above.

285.

WHETHER PROPERTY CAN BE SQUARED WITH JUSTICE.—When the injustice of property is strongly felt (and the hand of the great clock is once more at this place), we formulate two methods of relieving this injustice: either an equal distribution, or an abolition of private possession and a return to State ownership. The latter method is especially dear to the hearts of our Socialists, who are angry with that primitive Jew for saying, "Thou shalt not steal." In their view the eighth * commandment should rather run, "Thou shalt not possess."—The former method was frequently tried in antiquity, always indeed on a small scale, and yet with poor success. From this failure we too may learn. "Equal plots of land" is easily enough said, but how much bitterness is aroused by the necessary division and separation, by the loss of time-honoured possessions, how much piety is wounded and sacrificed! We uproot the foundation of morality when we uproot boundary-stones. Again, how much fresh bitterness among the new owners, how much envy and looking askance! For there have never been two

* The original, by a curious slip, has "seventh."—TR.

really equal plots of land, and if there were, man's envy of his neighbour would prevent him from believing in their equality. And how long would this equality, unhealthy and poisoned at the very roots, endure? In a few generations, by inheritance, here one plot would come to five owners, there five plots to one. Even supposing that men acquiesced in such abuses through the enactment of stern laws of inheritance, the same equal plots would indeed exist, but there would also be needy malcontents, owning nothing but dislike of their kinsmen and neighbours, and longing for a general upheaval.—If, however, by the second method we try to restore ownership to the community and make the individual but a temporary tenant, we interfere with agriculture. For man is opposed to all that is only a transitory possession, unblessed with his own care and sacrifice. With such property he behaves in freebooter fashion, as robber or as worthless spendthrift. When Plato declares that self-seeking would be removed with the abolition of property, we may answer him that, if self-seeking be taken away, man will no longer possess the four cardinal virtues either; as we must say that the most deadly plague could not injure mankind so terribly as if vanity were one day to disappear. Without vanity and self-seeking what are human virtues? By this I am far from meaning that these virtues are but varied names and masks for these two qualities. Plato's Utopian refrain, which is still sung by Socialists, rests upon a deficient knowledge of men. He lacked the historical science of moral emotions, the insight into the origin of the good and useful characteristics of the human soul. He believed, like all antiquity, in good and evil as in black and white —that is to say, in a radical difference between good and bad men and good and bad qualities.—In order that property may henceforth inspire more confidence and become more moral, we should keep open all the paths of work for small fortunes, but should prevent the effortless and sudden acquisition of wealth. Accordingly, we should take all the branches of transport and trade which favour the accumulation of large fortunes—especially, therefore, the money market—out of the hands of private persons or private companies, and look upon those who own too much, just as upon those who own nothing, as types fraught with danger to the community.

286.

THE VALUE OF LABOUR.—If we try to determine the value of labour by the amount of time, industry, good or bad will, constraint, inventiveness or laziness, honesty or make-believe bestowed upon it, the valuation can never be a just one. For the whole personality would have to be thrown into the scale, and this is impossible. Here the motto is, " Judge not! " But after all the cry for justice is the cry we now hear from those who are dissatisfied with the present valuation of labour. If we reflect further we find every person non-responsible for his product, the labour; hence merit can never be derived therefrom, and every labour is as good or as bad as it must be through this or that necessary concatenation of forces and weaknesses, abilities and desires. The worker is not at liberty to say whether he shall work or not, or to decide how he shall work. Only the standpoints of usefulness, wider and narrower, have created the valuation of labour. What we at present call justice does very well in this sphere as a highly refined utility, which does not only consider the moment and exploit the immediate opportunity, but looks to the permanence of all conditions, and thus also keeps in view the well-being of the worker, his physical and spiritual contentment : in order that he and his posterity may work well for our posterity and become trustworthy for longer periods than the individual span of human life. The *exploitation* of the worker was, as we now understand, a piece of folly, a robbery at the expense of the future, a jeopardisation of society. We almost have the war now, and in any case the expense of maintaining peace, of concluding treaties and winning confidence, will henceforth be very great, because the folly of the exploiters was very great and long-lasting.

287.

OF THE STUDY OF THE SOCIAL BODY.—The worst drawback for the modern student of economics and political science in Europe, and especially in Germany, is that the actual conditions, instead of exemplifying rules, illustrate exceptions or stages of transition and extinction. We must therefore learn to look beyond actually existing conditions and, for example, turn our eyes to distant North America, where we can still contemplate and investigate, if we will, the initial and normal movement of the social body. In Germany such a study requires arduous and historical research, or, as I have suggested, a telescope.

288.

HOW FAR MACHINERY HUMILIATES.—Machinery is impersonal; it robs the piece of work of its pride, of the individual merits and defects that cling to all work that is not machine-made—in other words, of its bit of humanity. Formerly, all buying from handicraftsmen meant a mark of distinction for their personalities, with whose productions people surrounded themselves. Furniture and dress accordingly became the symbols of mutual valuation and personal connection. Nowadays, on the other hand, we seem to live in the midst of anonymous and impersonal serfdom.—We must not buy the facilitation of labour too dear.

289.

CENTURY-OLD QUARANTINE.—Democratic institutions are centres of quarantine against the old plague of tyrannical desires. As such they are extremely useful and extremely tedious.

290.

THE MOST DANGEROUS PARTISAN.—The most dangerous partisan is he whose defection would involve the ruin of the whole party—in other words, the best partisan.

291.

DESTINY AND THE STOMACH.—A piece more or less of bread and butter in the jockey's body is occasionally the decisive factor in races and bets, and thus in the good and bad luck of thousands.—So long as the destiny of nations depends upon diplomats, the stomachs of diplomats will always be the object of patriotic misgivings. *Quousque tandem* ..

292.

THE VICTORY OF DEMOCRACY.—All political powers nowadays attempt to exploit the fear of Socialism for their own strengthening.   Yet in the long run democracy alone gains the advantage, for *all* parties are now compelled to flatter " the masses " and grant them facilities and liberties of all kinds, with the result that the masses finally become omnipotent.   The masses are as far as possible removed from Socialism as a doctrine of altering the acquisition of property. If once they get the steering-wheel into their hands, through great majorities in their Parliaments, they will attack with progressive taxation the whole dominant system of capitalists, merchants, and financiers, and will in fact slowly create a middle class which may forget Socialism like a disease that has been overcome.—The practical result of this increasing democratisation will next be a European league of nations, in which each individual nation, delimited by the proper geographical frontiers, has the position of a canton with its separate rights.   Small account will be taken of the historic memories of previously existing nations, because the pious affection for these memories will be gradually uprooted under the democratic régime, with all its craze for novelty and experiment. The corrections of frontiers that will prove necessary will be so carried out as to serve the interests of the great cantons and at the same time that of the whole federation, but not that of any venerable memories. To find the standpoints for these corrections will be the task of future diplomats, who will have to be at the same time students of civilisation, agriculturists, and commercial experts, with no armies but motives and utilities at their back. Then only will foreign and home politics be inseparably connected, whereas to-day the latter follows its haughty dictator, and gleans in sorry baskets the stubble that is left over from the harvest of the former.

293.

GOAL AND MEANS OF DEMOCRACY.—Democracy tries to create and guarantee independence for as many as possible in their opinions, way of life, and occupation. For this purpose democracy must withhold the political suffrage both from those who have nothing and from those who are really rich, as being the two intolerable classes of men. At the removal of these classes it must always work, because they are continually calling its task in question. In the same way democracy must prevent all measures that seem to aim at party organisation. For the three great foes of independence, in that threefold sense, are the have-nots, the rich, and the parties.—I speak of democracy as of a thing to come. What at present goes by that name is distinguished from older forms of government only by the fact that it drives with new horses; the roads and the wheels are the same as of yore.—Has the danger really become less with *these* conveyances of the commonwealth?

294.

DISCRETION AND SUCCESS.—That great quality of discretion, which is fundamentally the virtue of virtues, their ancestress and queen, has in common life by no means always success on its side. The wooer would find himself deceived if he had wooed that virtue only for the sake of success. For it is rated by practical people as suspicious, and is confused with cunning and hypocrisy: he who obviously lacks discretion, the man who quickly grasps and sometimes misses his grasp, has prejudice on his side—he is an honest, trustworthy fellow. Practical people, accordingly, do not like the prudent man, thinking he is to them a danger. Moreover, we often assume the prudent man to be anxious, preoccupied, pedantic—unpractical, butterfly people find him uncomfortable, because he does not live in their happy-go-lucky way, without thinking of actions and duties; he appears among them as their embodied conscience, and the bright day is dimmed to their eyes before his gaze. Thus when success and popularity fail him, he may often say by way of private consolation, "So high are the taxes you have to pay for the possession of the most precious of human commodities—still it is worth the price!"

295.

ET IN ARCADIA EGO. — I looked down, over waves of hills, to a milky-green lake, through firs and pines austere with age; rocky crags of all shapes about me, the soil gay with flowers and grasses. A herd of cattle moved, stretched, and expanded itself before me ; single cows and groups in the distance, in the clearest evening light, hard by the forest of pines ; others nearer and darker ; all in calm and eventide contentment. My watch pointed to half-past six. The bull of the herd had stepped into the white foaming brook, and went forward slowly, now striving against, now giving way to his tempestuous course; thus, no doubt, he took his sort of fierce pleasure. Two dark brown beings, of Bergamasque origin, tended the herd, the girl dressed almost like a boy. On the left, over-hanging cliffs and fields of snow above broad belts of woodland ; to the right, two enormous ice-covered peaks, high above me, shimmering in the veil of the sunny haze—all large, silent, and bright. The beauty of the whole was awe-inspiring and induced to a mute worship of the moment and its revelation. Unconsciously, as if nothing could be more natural, you peopled this pure, clear world of light (which had no trace of yearning, of expectancy, of looking forward or backward) with Greek heroes. You felt it all as Poussin and his school felt—at once heroic and idyllic.—So individual men too have lived, con-stantly feeling themselves in the world and the world in themselves, and among them one of the greatest men, the inventor of a heroico-idyllic form of philosophy—Epicurus.

296.

COUNTING AND MEASURING.—The art of seeing many things, of weighing one with another, of reckoning one thing with another and constructing from them a rapid conclusion, a fairly correct sum —that goes to make a great politician or general or merchant. This quality is, in fact, a power of speedy mental calculation. The art of seeing *one* thing alone, of finding therein the sole motive for action, the guiding principle of all other action, goes to make the hero and also the fanatic. This quality means a dexterity in measuring with one scale.

297.

NOT TO SEE TOO SOON.—As long as we undergo some experience, we must give ourselves up to the experience and shut our eyes—in other words, not become observers of what we are undergoing. For to observe would disturb good digestion of the experience, and instead of wisdom we should gain nothing but dyspepsia.

298.

FROM THE PRACTICE OF THE WISE.—To become wise we must *will* to undergo certain experiences, and accordingly leap into their jaws. This, it is true, is very dangerous. Many a " sage " has been eaten up in the process.

299.

EXHAUSTION OF THE INTELLECT.—Our occasional coldness and indifference towards people, which is imputed to us as hardness and defect of character, is often only an exhaustion of the intellect. In this state other men are to us, as we are to ourselves, tedious or immaterial.

300.

" THE ONE THING NEEDFUL."—If we are clever, the one thing we need is to have joy in our hearts. " Ah," adds some one, " if we are clever, the best thing we can do is to be wise."

301.

A SIGN OF LOVE.—Some one said, " There are two persons about whom I have never thought deeply. That is a sign of my love for them."

302.

HOW WE SEEK TO IMPROVE BAD ARGUMENTS. —Many a man adds a bit of his personality to his bad arguments, as if they would thus go better and change into straight and good arguments. In the same way, players at skittles, even after a throw, try to give a direction to the ball by turns and gestures.

303.

HONESTY.—It is but a small thing to be a pattern sort of man with regard to rights and property—for instance (to name trifling points, which of course give a better proof of this sort of pattern nature than great examples), if as a boy one never steals fruit from another's orchard, and as a man never walks on unmown fields. It is but little; you are then still only a " law-abiding person," with just that degree of morality of which a " society," a group of human beings, is capable.

304.

" MAN ! "—What is the vanity of the vainest individual as compared with the vanity which the most modest person feels when he thinks of his position in nature and in the world as " Man ! "

305.

THE MOST NECESSARY GYMNASTIC.—Through deficiency in self-control in small matters a similar deficiency on great occasions slowly arises. Every day on which we have not at least once denied ourselves some *trifle* is turned to bad use and a danger to the next day. This gymnastic is indispensable if we wish to maintain the joy of being our own master.

306.

LOSING OURSELVES.—When we have first found ourselves, we must understand how from time to time to *lose* ourselves and then to find ourselves again.—This is true on the assumption that we are thinkers. A thinker finds it a drawback always to be tied to one person.

307.

WHEN IT IS NECESSARY TO PART.—You must, for a time at least, part from that which you want to know and measure. Only when you have left a city do you see how high its towers rise above its houses.

308.

AT NOONTIDE.—He to whom an active and stormy morning of life is allotted, at the noontide of life feels his soul overcome by a strange longing for a rest that may last for months and years. All grows silent around him, voices sound farther and farther in the distance, the sun shines straight down upon him. On a hidden woodland sward he sees the great God Pan sleeping, and with Pan Nature seems to him to have gone to sleep with an expression of eternity on their faces. He wants nothing, he troubles about nothing ; his heart stands still, only his eye lives. It is a death with waking eyes. Then man sees much that he never saw before, and, so far as his eye can reach, all is woven into and as it were buried in a net of light. He feels happy, but it is a heavy, very heavy kind of happiness.—Then at last the wind stirs in the trees, noontide is over, life carries him away again, life with its blind eyes, and its tempestuous retinue behind it — desire, illusion, oblivion, enjoyment, destruction, decay. And so comes evening, more stormy and more active than was even the morning.—To the really active man these prolonged phases of cognition seem almost uncanny and morbid, but not unpleasant.

309.

To Beware of One's Portrait-Painter.—A great painter, who in a portrait has revealed and put on canvas the fullest expression and look of which a man is capable, will almost always think, when he sees the man later in real life, that he is only looking at a caricature.

310.

The Two Principles of the New Life.—*First Principle*: to arrange one's life on the most secure and tangible basis, not as hitherto upon the most distant, undetermined, and cloudy foundation. *Second Principle*: to establish the rank of the nearest and nearer things, and of the more and less secure, before one arranges one's life and directs it to a final end.

311.

Dangerous Irritability.—Talented men who are at the same time *idle* will always appear somewhat irritated when one of their friends has accomplished a thorough piece of work. Their jealousy is awakened, they are ashamed of their own laziness, or rather, they fear that their active friend will now despise them even more than before. In such a mood they criticise the new achievement, and, to the utter astonishment of the author, their criticism becomes a revenge.

312.

Destructions of Illusions. — Illusions are certainly expensive amusements; but the destruc-

tion of illusions is still more expensive, if looked
upon as an amusement, as it undoubtedly is by some
people.

313.

THE MONOTONE OF THE " SAGE."—Cows sometimes have a look of wondering which stops short
on the path to questioning. In the eye of the
higher intelligence, on the other hand, the *nil admi-
rari* is spread out like the monotony of the cloudless sky.

314.

NOT TO BE ILL TOO LONG.—We should beware
of being ill too long. The lookers-on become impatient of their customary duty of showing sympathy, because they find it too much trouble to
maintain the appearance of this emotion for any
length of time. Then they immediately pass to
suspicion of our character, with the conclusion:
" You deserve to be ill, and we need no longer be
at pains to show our sympathy."

315.

A HINT TO ENTHUSIASTS. — He who likes to
be carried away, and would fain be carried on high,
must beware lest he become too heavy. For instance, he must not learn much, and especially not
let himself be crammed with science. Science
makes men ponderous—take care, ye enthusiasts!

316.

KNOWLEDGE OF HOW TO SURPRISE ONESELF.
—He who would see himself as he is, must know

how to *surprise* himself, torch in hand. For with
the mind it is as with the body: whoever is accustomed to look at himself in the glass forgets
his ugliness, and only recognises it again by means
of the portrait-painter. Yet he even grows used
to the picture and forgets his ugliness all over
again.—Herein we see the universal law that man
cannot endure unalterable ugliness, unless for a
moment. He forgets or denies it in all cases.—The
moralists must reckon upon that "moment" for
bringing forward their truths.

317.

OPINIONS AND FISH.—We are possessors of our
opinions as of fish—that is, in so far as we are possessors of a fish pond. We must go fishing and
have luck—then we have *our* fish, *our* opinions. I
speak here of live opinions, of live fish. Others are
content to possess a cabinet of fossils—and, in their
head, "convictions."

318.

SIGNS OF FREEDOM AND SERVITUDE. — To
satisfy one's needs so far as possible oneself, even
if imperfectly, is the path towards freedom in mind
and personality. To satisfy many even superfluous
needs, and that as fully as possible, is a training
for servitude. The Sophist Hippias, who himself
earned and made all that he wore within and without, is the representative of the highest freedom of
mind and personality. It does not matter whether

all is done equally well and perfectly—pride can repair the damaged places.

319.

BELIEF IN ONESELF.—In our times we mistrust every one who believes in himself. Formerly this was enough to make people believe in one. The recipe for finding faith now runs: "Spare not thyself! In order to set thy opinion in a credible light, thou must first set fire to thy own hut!"

320.

AT ONCE RICHER AND POORER.—I know a man who accustomed himself even in childhood to think well of the intellectuality of mankind—in other words, of their real devotion as regards things of the intellect, their unselfish preference for that which is recognised as true—but who had at the same time a modest or even depreciatory view of his own brain (judgment, memory, presence of mind, imagination). He set no value on himself when he compared himself with others. Now in the course of years he was compelled, first once and then in a hundred ways, to revise this verdict. One would have thought he would be thoroughly satisfied and delighted. Such, in fact, was to some extent the case, but, as he once said, "Yet a bitterness of the deepest dye is mingled with my feeling, such as I did not know in earlier life; for since I learnt to value men and myself more correctly, my intellect seems to me of less use. I scarcely think I can now do any good at all with it, because the minds of others cannot understand the good. I now always see before me the frightful gulf between those who could give help and those who need help.   So I am troubled by the misfortune of having my intellect to myself and of being forced to enjoy it alone so far as it can give any enjoyment.   But to give is more blessed than to possess, and what is the richest man in the solitude of a desert? " *

321.

HOW WE SHOULD ATTACK. — The reasons for which men believe or do not believe are in very few people as strong as they might be.   As a rule, in order to shake a belief it is far from necessary to use the heaviest weapon of attack.   Many attain their object by merely making the attack with some noise— in fact, pop-guns are often enough.   In dealing with very vain persons, the semblance of a strong attack is enough.   They think they are being taken quite seriously, and readily give way.

322.

DEATH.—Through the certain prospect of death a precious, fragrant drop of frivolity might be mixed with every life—and now, you singular druggist-souls, you have made of death a drop of poison, unpleasant to taste, which makes the whole of life hideous.

323.

REPENTANCE.—Never allow repentance free play,

---

* Clearly autobiographical.   Nietzsche, like all great men, passed through a period of modesty and doubt.—TR.

but say at once to yourself, " That would be adding a second piece of folly to the first." If you have worked evil, you must bethink yourself of doing good. If you are punished for your actions, submit to the punishment with the feeling that by this very submission you are somehow doing good, in that you are deterring others from falling into the same error. Every malefactor who is punished has a right to consider himself a benefactor to mankind.

324.

BECOMING A THINKER.—How can any one become a thinker if he does not spend at least a third part of the day without passions, men, and books?

325.

THE BEST REMEDY.—A little health on and off is the best remedy for the invalid.

326.

DON'T TOUCH.—There are dreadful people who, instead of solving a problem, complicate it for those who deal with it and make it harder to solve.* Whoever does not know how to hit the nail on the head should be entreated not to hit the nail at all.

327.

FORGETTING NATURE. — We speak of Nature, and, in doing so, forget ourselves : we ourselves are

---

* Nietzsche here alludes to his own countrymen.—TR.

Nature, *quand même.* — Consequently, Nature is something quite different from what we feel on hearing her name pronounced.

328.

PROFUNDITY AND ENNUI.—In the case of profound men, as of deep wells, it takes a long time before anything that is thrown into them reaches the bottom.   The spectators, who generally do not wait long enough, too readily look upon such a man as callous and hard—or even as boring.

329.

WHEN IT IS TIME TO VOW FIDELITY TO ONESELF.—We sometimes go astray in an intellectual direction which does not correspond to our talents. For a time we struggle heroically against wind and tide, really against ourselves; but finally we become weary and we pant.   What we accomplish gives us no real pleasure, since we think that we have paid too heavy a price for these successes.   We even despair of our productivity, of our future, perhaps in the midst of victory.—Finally, finally we turn back—and then the wind swells our sails and bears us into our smooth water.   What bliss!   How certain of victory we feel!   Only now do we know what we are and what we intend, and now we vow fidelity to ourselves, and have a right to do so—as men that know.

330.

WEATHER PROPHETS.—Just as the clouds reveal to us the direction of the wind high above our heads, so the lightest and freest spirits give signs of future weather by their course.   The wind in the valley and the market-place opinions of to-day have no significance for the future, but only for the past.

331.

CONTINUAL ACCELERATION.—Those who begin slowly and find it hard to become familiar with a subject, sometimes acquire afterwards the quality of continual acceleration—so that in the end no one knows where the current will take them.

332.

THE THREE GOOD THINGS.—Greatness, calm, sunlight—these three embrace all that a thinker desires and also demands of himself: his hopes and duties, his claims in the intellectual and moral sphere, nay even in his daily manner of life and the scenic background of his residence.   Corresponding to these three things are, firstly thoughts that exalt, secondly thoughts that soothe, and thirdly thoughts that illuminate—but, fourthly, thoughts that share in all these three qualities, in which all earthly things are transfigured.   This is the kingdom of the great *trinity of joy*.

333.

DYING FOR "TRUTH."—We should not let ourselves be burnt for our opinions—we are not so certain of them as all that.   But we might let ourselves be burnt for the right of possessing and changing our opinions.

334.

MARKET VALUE.—If we wish to pass exactly for what we are, we must be something that has its market value. As, however, only objects in common use have a market value, this desire is the consequence either of shrewd modesty or of stupid immodesty.

335.

MORAL FOR BUILDERS.—We must remove the scaffolding when the house has been built.

336.

SOPHOCLEANISM.—Who poured more water into wine than the Greeks? Sobriety and grace combined—that was the aristocratic privilege of the Athenian in the time of Sophocles and after. Imitate that whoever can ! In life and in work !

337.

HEROISM.—The heroic consists in doing something great (or in nobly *not* doing something) without feeling oneself to be in competition *with* or *before* others. The hero carries with him, wherever he goes, the wilderness and the holy land with inviolable precincts.

338.

FINDING OUR " DOUBLE " IN NATURE.—In some country places we rediscover ourselves, with a delightful shudder : it is the pleasantest way of finding our " double."—How happy must he be who has that feeling just here, in this perpetually sunny October air, in this happy elfin play of the wind from morn till eve, in this clearest of atmospheres and mildest of temperatures, in all the serious yet cheerful landscape of hill, lake, and forest on this plateau, which has encamped fearlessly next to the terrors of eternal snow : here, where Italy and Finland have joined hands, and where the home of all the silver colour-tones of Nature seems to be established. How happy must he be who can say, " True, there are many grander and finer pieces of scenery, but this is so familiar and intimate to me, related by blood, nay even more to me ! "

339.

AFFABILITY OF THE SAGE.—The sage will unconsciously be affable in his intercourse with other men, as a prince would be, and will readily treat them as equals, in spite of all differences of talent, rank, and character. For this characteristic, however, so soon as people notice it, he is most heavily censured.

340.

GOLD.—All that is gold does not glitter. A soft sheen characterises the most precious metal.

341.

WHEEL AND DRAG.—The wheel and the drag have different duties, but also one in common —that of hurting each other.

342.

DISTURBANCES OF THE THINKER.—All that interrupts the thinker in his thoughts (disturbs him, as people say) must be regarded by him calmly, as a new model who comes in by the door to offer himself to the artist. Interruptions are the ravens which bring food to the recluse.

343.

BEING VERY CLEVER.—Being very clever keeps men young, but they must put up with being considered, for that very reason, older than they are. For men read the handwriting of the intellect as signs of *experience*—that is, of having lived much and evilly, of suffering, error, and repentance. Hence, if we are very clever and show it, we appear to them older and wickeder than we are.

344.

HOW WE MUST CONQUER.—We ought not to desire victory if we only have the prospect of overcoming our opponent by a hair's breadth. A good victory makes the vanquished rejoice, and must have about it something divine which spares *humiliation*.

345.

AN ILLUSION OF SUPERIOR MINDS.—Superior minds find it difficult to free themselves from an illusion; for they imagine that they excite envy among the mediocre and are looked upon as ex-

ceptions.   As a matter of fact, however, they are
looked upon as superfluous, as something that would
not be missed if it did not exist.

346.

DEMANDED BY CLEANLINESS.—Changing opinions is in some natures as much demanded by cleanliness as changing clothes.   In the case of other
natures it is only demanded by vanity.

347.

ALSO WORTHY OF A HERO.—Here is a hero who
did nothing but shake the tree as soon as the fruits
were ripe.   Do you think that too small a thing?
Well, just look at the tree that he shook.

348.

A GAUGE FOR WISDOM.—The growth of wisdom
may be gauged exactly by the diminution of ill-
temper.

349.

EXPRESSING AN ERROR DISAGREEABLY.—It is
not to every one's taste to hear truth pleasantly expressed.   But let no one at least believe that error
will become truth if it is disagreeably expressed.

350.

THE GOLDEN MAXIM.— Man has been bound
with many chains, in order that he may forget to

comport himself like an animal. And indeed he
has become more gentle, more intellectual, more
joyous, more meditative than any animal. But now
he still suffers from having carried his chains so long,
from having been so long without pure air and free
movement—these chains, however, are, as I repeat
again and again, the ponderous and significant
errors of moral, religious, and metaphysical ideas.
Only when the disease of chains is overcome is the
first great goal reached—the separation of man from
the brute. At present we stand in the midst of our
work of removing the chains, and in doing so we
need the strictest precautions. Only the ennobled
man may be granted freedom of spirit; to him
alone comes the alleviation of life and heals his
wounds; he is the first who can say that he lives
for the sake of joy, with no other aim; in any other
mouth, his motto of " Peace around me and good-
will towards all the most familiar things," would be
dangerous.—In this motto for single individuals he
is thinking of an ancient saying, magnificent and
pathetic, which applied to all, and has remained
standing above all mankind, as a motto and a
beacon whereby shall perish all who adorn their
banner too early—the rock on which Christianity
foundered. It is not even yet time, it seems, for *all
men* to have the lot of those shepherds who saw the
heavens lit up above them and heard the words:
"Peace on earth and goodwill to one another among
men."—It is still the age of the individual.

     *   *   *   *   *   *

The Shadow: Of all that you have enunciated, nothing pleased me more than one promise: "Ye want again to be good neighbours to the most familiar things." This will be to the advantage of us poor shadows too. For do but confess that you have hitherto been only too fond of reviling us.

The Wanderer: Reviling? But why did you never defend yourselves? After all, you were very close to our ears.

The Shadow: It seemed to us that we were too near you to have a right to talk of ourselves.

The Wanderer: What delicacy! Ah, you shadows are "better men "* than we, I can see that.

The Shadow: And yet you called us "importunate"—us, who know one thing at least extremely well: how to be silent and to wait—no Englishman knows it better. It is true we are very, very often in the retinue of men, but never as their bondsmen. When man shuns light, we shun man—so far, at least, we are free.

The Wanderer: Ah, light shuns man far oftener, and then also you abandon him.

The Shadow: It has often pained me to leave you. I am eager for knowledge, and much in man has remained obscure to me, because I cannot always be in his company. At the price of complete knowledge of man I would gladly be your slave.

The Wanderer: Do you know, do I know, whether you would not then unwittingly become master in-

---

* An allusion to the poem "Der Wilde" (The Savage) by Säume, which ends with the line, "Sehet, wir wilden sind doch bessere Menschen" (Behold, after all, we savages are better men).—TR.

stead of slave? Or would remain a slave indeed, but would lead a life of humiliation and disgust because you despised your master? Let us both be content with freedom such as you have enjoyed up to now—you and I! For the sight of a being not free would embitter my greatest joys; all that is best would be repugnant to me if any one had to share it with me —I will not hear of any slaves about me. That is why I do not care for the dog, that lazy, tail-wagging parasite, who first became " doggish" as the slave of man, and of whom they still say that he is loyal to his master and follows him like——

The Shadow: Like his shadow, they say. Perhaps I have already followed you too long to-day? It has been the longest day, but we are nearing the end; be patient a little more! The grass is damp; I am feeling chilly.

The Wanderer: Oh, is it already time to part? And I had to hurt you in the end—I saw you became darker.

The Shadow: I blushed the only colour I have at command. I remembered that I had often lain at your feet like a dog, and that you then——

The Wanderer: Can I not with all speed do something to please you? Have you no wish?

The Shadow: None, except perhaps the wish that the philosophic " dog "* expressed to Alexander the Great—just move a little out of my light; I feel cold.

The Wanderer: What am I to do?

----

* Diogenes, founder of the Cynic school, which derived its name from κυών (dog).—TR.

The Shadow : Walk under those fir-trees and look around you towards the mountains; the sun is sinking.

The Wanderer : Where are you? Where are you ?

.

THE WORKS OF
FRIEDRICH NIETZSCHE.

First Complete and Authorised English Translation, in 18 Volumes.

EDITED BY DR OSCAR LEVY.

THE MACMILLAN COMPANY, PUBLISHERS, NEW YORK.